ALSO BY BILL GERTZ

Betrayal:
How the Clinton Administration
Undermined American Security

The China Threat:
How the People's Republic Targets America

Breakdown:
How America's Intelligence Failures Led to September 11

Treachery:
How America's Friends and Foes
Are Secretly Arming Our Enemies

Enemies:
How America's Foes Steal Our Vital Secrets—
and How We Let It Happen

The Failure Factory:
How Unelected Bureaucrats, Liberal Democrats, and
Big-Government Republicans Are Undermining
America's Security and Leading Us to War

iWAR

WAR AND PEACE IN THE INFORMATION AGE

BILL GERTZ

THRESHOLD EDITIONS

NEW YORK   LONDON   TORONTO   SYDNEY   NEW DELHI

To American warriors

Threshold Editions
An Imprint of Simon & Schuster, Inc.
1230 Avenue of the Americas
New York, NY 10020

First Threshold Editions paperback edition July 2017

THRESHOLD EDITIONS and colophon are trademarks of Simon & Schuster, Inc.

For information about special discounts for bulk purchases, please contact Simon & Schuster Special Sales at 1-866-506-1949 or business@simonandschuster.com.

The Simon & Schuster Speakers Bureau can bring authors to your live event. For more information, or to book an event, contact the Simon & Schuster Speakers Bureau at 1-866-248-3049 or visit our website at www.simonspeakers.com.

Interior design by Akasha Archer

Manufactured in the United States of America

10 9 8 7 6 5 4 3 2 1

Library of Congress Cataloging-in-Publication Data is available.

ISBN 978-1-5011-5496-6
ISBN 978-1-5011-5498-0 (pbk)
ISBN 978-1-5011-5499-7 (ebook)

CONTENTS

War is essentially a clash of purposes. Only derivatively is it a clash of arms. Peace and war are two sides of the same coin. Failing to grasp that makes it impossible to understand the event that ends war and ushers in peace, namely victory.

—ANGELO CODEVILLA, NATIONAL SECURITY STRATEGIST, *ADVICE TO WAR PRESIDENTS*, 2009

PREFACE

Where We Are Today

The surprise election of Donald Trump as president in November 2016 catapulted the danger of information warfare to the forefront of American politics. What was widely viewed as the all-but-certain election of Hillary Clinton as the successor to President Barack Obama was not to be. The failure of the Clinton election campaign triggered an avalanche of political recrimination from Democrats who remained certain that Russia stole the election from Clinton and helped Trump take up residence in the White House.

A joint intelligence assessment produced in January 2017 by the National Security Agency, FBI, and CIA concluded that Russian intelligence services, directed by Russian president Vladimir Putin, had carried out a covert influence operation using cyberattacks to steal emails and documents from political figures and institutions and weaponize the stolen data by releasing it to Kremlin-friendly media outlets. The objective was to improve Trump's election chances while discrediting Clinton and portraying her unfavorably. The report said that the campaign was unprecedented and "demonstrated a significant escalation in directness, level of activity, and scope of effort compared to previous operations."

By the spring, investigations into Russian cyber-enabled political influence operations had produced no evidence linking the Trump campaign to Moscow. Undeterred, Democrats nonetheless promoted the false narrative of collusion with Russia in a bid to claim that the new administration was illegitimate. Their narrative largely was based on a widely discredited private intelligence dossier produced by a former British intelligence officer, Christopher Steele. The thirty-five-page dossier was financed by the Democratic-linked Fusion GPS opposition research firm. It claimed—falsely—that three men connected to the Trump campaign held meetings with Russians and were guilty of various misdeeds. Most of the dossier's allegations were shown to be false. The document bore all the hallmarks of a classic Russian disinformation—the blending of false and true information. Congressional Democrats, nonetheless, used the dossier in a push for creating a special commission to investigate the alleged Trump–Moscow ties.

Trump as president continued the use of Twitter as one of his most effective political tools, engaging in early morning Twitter storms to promote his policies and criticize his opponents, especially what he termed hostile "fake media"—the liberal press that took after the new president with vengeance.

On China, Trump effectively challenged China's unrelenting information operations designed to weaken the United States by striking out against one of the foundations of American foreign policy. After angering Beijing by taking a congratulatory tele-

phone call from Taiwan's president, Trump struck out against
the core of China's relationship with the United States as outlined in communiqués from the 1980s. Trump tweeted that the
United States might abandon its decades-long position known
as the One-China Policy, which shifted American diplomatic
recognition from Taiwan to Beijing, only to back off the threatened policy shift under Chinese pressure.

Trump's most impressive information operation took place
during his early April summit with Chinese supreme leader Xi
Jinping. Playing to Chinese fears of U.S. military intervention in
Asia against an increasingly hostile North Korea, the president
ordered a cruise missile strike on a Syrian air base the same night
he dined with Xi at the Mar-a-Lago resort. The message to Beijing was unmistakable: The new president is unpredictable and
not to be trifled with.

Among the more sensational Twitter strikes from Trump
came in March: "Terrible! Just found out that Obama had my
'wires tapped' in Trump Tower just before the victory. Nothing
found. This is McCarthyism!"

The allegation set off a potential scandal of improper domestic political spying by the Obama administration. The wiretapping tweet initially drew guffaws from Trump opponents.
FBI Director James Comey, still reeling from his high-profile
intervention in the presidential campaign, once again took center stage. In testimony before the House intelligence panel in
March, Comey revealed that bureau counterintelligence agents
were in fact looking into ties between Trump associates and
Russia. But the probe was limited to intelligence gathering and
did not appear focused on criminal wrongdoing.

But on the Trump wiretapping claim, Comey had this to say: "With respect to the president's tweets about alleged wiretapping directed at him by the prior administration, I have no information that supports those tweets, and we have looked carefully inside the FBI."

The day after the categorical denial, however, Representative Devin Nunes, chairman of the House Permanent Select Committee on Intelligence, appeared to contradict Comey in producing another sensational disclosure. Dozens of highly classified intelligence reports viewed by Nunes at a secure office in the White House complex had revealed the names of Americans who had been "unmasked." The unmasking violated privacy controls used in foreign intelligence reports targeting foreign officials that had swept up conversations with Americans. Nunes, a California Republican, suggested that the reports had revealed the outlines of something close to what Trump had claimed in his controversial tweet, namely, that the Obama administration had engaged in a domestic political spying operation against the Trump transition team using a three-month-long foreign electronic intelligence operation as cover.

"What I've read seems to be some level of surveillance activity, perhaps legal, but I don't know that it's right and I don't know if the American people would be comfortable with what I've read," Nunes said.

The Nunes disclosures set off a competing Republican political narrative. And they fueled Republican anger at what appeared to be political leaks from Obama holdovers within the Trump administration who had released highly classified communications intercepts obtained by the NSA. The intercepts revealed that the new White House National Security Adviser, retired Army Lieutenant

General Michael Flynn, in an intercepted phone conversation with the Russian ambassador to the United States, had discussed U.S. sanctions on Russia that Moscow was working to have lifted. Disclosure of the intercept prompted Flynn's resignation, since the conversation contradicted his assertions to Vice President Mike Pence that no such discussions had been held. The vice president had gone on a Sunday news show television appearance and announced falsely that Flynn had not discussed sanctions with the ambassador, Sergey Kislyak.

North Korea showed itself a continuing information warfare threat. And *iWar*'s proposal to wage information warfare against the regime of North Korean dictator Kim Jong Un may have prompted Kim to strike out. The proposal called for using Kim's estranged brother, Kim Jong Nam, as a leader-in-waiting replacement while the country is flooded with laptops and handheld devices that could form a base for information operations. Weeks after the *iWar* proposal was made public, North Korea's Ministry of State Security carried out the assassination of Kim Jong Nam as he walked through the airport in Kuala Lumpur, Malaysia. Two women carrying components of the deadly nerve agent VX walked up to Kim and wiped the toxic agent on his face during the attack. He died before reaching the hospital.

Social media gave new prominence to information warfare threats. The social media giant Facebook published a report in April warning that information operations are not limited to technical cyber intrusions and theft. The company's report on "information operations" focused on the Russian influence operations during the election. It turns out that Facebook was part of information battle space for Moscow that created fake personas on Facebook to amplify data stolen by the Russians. Pages also were created to amplify news stories and direct people to stolen documents and emails.

Facebook warned that hostile actors are using social media for information warfare in attempting to distort public discourse, recruit supporters and financiers, and affect the outcome of political or military activities. "We have had to expand our security focus from traditional abusive behavior, such as account hacking, malware, spam and financial scams, to include more subtle and insidious forms of misuse, including attempts to manipulate civic discourse and deceive people," the report states.

The Russian election subversion activities would lead to the expulsion of thirty-nine Russian intelligence operatives from the United States. It would be the only substantive action taken by Obama in response to eight years of cyber- and information warfare attacks.

The information warfare programs conducted by Russia, China, Iran, North Korea and Islamic terrorists against the United States and American allies continue and are becoming more brazen. And there are some indications that both the Trump administration and Congress have begun to recognize the need to do something about it.

The publication of *iWar* has produced a greater awareness of information threats. But much work remains to be done to counter the dangers.

—Bill Gertz
April 2017

INTRODUCTION

Suppose They Gave a War and Nobody Knew

The U.S. side has failed to show up for the war of ideas.
Strategic communication or public diplomacy, the purpose
of which is to win such wars, is the single weakest
area of U.S. government performance since 9/11.
—ROBERT R. REILLY, FORMER DIRECTOR,
VOICE OF AMERICA

America is at war, but most Americans don't know it. Major world powers such as China and Russia, along with rogue states including Iran and North Korea and the Islamic State terrorist group, are engaged in relentless covert information warfare. The current stage of this virtual conflict involves salvos and sorties fired from computers and handheld devices with the ultimate goal of defeating and destroying the American nation and, more important, its ideals and values.

To be clear, deadly kinetic warfare is not over, as the ongoing conflicts in Afghanistan, Iran, Syria, and elsewhere attest. And the deadly rampage of the Islamic State shows few signs of abating. But this new form of warfare emerging in the new millennium is part of the Information Age, which has come to dominate our lives.

The central idea behind *iWar: War and Peace in the Information Age* is that warfare in the twenty-first century will be dominated by information operations: nonkinetic conflict waged in the digital realm. By nonkinetic, I mean warfare involving weapons that do not always produce the kind of physical damage associated with the arms and weaponry of traditional military warfare. I divide this new type of conflict roughly into two types: technical cyberattacks on networks that run everything from our electrical grids to our financial transactions, and content-oriented, sophisticated information war that uses a wide array of information tools as weapons. Content attack operations employ media warfare, legal warfare, psychological warfare, traditional public diplomacy, and strategic communications along with secret or semi-secret operations such as disinformation—the use of false and misleading information—and covert influence activities. All these are designed to achieve strategic objectives without resorting to direct military force.

What is equally clear is that under the policies of President Barack Obama, the United States has been dangerously disarmed in the information warfare sphere and has been rendered incapable of countering this emerging strategic threat. Obama adopted security and foreign policies based on the liberal progressive misunderstanding that threats could be wished away with high-minded policies that foolishly sought to redefine adversaries as friends while distancing America from its traditional friends and allies abroad. The result has been a national disaster that could threaten American interests and the security of Americans for a generation, as both nation-states and nonstate terrorist and criminal groups act with seeming impunity around the world.

The ultimate danger is that the peace and security of the United States, once secured by two oceans and friendly neighbors to the north and south, is quickly becoming a thing of the past.

As the utility of conventional armed warfare and high-end nuclear war diminishes, these new forms of conflict are being carried out through information operations, as nations seek to advance political and strategic objectives without the physical destruction that accompanies traditional forms of warfare.

Worse still, the United States government and the public remain completely in the dark about this new and potentially existential threat facing the country and its interests. Under Obama and his administration, the American people have been inundated by a false political narrative that has come to dominate both government and elite American strategic thinking. This narrative argues that the world has evolved past traditional rivalries and the concept of national interest itself. Instead, the Obama worldview asserted—falsely—that we currently live in a cosmopolitan dreamworld of global cooperation and shared values that regards international peace and harmony as a common aspiration of all nations.

This naïve approach to world affairs under which all peoples of the world can now sit around the proverbial campfire and sing "Kumbaya" has been promoted by the president and his ideologically driven aides with policies that deliberately abrogated American world leadership. It is an ideology based on a destructive liberal, left-wing political view that argues that the underlying cause of all the world's problems is the world geopolitical system dominated by the American superpower, a superpower that seeks to promote its brand of freedom and democracy for all.

Much of the problem can be traced to a traditional news media that has failed to understand foreign information threats and done little to expose them.

Unfortunately, this postmodern worldview has produced not a more peaceful planet, but a new world disorder. China, a nuclear-armed communist dictatorship despite its socialist economic reforms, is advancing its vision of an antidemocratic and anticapitalist political and economic system at the same time it is working to undermine and ultimately destroy the U.S.-led international system based on American concepts of freedom and individual liberty as the path to prosperity.

Russia has reemerged from the Cold War era as a new aggressor, with its leader, Vladimir Putin, seeking to reassert Soviet-style hegemony—and to undermine U.S. leadership and influence.

Information warfare carried out by the Islamist regime in Iran, the world's deadliest state sponsor of global terrorism, has deceived Obama in seeking to emerge from the chaos of the Middle East as the dominant regional power, and North Korea in recent decades has been given free rein to develop nuclear weapons and missile delivery systems unimpeded, a development that not only perpetuates its crimes-against-humanity regime but poses growing threats to both regional states and the U.S. homeland—the ultimate target of Pyongyang's growing arsenal of nuclear missiles.

Social media has emerged as the newest platform in the forefront of information warfare. Twitter, the 140-character microblog for disseminating news and information, boasts 320 million users—nearly 80 percent located outside the United States. Social media giant Facebook has 1.59 billion users—nearly a quarter of the world's population, and it too reports that more than 83 percent of its users reside outside the United States. Other media such as LinkedIn (255 million), Pinterest (250 million), Google+ (120 million), Tumblr (110 million), and Instagram (100 million) are among the new platforms in the emerging landscape of information warfare.

Few outside the secretive world of U.S. intelligence agencies know that months before the September 11, 2012, terrorist attack in Benghazi, Libya, that killed a U.S. ambassador and three other Americans, the Islamist militias that carried out the deadly attacks on CIA and State Department facilities were posting photos of the arms and equipment they were sending to fellow Islamist rebels fighting in Syria's civil war, the new spawning ground for global terrorism.

Information warfare is rapidly becoming the new mode of strategic international conflict with the expansion of the Internet and other information-based networks and technology. Information warfare is the extension of traditional conflict using computer-origin cyberattacks, strategic propaganda and disinformation operations, the use of laws and legal systems to wage warfare, media warfare, and covert intelligence operations that seek to advance strategic objectives. In military terms, it is defined as the use of information-related capabilities to influence, disrupt, corrupt, or usurp the decision-making capabilities of adversaries and potential adversaries.

China's communist leaders, steeped in ancient strategy, represent the current state of the art of information warfare, as seen in Beijing's decades-long strategic deception campaign to falsely convince world publics that Beijing poses no threat. The campaign has been so successful that for decades the highest levels of the U.S. government and intelligence services were deceived, as when the director of the Pentagon's Defense Intelligence Agency (DIA) in the late 1990s told me that China posed no threat to the United States because Chinese leaders had said so. It was a glaring example of the effectiveness of information warfare strategic deception.

Pivotal to the rise of foreign information warfare programs has been the failure of American public diplomacy and counter-disinformation efforts.

After the fall of the Soviet Union in 1991, U.S. government information programs proved nothing less than disastrous. This failure accelerated in 1999, when the once-powerful U.S. Information Agency (USIA), the large federal government system that provided truthful and relevant information to world publics starved for such information under dictatorial regimes, was shut down and its functions folded into the State Department. Since that time, American public diplomacy and strategic information warfare capabilities have declined or been eliminated. The ones remaining are ill-suited to challenges and confrontations posed by today's foreign information threats, which have increased sharply in both technical capability as well as impact over the past two decades.

Today, the scourge of political correctness in American society is pervasive and represents a dangerous political ideology confronting the country. Political correctness has become a leftist ideology defined as policies, language, and measures that go to extreme lengths to avoid offending specific groups being promoted by the Left as part of a political narrative aimed at producing liberal or progressive changes in society. From Hollywood to the news media to corporate boardrooms, free speech and honest political discourse and debate have been stifled through the false ideology dominated by the use of liberal left bromides that have turned the phrase "Land of the free, home of the brave" into "Watch what you say and fear any politically incorrect utterance."

Without a dedicated agency like USIA, and hamstrung by political correctness, strategic efforts to extend the American dream of a world based on principles and values of democracy, equality, and freedom have foundered. Instead, the remaining entity engaged in promoting U.S. policies abroad is the Broadcasting Board of Governors, a small group composed mainly of inexperienced communicators who oversee official U.S. radio broadcasts. The quality and quantity of those broadcasts and U.S. democracy and freedom promotion efforts declined sharply after the demise in 1999 of USIA, which, while limited in scope, had bolstered the democratic revolutions that emerged in the aftermath of the Soviet collapse in 1991.

In the early 1980s, when I was working as a reporter for the *Washington Times,* cutting-edge technology in the newsroom consisted of IBM Selectric typewriters. The typewriters soon were replaced by large, early-generation desktop computers equipped with cathode-ray tube displays. The first portable computers followed and were bulky, heavy, and the size of a small suitcase. They eventually were replaced by the first truly portable computing devices made by RadioShack and designated TRS-80 computers, affectionately nicknamed "Trash 80s." These first laptop computers carried almost no memory and used small, difficult-to-see liquid crystal screens about four by ten inches in size. But the TRS-80 represented a sea change for the communications revolution taking place at that time. For the first time in history, reporters could remotely file digital text stories from a small, portable device through telephone lines connected directly to the computer. The electronic grinding noise made by the often-iffy phone connection was an adventure in communications. But the process eliminated the slow and cumbersome process of having to retype newspaper hard copy from facsimile pages, or from voice dictation, in filing news stories remotely. The digitization process would revolutionize the news business within a few short years.

I have been covering national security affairs for more than three decades. Over that period I have developed a reputation as one of the most well-sourced news reporters in the world, and someone who remains on the leading edge of some of the world's important stories. Information warfare is only now emerging as one of those strategically important stories.

During my career, I have been extremely fortunate to have the front-row seat I had in the dawning of the Information Age. I covered some of the most important stories of the Cold War, ranging from the threat of nuclear annihilation and efforts to prevent it, to the clandestine spy wars waged relentlessly between the United States and the aggressive intelligence services of the communist world.

One indicator of my success is the frequent denunciations both domestically and internationally for regularly breaking major news stories. Vyacheslav Trubnikov, director of the Russian Foreign Intelligence Service between 1996 and 2000, once called me a "tool of the CIA" for an exposé on Russian intelligence operations in the Balkans. For reports exposing Chinese military activities, the official Chinese state news agency, Xinhua, disparaged me as the number-one "anti-China expert" in the world. (For the record, I remain very much pro-China—pro-Chinese people.) Former CIA director R. James Woolsey had this to say: "When I was DCI [Director of Central Intelligence] Bill used to drive me crazy because I couldn't figure out where the leaks were coming from. Now that I've been outside for two years, I read him religiously to find out what's going on." And former defense secretary Donald Rumsfeld once told me, "You're drilling holes in the Pentagon and sucking out information." I do not think the remark was meant as a compliment, but as a news reporter that certainly has been one key part of the job.

Today's ubiquitous handheld information devices remain the cutting edge—for now—of the Information Age. Today's cell phones, tablets, and computers possess more computing power than room-sized supercomputers of the 1990s. These small devices have come to dominate our lives. And they also are transforming our lives, as we become intricately connected to these advanced and increasingly sophisticated information and communication machines. Yet even with these technological marvels that we so take for granted in our daily lives, we are in the early stages of seeing the application of their full potential. The possibilities seem limitless. The Internet of Things will be the next level of our expanding electronic connectivity beyond computers and cell phones, and will further integrate our electronic devices. And it's not just things, but services. Using the ride-sharing app Uber to get from place to place has already become a verb. Future networks will reach into the myriad of micromechanical devices, from our cars and the elements of our cars, to our home appliances to thousands of other devices that will be part of our fully digital universe.

Information dominates our lives and has revolutionized the way we work and play—and soon how we wage war. It affects everything from how we communicate, educate, and inform to how we do business and entertain ourselves. Unfortunately, the dark side of the technology is that it is changing the nature of modern warfare.

Perhaps the most visible element of the information warfare revolution is cyberwarfare. Cyberattacks, once limited to hackers defacing websites with banners proclaiming some political cause, are becoming increasingly dangerous and destructive. Sophisticated intelligence services like those employed by China and Russia currently are capable of causing widespread destruction that potentially could produce mass casualties like those seen in previous major wars. Russia's spy services were caught hacking American political organizations and using the stolen emails, audio, and documents to try to influence the outcome of the 2016 presidential election. China already has infiltrated U.S. information networks on a grand scale and is believed to be preparing for future warfare that will involve computer-based attacks capable of shutting down U.S. electrical power grids, or destroying the networks used by financial institutions, thus crippling our ability to function as a nation and disrupting civil society in ways we have yet to fully fathom.

The Internet itself was shown to be vulnerable to cyberattack. On October 21, 2016, major portions of the Internet in the United States were shut down in massive denial of service attacks. Three waves of escalating automated attacks conducted millions of attempts to remotely access server farms at a key Internet firm in New Hampshire called Dyn. The attempts crushed the company's data-handling capability, and its servers failed, causing massive Internet outages on the East Coast and eventually the West Coast. Dyn provides Internet services for thousands of websites, including six percent of Fortune 500 companies, and the shutdown produced outages at Twitter, Spotify, Amazon AWS, Amazon Ads, Reddit, PayPal, and other major players. No data was stolen but the action represented the first major cyberattack involving the Internet of Things. Instead of using hijacked computers, the unknown hackers hijacked tens of millions of different connected devices infected with malware, including webcams, security cameras, DVRs, smart TVs, routers, and similar devices and used them to conduct remote access attempts at Dyn. Authorities said the attack coincided with the release of malicious distributed denial of service (DDOS) software called Mirai.

Aside from a failure to counter information warfare, one bright spot is the United States' program to prepare for one part of information warfare—cyberwarfare. Still, that capability has remained limited by the imposition of government policies designed to wish away information threats as somehow inconvenient relics of an earlier age. Our capability to wage information warfare—both cyber and content—also has been weakened by legal and bureaucratic impediments that have left the nation extremely vulnerable to widespread destructive cyberattacks that could kill millions.

In 2016, American government leaders and policies remained locked in destructive self-denial about these threats. The dominant thinking within government was that this is a time when adversaries are things of the past.

The central challenge for the twenty-first century will be

to harness the tools of the American technological and information revolution for good. And more important, to oppose evil. Yes, the terms *good* and *evil* may sound anachronistic to newer generations raised on value-neutral liberal leftism. But the nation as a whole urgently needs to return to the values of freedom and justice for all, which have been lost in the cacophony of acrimonious political debate so prevalent today.

To remedy the problems and counter the threats outlined in this book, I am proposing a series of concrete plans and actions for creating "Information America," a U.S. Information Agency–like organization designed for the twenty-first century and tooled for the Information Age and the threats it poses. The organization will promote fundamental American ideals and values, while working to counter lies and disinformation, using truth and facts as the ultimate weapons of information war. The task is urgent in a world racked by violence and hatred. Creating effective information-based capabilities offers the promise of solving some of the world's most pressing problems through the use of information as a strategic tool to promote peace and freedom.

WORLD WAR C

Munitions of the Mind

Cyberspace has become a full-blown war zone as governments across the globe clash for digital supremacy in a new, mostly invisible theater of operations.
—FireEye, "World War C: Understanding Nation-State Motives Behind Today's Advanced Cyber Attacks"

The world today is on fire and social media networks are providing the fuel to keep it burning. From the 2009 Green Revolution in Iran, which brought thousands into the streets to protest corrupt elections, to dissidents in China pressing democratic political reform, to the Arab Spring, which morphed into the horrors of the Syrian civil war, social media is emerging as the new front in global information conflict.

The al Qaeda–inspired terrorist attack at Foot Hood, Texas, in 2009, and the Islamic State–backed terrorist attacks in San Bernardino, California, in 2015 and Orlando, Florida, in 2016 were all linked to overseas terrorism through social media. They are signs that more and increasingly deadly terrorists attacks—suicide bombings and shootings—are likely to be unleashed against the United States *inside* the country, despite the best efforts of American security authorities to try to stop them. The danger is real and must be recognized and countered through a concerted campaign against these threats on social media.

A key information warfare ploy of America's Islamist enemies has involved exploiting Western governments' indecision over what to do in response to mass killings and other deadly humanitarian disasters. The Islamists have adopted a coordinated strategy aimed at destabilizing and ultimately defeating the West with the ultimate objective of imposing an Islamic supremacist world order. The terrorists are waging jihad, or Islamic holy war, through their bombings, shootings, and other deadly attacks to create as much mayhem as possible. The strategy is based on their view that Western leaders lack the will to take the necessary steps to challenge both their actions and their ideology. Instead, the Islamists seek to provoke military responses by their non-Muslim targets that cost lives, deplete resources, and produce a kind of ideological disarmament in the West. In so doing, the enemies have manipulated the United States into hastening its own demise.

The use of Syrian refugees is a case in point. As millions of Syrians fled the Middle East and streamed into Europe beginning in 2015, little regard was given to the potential use of these refugee flows for the infiltration by Islamist terrorists and their sympathizers. Some of the worst fears were realized on New Year's Eve 2015 in Cologne, Germany, when around one thousand drunk and aggressive refugees went on a rape spree, sexually assaulting some eighty women at a central railway station.

Can similar attacks be expected in the United States? President Barack Obama by August 2016 had admitted 10,000 Syrian refugees, as more than 30,000 others waited for entry. While many of the refugees harbor no ill will, their ranks include Islamists who are either planning to conduct terrorists attacks or will be recruited to do so in the future. The Department of Homeland Security's Citizenship and Immigration Services chief, Matthew Emrich, told a Senate Judiciary Committee hearing that there was no way to properly screen the incoming Syrians for terrorist ties because of a lack of intelligence and an inability to check their backgrounds.

Around the same time the United States reached its 10,000-Syrian-refugees mark, the U.S. Southern Command, the military command responsible for Latin and South America, issued one of its most alarming warnings. The Southcom J-2 intelligence directorate reported in a secret dispatch that Sunni extremists from the Middle East and elsewhere were entering the United States with ease. According to officials familiar with the warning, the report was ignored because it conflicted with the Obama administration's policy of promoting emigration by Syrians and the president's personal sympathy toward Islam.

Britain's government-run British Broadcasting Corporation, in an internal analysis provided to the CIA, warned in 2013 that social media was becoming a major weapon for Islamic terrorists. "The adoption of Twitter by Arabic-speaking jihad supporters has massively changed the landscape of the online jihad over the past year, presenting both opportunities and challenges for media jihad operatives," the BBC said. "Originally embraced as a means of spreading the jihadist message to a wider audience, Twitter has now become an established feature of the online jihad." Jihad is the Islamic concept of holy war and has been used by terrorists to conduct deadly and indiscriminate attacks in advancing the cause of creating a world dominated by Islam. According to an Islamic State magazine, *Dabiq*, the name *Islam* is derived from the Arabic words *istislam* and *salamah*, or submission and sincerity. "This is the essence of Islam, to submit to Allah sincerely (i.e., to Him alone)," the magazine stated.

The BBC in January 2016 revealed even more sophisticated Islamic State media operations that are used to project the group's power and create the fiction that it is a fully functioning state.

"A distinct feature of IS's media operation is its agility and ability to respond quickly to events, often outperforming state media in the Middle East," the BBC said. "This has been enabled by the group's sophisticated use of social media and a network of dedicated online supporters who amplify IS's message. Despite an ongoing clampdown on IS-affiliated accounts on Twitter and other platforms, the group's material continues to surface in a timely manner. Exploitation of the messaging app Telegram has helped the group secure a more stable and resilient mechanism for distributing its propaganda."

Telegram is a Russian-produced messaging application that has become a key tool for Islamic State terrorists seeking to block surveillance and spying by U.S. and other intelligence services. It uses a strong data encryption that while not unbreakable is difficult to unscramble. Telegram forums used by the group include both propaganda and instructional materials, such as how to avoid being identified online.

Communications are not the only use of social media. Islamic State supporters sought to instill panic after the March 2016 terror attacks in Brussels, Belgium. Several jihadist Twitter accounts from Islamic State sympathizers spread rumors of further attacks throughout the city. The tweets included statements saying not to take victims to Brussels's St. Pierre hospital, as bombs had been planted there, and that bombs were planted at the Free University. "URGENT / Several bombs placed at European Commission! Evacuate urgently or die!" a third tweet warned.

Civil war in Syria revealed as never before the integration of both information warfare and traditional armed conflict. The Internet and social media are being used there by the Islamic State and other terrorist groups as a command-and-control platform for its forces to communicate orders, dispatch forces, synchronize military activities, and gather intelligence. Terrorists also can crowdsource—seek support from online users—their campaigns on social media to learn the best methods for building bombs and explosives, attacking targets, and even developing high-technology arms, such as unmanned aerial vehicles.

Modern warfare is shifting away from large-scale territorial conflicts between the military forces of nation-states to different forms of organized violence—including the lower-level and middle-level insurgencies and internal conflicts like those in Afghanistan and Syria. Social media also is fueling the information conflicts waged by Russia in Ukraine, and China in its maritime and territorial disputes along its periphery.

Warfare by conventional military forces to achieve victory over other conventional forces is becoming less common. Instead, information-dominated activities, such as cyberattacks, influence operations, and propaganda and disinformation attacks are dominating the modern battlefield in a bid to control and influence populations according to desired ends.

The United States and the West have failed utterly to recognize this danger while their governments continue to rely heavily on military forces for achieving state goals, despite the fact that the military is ill-suited to resolving these conflicts.

The debacle of Afghanistan highlights the problem. More than a decade and tens of billions of dollars in military activities have produced nothing approaching a stable, Western-oriented state in the mountainous and backward Southwest Asian country, which remains as prone to terrorist control as it was when al Qaeda first made the country its headquarters in the 1990s.

Social media networks currently are among the most potent arms, what Thomas Elkjer Nissen of the Royal Danish Defence College has called the "weaponization of social media." Instead of simply destroying targets with bombs and other weapons to produce desired military effects, modern warfare is moving to the Internet and information networks like social media, while employing a broad array of nonmilitary methods—political, economic, social, psychological, cyber—to produce effects that in the past were the domain of military force. Nissen identified the militarization of social media—by both states and nonstate groups—as intelligence gathering, targeting, psychological warfare, cyberattacks, and command and control.

U.S. military information warfare programs and operations have been hampered by a destructive internal debate over informing and influencing target audiences. The military in this field has been dominated by those who advocate limiting information operations to informing, through public affairs and other media activities. The influence operations as a result have been reduced to almost zero, because the use of information influence tools may involve lying or deceiving targets and thus would represent official government lying, something currently banned in most liberal democracies as a core principle.

That must change if the United States is to prevail over its adversaries in the Information Age, as states like China, Russia, Iran, and many others routinely and systematically use lies and deception as policies authorized and deployed in pursuit of strategic goals. As mentioned, the Islamic

State also uses lies and deception in its operations against the civilized world, based on the Islamic tenet that lying to infidels—anyone who is not Muslim—is not only permitted but required in pursuit of jihad and the establishment of a global Islamic-controlled world. Psychological warfare operations aimed at influencing global publics figure prominently in this new warfare waged extensively through social media networks, what have been called "munitions of the mind"— using media to persuade people to think and act in ways that benefit those using psychological warfare operations.

The Information Age and new technology for the first time have given adversaries the tools to communicate directly with target audiences to achieve strategic objectives after a time in the past when they were blocked by traditional media controls on information.

Social media warfare is intricately connected to technology, especially the handheld communications device. Fifty years ago, on September 8, 1966, the popular science fiction TV series *Star Trek* broadcast its first episode. Ten minutes into the show, Starship captain James T. Kirk reached into his pocket and flipped open a small, handheld device with a gold mesh cover accompanied by a small electronic chirp. "Transporter room," Kirk called, "lock on to us. Three beaming up." Kirk's communicator marveled us as a science fiction pipe dream of a small, portable device capable of making personal communications without wires in an instant. It would take Motorola engineer Martin Cooper another seven years to make the first personal cell phone call while walking the streets of Manhattan. Cooper took his inspiration for mobile phones from the Star Trek communicator.

Within a few decades, mobile communications devices rapidly evolved into the powerful handheld ones that have become ubiquitous and by 2016 represented the leading edge of the Information Age. An iPhone 7 packs more computing power than a gigantic Cray-2 supercomputer did in 1985. More than the hardware, the use of our handheld devices today is expanding the frontiers of the Internet through the use of the World Wide Web's most popular feature: social media—information tools that facilitate everything from how we communicate to how we interact with society at large. The new media platforms are impacting all aspects of our lives, from business, to politics, to science, to relationships, and of course to journalism and the news business. It is impacting our lives in ways that were only imagined in the realm of science fiction of the 1960s.

Facebook and Twitter have emerged as the dominant social media, hosting hundreds of millions of users who interact almost constantly. Many other platforms also are popular and newer and different social media are expected to emerge in the near future. As a veteran newspaper reporter and proverbial ink-stained wretch, I have come to conclude that no other type of media on the Internet claims as much of our time and attention as social media. And these platforms are making us more interconnected, communicative, and engaged than at any other time in human history.

According to the business website eBizMBA, the top

fifteen social media sites log more than 2.5 billion unique visitors, a staggering number of interactive users. In addition to Facebook and Twitter, with 1.1 billion and 310 million users, respectively, other major platforms include LinkedIn (250 million), Pinterest (250 million), Google+ (120 million), Tumblr (110 million), Instagram (100 million), VKontakte, or VK (80 million), and Flickr (65 million). Other social media powerhouses: Vine (42 million), Meetup (40 million), Tagged (38 million), ASKfm (37 million), MeetMe (15.5 million), and Classmates (15 million).

The activities on these platforms range from blogging with family and friends to promoting news and commercial interests, such as seen in the Facebook and Google+ model, to microblogging, as shown by Twitter, which mixes short messages with links to other content. LinkedIn is more commonly used by business professionals for networking, and Instagram and Flickr support avid photo and video aficionados.

After Twitter's emergence in 2006 I considered the 140-character social media outlet as the most important emerging tool for news dissemination and an extremely valuable source of unfiltered news and information that can be available in my handheld nearly instantaneously. In the past, getting rapid news and information was limited to listening to the radio or watching breaking news on cable television. That model was shattered for me in the spring of 2013 as I sat on the balcony of my brother's Northern California home overlooking San Francisco when the Associated Press first reported details in my heavily news-oriented Twitter feed announcing an explosion near the finish line of the Boston Marathon. Within minutes of the April 15 terrorist attack, I knew something terrible had happened and immediately began working the story of how the two émigré brothers from Russia had become radical jihadists and set off home-made pressure-cooker bombs built from instructions posted online in an al Qaeda magazine.

Another example of a revolutionary news report for the Twitter news hall of fame, if such a place were created, would be the tweet from Pakistan by Sohaib Athar on May 1, 2011: "Helicopter hovering above Abbottabad at 1AM (is a rare event)." Athar inadvertently had disclosed the biggest news scoop of the decade, which would later be revealed as the daring U.S. Navy SEAL special operations raid to kill al Qaeda terror leader Osama bin Laden, the mastermind be-hind the September 11, 2001, terrorist attacks in New York and Washington, D.C.

The explosion of social media, unfortunately, is not limited to disseminating news, texting our friends, posting thoughts about the hamburger we ate for lunch, or sharing hilarious cat videos. Social media is rapidly becoming the new battleground in a larger information war being waged by a variety of states and enemies.

Today, a war of words unlike any previous conflict in history is playing out on social media platforms around the world. From Islamic State terrorists in Syria, to dissident Chinese Communist Party members, to Russian democrats opposing the authoritarian rule of Russian leader Vladimir Putin, social media has become a new engine of information warfare to support democratic causes, as entrenched dictators seek to harness media platforms for their own purposes, mainly to constrain freedoms and democracy, or to perpetuate authoritarian rule.

Within a decade, the social media revolution produced worldwide upheaval, beginning with Iran's pro-reform Green Revolution in 2009, when thousands of Iranians took to the streets to protest rigged elections. The protests sparked what would become the Arab Spring, which began in December 2010 with demonstrations against corruption and political repression in Tunisia, which brought down the government in Tunis after a street vendor set himself on fire to protest police confiscating his unlicensed produce cart. Within months, governments and rulers throughout North Africa and the Middle East were toppled in Egypt, Libya, and Yemen.

Protests and civil unrest spread to Bahrain, Algeria, Iraq, Jordan, Kuwait, Morocco, and Sudan. Perhaps the most devastating upheaval of the Arab Spring occurred in Syria, where unrest set in motion a deadly chain of events leading to the rise of an ultraviolent offshoot of al Qaeda, what became known as the Islamic State. All the Arab Spring upheavals were facilitated by social media, specifically Facebook and Twitter, which publicized the events and inspired people to take to the streets by the thousands. By 2016, Libya had been transformed into a failed state and a new safe haven for Islamist terrorists. Syria's civil war has claimed more than 200,000 lives and spawned the Islamic State takeover of an area the size of New England, with some 6 million people living under its control. The Islamic State was the first terrorist group to emerge from the shadows of covert suicide and bombing attacks into a group declaring an expansionist goal of seizing and holding territory and seeking further gains. By mid-2016, the group was pulling down some $4 million a day through taxes imposed on people under its control and through oil sales and other financial activities.

Studies showed that social media helped trigger the Arab Spring protests by allowing participants to coordinate protests. As journalist Malcolm Gladwell noted in the *New Yorker*, social media made *how* information was communicated more important than *what* was communicated. Of Mao's notion that political power grows from the barrel of a gun, today's social media aficionados would likely note: "Whoa. Did you see what Mao just tweeted?"

Social media warfare is not limited to events overseas. In the United States, the 2016 presidential campaign unleashed one of the most bitter and hostile political battles in recent history. Candidates took to Twitter and Facebook to attack and discredit rivals for the highest U.S. office.

Establishment political candidates for both the Democratic and Republican parties who could not master the 140-character virtual machine gun of Twitter quickly found themselves outgunned by social media warriors supporting outliers on the Republican side like Senator Ted Cruz and the eventual nominee, businessman Donald Trump, and Democratic candidate and self-declared socialist revolutionary Senator Bernie Sanders.

But it was the New York real estate mogul Trump, using a masterful strategy of provocation, exaggeration, hyperbole, and verbal assault, who will be remembered for scoring political breakthroughs at key points early in the campaign that eventually produced his Republican nomination. For the first time since Dwight D. Eisenhower, a noncareer politician captured a major party nomination. Trump used Twitter like a bulldozer, ravaging opponents or anyone else he disliked with what the *New York Times* called "pithy, mean, and powerful" word blasts. Analysis by the online media outlet *Slate* revealed his genius for social media warfare in Trump's ability to use three Aristotelian modes of persuasion, in tweets that captured appeals to logos, ethos, and pathos— logic, credibility, and emotion. Practically, this played out by using a statement of fact, followed by criticism of opponents' credibility and then an emotional coup de grace, most often enhanced by the use of biting humor thrown in. Perhaps one of Trump's most devastating tweets targeted *Huffington Post* editor Arianna Huffington, hit with this famous missive in 2012: "@ariannahuff is unattractive both inside and out. I fully understand why her former husband left her for a man—he made a good decision." Typical of the approach was Trump's tweet after one presidential debate: "Wow, @CNN got caught fixing their 'focus group' in order to make Crooked Hillary look better. Really pathetic and totally dishonest!"

Trump's use of social media warfare will set the tone for

political campaigns for years to come. Republican rivals were picked off one by one during the primaries, leaving the moderate Republican governor from Ohio, John Kasich, who appealed to many middle-of-the-road Republicans, without a fighting chance. "Unfortunately, in the world in which we live there are concepts of truth, truthiness, reality, wikiality—wikiality being the thing most people believe, not necessarily the reality of the situation," says Shelly Palmer, a social media and technology expert. "And what we've learned since the dawn of social media is, to steal a line from mathematics, the narrative that wins is not the one that can draw the line of best fit to the truth, but the one that is inside the blanket that comforts the listener," he told me.

Social media has spawned an age when technology has allowed people to filter news and information to suit their tastes and beliefs, creating multiple realities and truths. The filtered state is so secure, one no longer needs to venture outside one's informational comfort zone. "The concept of truth no longer exists," Palmer says. "It's the concept of belief systems and ideology which make you tribal in a way that is actually more tribal than ever in history and it's electronically filtered from other tribes. That is fascinating." Kasich provided an example of a politician who failed to grasp the power of social media to communicate his political message and tenets to potential voters. As Palmer put it: "This guy was invisible because he's not controversial. He gets no attention because in the twenty-first century—warfare or otherwise—it's important to be important, and he is not."

Facebook, the largest social media outlet, boasts of its

ability to connect family and friends with blogs, photos, and videos, and of allowing commercial entities to promote their business. For the news business, Facebook outpaces all other social media in its ability to reach millions of readers. Facebook has come under fire from some critics over its policies and its founder, Mark Zuckerberg, who so craved recognition from communist China and its market of 1.3 billion people that he asked Chinese supreme leader Xi Jinping to name the child Zuckerberg and his wife were expecting (Xi declined). Internet news pioneer Matt Drudge, whose website *Drudge Report* dominates both old and new media in terms of reaching millions of readers, sees a different picture of Facebook, Twitter, and other corporatist social media giants. Drudge believes social media is stifling Internet freedoms by using technology controls that prevent free speech and expression, and negatively influencing world populations. The famed Internet mogul emerged from years of self-imposed obscurity in October 2015 to rail against what he termed the ghettoization of the Internet under big social media powers that exercise control through a dangerous groupthink. "This whole social media stuff is bogus," Drudge told Alex Jones, the popular Internet radio host on the website Infowars. "Facebook has two billion users? This is garbage, this is designed to demoralize the individual."

Facebook would also come under fire in 2016 amid accusations of censoring news articles posted on its platform by conservatives and libertarians. Facebook also prevents "friends" who connect with outlets or people on their platform from reaching outside their group, which is limited to five thousand friends; for more than that, a user must then set up a public Facebook page that controls what followers and supporters the user can reach. Additionally, if public users want to reach the hundreds of thousands of supporters of their Facebook pages with news or other information, they must pay large sums to Facebook, because the social media platform strictly controls the technology and prevents free interaction with its 1.1 billion users. Like a technology prophet, Drudge offered this ominous declaration: "I'm just warning this country: Don't get into this false sense that you are an individual when you're on Facebook. No, you're not; you're a pawn in their scheme."

Facebook was criticized for engaging in partisan politics during the 2016 presidential election campaign when someone from inside the company posted online an internal company listing of proposed questions to ask Zuckerberg during an employee meeting on March 4. One of the questions posed was "What responsibility does Facebook have to help prevent President Trump in 2017?" The question pointed to the company's political outlook and how that would affect its 1.1 billion users. As a privately owned entity, Facebook has the power to allow or block any content. The posting raised questions about what happens when a social media giant operating in the United States and internationally decides to adopt a political viewpoint and act on it. Facebook hosted at least two sites promoting Trump for president, and other presidential contenders relied on it to influence voters.

• • •

On the terrorism social media front, the Islamic State's efficient use of social media sites for its operations created new challenges for American counterterrorism officials. Beginning in 2013, Facebook and Twitter executives struggled to deal with competing demands from U.S. intelligence agencies to allow spying on Islamic State (IS) operatives and sympathizers who were using social media in ways that were yielding valuable intelligence on operations and leaders. Others in government argued social media is assisting Islamists in advancing terrorist goals and that they should not be allowed to use the microblog and blog forums to spread propaganda, recruit members, and communicate in the field and worldwide. As a result of the shift by terrorists to using social media, U.S. and other Western intelligence agencies now devote hundreds of personnel and millions of dollars in resources to monitoring social media for key indicators of terrorists' plans and strategies, mainly to try to determine if major attacks are being planned and what the targets are likely to be. As the number, scale, and geographic location of the major IS attacks of 2015 and 2016 demonstrated, intelligence agencies have not been able to effectively tap into social media in seeking to forestall mass killings and bombings. Paris, San Bernardino, Brussels, Baghdad, and Kabul all suffered major IS-related attacks. From 2013 through July 2016, the death toll from IS attacks numbered more than 3,000 killed and more than 6,300 injured.

A review of open-source intelligence reporting reveals that Western intelligence services are struggling to balance the need to keep track of terrorist group members and their statements with actions by Twitter and Facebook to shut down the accounts for advocating violence or otherwise promoting illegal terrorist activities. Spy agencies use their access to classified intelligence—mostly electronic collection by the National Security Agency—to identify key terrorist leaders and operators and communicate to Facebook and Twitter that certain people should not be shut down. For the terrorist sympathizers—those not directly involved in terrorist activities—intelligence agencies recognize that these people are propagandists who are supporting the cause and must be countered in different ways.

Social media postings on Twitter and Facebook by key players in the terrorist underworld often provide clues to online friends' and followers' locations and in some cases the postings can be traced electronically. "They often come to us and say, 'Do not take down these accounts,'" one social media executive told me of U.S. government spying efforts. Terrorists also use YouTube to post videos. Syrian Islamic State terrorists have utilized the technique to great effect over the course of their operations in Syria and Iraq, uploading gruesome videos showing Islamists beheading people, carrying out mass executions, burning people alive, and running over victims with tanks—all for the shock value of showing the ideological commitment to do what is needed to advance the cause of jihad against the West. Twitter and Facebook executives declined to discuss on the record their policies for dealing with online terrorists. However, spokesmen for both companies told me they try to balance concerns for security and stopping criminal activity with the need for free speech and openness. Additionally, Twitter and Facebook would not talk about interaction with governments on counterterrorism. They instead pointed to online policy statements governing the sharing of members' data with law enforcement and implicitly with U.S. intelligence agencies. Both companies require court orders or subpoenas before granting access to user data. Search warrants are needed for access to communications. Twitter user profile data is all public, as are tweets. Facebook's format allows private social interaction, although it remains a very open medium with few restrictions on content or users.

"At Facebook, we have rules that bar direct statements of hate, attacks on private individuals and groups, and the promotion of terrorism," a Facebook spokesman told me. "Where hateful content is posted and reported, Facebook removes it and disables accounts of those responsible." The problem for both Twitter and Facebook is the vast numbers of accounts and huge numbers of postings. Neither company actively monitors the millions of tweets and billions of Facebook postings placed online each day. Facebook users post an estimated 4.75 billion pieces of content every day. The company could not provide statistics for the number of reports of abuse by Islamists. Instead, the company relies exclusively on users to report abuses of Facebook's terms of service.

Facebook has teams of specialists who respond to reports of abuse and review the cases. "When that happens, a user operations team reviews that content and sees if it violates the terms of service," the spokesman said. "If it does, it will be taken down quickly and the user is notified."

Like Facebook, Twitter does not actively monitor content and relies on users to report cases of abuse amid the more than 500 million tweets posted every day, in more than thirty-six languages. Twitter receives hundreds of abuse reports daily, often with requests to close accounts. Several Twitter teams operating in different time zones also review the reports. In many cases the requests are dismissed because the reports falsely identified violations of the terms of service. Twitter also seeks to promote free speech, within its rules. The company operates globally and as a result has agreed to comply with the laws of the countries where it operates. For example, Germany, because of its Nazi past, imposes stricter laws against anti-Semitism than the United States. So the company applies filters specific to content posted in Germany to block anti-Semitic tweets. Twitter teams that review objectionable content are made up of a variety of security experts, civil liberties advocates, linguists, and others who consult on reported abuses.

Social media remains a key tool in information warfare to influence publics and create what have been dubbed weapons of mass disruption. "Low-cost, easily accessible social media tools act as a force multiplier by increasing networking and organizing capabilities," says Catherine A. Theohary, an information security specialist at the U.S. Congressional Research Service. "The ability to rapidly disseminate graphic images and ideas to shape the public narrative transforms social media into a strategic weapon in the hands of terrorists, insurgent groups, or governments engaged in conflict."

"ISIL is the first social media–fueled terrorist group,"

Secretary of Defense Ashton Carter said in April 2016. While its predecessor, al Qaeda, relied more on the Internet, the Islamic State has shifted to the use of social media. "These guys are able to go out and troll for people who are dissatisfied here and there," Carter said. The defense secretary could not answer how the military was working to deal with the problem of terrorists' use of social media for information warfare. Instead he resorted to the oft-stated claim that the group will be destroyed, first in Syria and Iraq. "So we need to destroy that idea by defeating ISIL in Iraq and Syria, and we're busy doing that," Carter said, noting the group was spreading to Europe, Asia, and other parts of the world. Social media, he noted, provides the group with a new tool.

Asked how to stop the terrorist group, Carter said there are two ways. One is to destroy them physically through military and intelligence operations, what he termed "the old-fashioned way."

"And the other," Carter said, "is we have to get better at countering social media, and it's partly by telling our own story, which is basically the truth, but it's also partly by not allowing these guys to use the Internet to do command control, to dominate populations, to take money from other people, pass money around the world, and we're doing that right now. Our cyber command, this is their first big operation in cyber, is to go into Iraq and Syria and take that tool away from these characters in Iraq and Syria, and that's what we're working on now." It is not clear whether the cyber military operations are producing the desired effects.

The notion of "telling the story" has been failing for the

United States and is a remnant of the twentieth century's ideological battle against Soviet communism. Islamists' use of social media shows no signs of being limited or countered, despite the efforts of U.S. intelligence agencies and the State Department, which created an office called the Center for Strategic Counterterrorism Communications (see Chapter 9). Terrorists are above all ideological information warriors, and efforts to defeat this enemy will require much more than is currently being done. "We are in a long war," declared Abu Firas al-Suri on social media used by the al Qaeda–affiliated Syrian rebel group Al-Nusra Front. "This war will not end in months nor years, this war could last for decades." In April 2016, al-Suri's role in the long war was cut short after he was killed in a U.S. air strike in Syria.

In China, Beijing's leaders have blocked U.S. social media outlets through censorship technology and in other cases used their political leverage to influence American social media. Twitter came under fire for naming as its managing director in that country Kathy Chen, who according to her LinkedIn profile once worked as general manager for a joint venture software company whose partner was the Ministry of State Security—China's civilian intelligence service. The company produced filtering software designed to block content from the anticommunist international movement Falun Gong. She also worked for a research institute affiliated with the People's Liberation Army, as the Chinese military is known. The intelligence and military credentials are indications that China's government will control Twitter in China. Chen announced in tweets issued after her appointment that she looked forward to working with Xinhua, the state news agency. The clearest sign of the problem was disclosed in an April 2016 report in the Communist Party–controlled *Global Times* newspaper that defended Chen. "Strong opposition against appointing Chen is an affair between the company and some of its users," the newspaper stated. "It brings no damage to the Chinese mainland and is not something we need to worry about. The incident gives us a glimpse into how extreme and ridiculous the overseas anti-China circle can be." A recommendation from one of the Communist Party's most xenophobic and anti-American propaganda organs should be a disqualification for the Twitter executive.

Twitter is banned in China, but the appointment of a government-linked director signaled that the social media site was preparing to pander to what has been called the Great Firewall of China—the Chinese government program to block uncontrolled content from reaching China's 600 million Internet users. *Global Times* said Twitter will not become another Weibo, the hugely popular microblogging service in China that is tightly controlled by the government. But the state-run outlet warned that if Twitter entered the Chinese market, "certain adjustments according to Chinese law would be necessary."

The appointment prompted Australian-based Chinese human rights activist Badiucao to post one of his biting social commentary artworks showing the Twitter bluebird logo being impaled by a yellow star like the one contained in the flag of the People's Republic of China. "Twitter is already dead," Badiucao proclaimed on the artwork. Outside the United States, China is one of two countries that have adopted near-paranoid obsessions with the revolutionary appeal of social media for protesters seeking to oust authoritarian regimes and replace them with more democratic systems. Like Twitter, Facebook is working diligently to convince China to allow the social media platform to operate freely in that communist country, something Beijing's propaganda officials as of 2016 had refused, fearing the power of a free and open platform to boost efforts—both within the Communist Party and outside the party and the country—to promote genuine democratic political reform in China.

Social media networks emerged in the United States as an outgrowth of the Internet and email. By 2016 they had become the preferred weapon in a new kind of information warfare that is still in its infancy. Understanding social media warfare is a strategic imperative if threats posed by nation-states like China and Russia and nonstate threats like Islamic terrorism are to be neutralized.

2

NORTH KOREA

Eternal Leader's Rocket Becomes Glorious Submarine to Fool Puppet Forces

We've obtained all your internal data including your secrets and top secrets. If you don't obey us, we'll release data shown below to the world.
—MESSAGE DISPLAYED ON HACKED COMPUTERS OF SONY PICTURES ENTERTAINMENT, NOVEMBER 24, 2014

The year is 2038 and Supreme Leader of North Korea Kim Jue Ae, daughter of the late Kim Jong Un, has taken power despite her young age. At twenty-five, Kim became the fourth hereditary communist dictator from the Kim family to take power—shortly after her father died mysteriously in a train crash many intelligence services suspect was the clandestine work of Chinese special forces. China's leaders had grown weary of the unpredictability of Kim Jong Un, who too frequently brandished his nuclear arsenal, and finally got him out of the way. The new leader actually was little more than a puppet of several North Korean military officers Beijing carefully had cultivated as agents for years. Unknown to the Chinese was that a secret faction inside the Korean People's Army maintained fanatical loyalty to the dead Kim and now planned to take revenge. On January 8, 2038, the KPA officers set in motion a dangerous plot to destroy the ruling Communist Party of China.

"Launch missiles!" the renegade North Korean commander ordered. One second later, a North Korean Sang-O-class (Shark-class) submarine hiding underwater near the U.S. island of Guam in the South Pacific fired two intermediate-range KN-21 missiles. The missile warheads traversed the 2,500-mile distance flawlessly, detonating several thousand feet above the leadership compound in central Beijing known as Zhongnanhai just as Supreme Leader Bo Guagua, son of the late neo-Maoist leader Bo Xilai, was leading a meeting of the nine-member Standing Committee of the Politburo of the Communist Party of China, the apex of power. The blasts from the 250-kiloton nuclear warheads destroyed the compound and everyone in it as well as all buildings within a ten-mile radius. The blast and subsequent firestorm killed millions more in the Chinese capital.

The North Koreans had planned the operation using cyberattacks that disabled key Chinese missile defense sensors. The missiles and warheads were outfitted with special electronic masking transmitters that made the missiles appear on a few operating Chinese radar and sensors exactly as U.S.-made Trident III submarine-launched ballistic missiles.

North Korean cyberwarfare specialists also broadcast coded English-language radio communications designed to deceive the Chinese military into believing the missiles had been launched from the USS Texas, one of the United States' newest ballistic missile submarines.

North Korean intelligence had succeeded in covertly penetrating the Chinese military command structure and using sophisticated cyberwarfare operations that convinced surviving Chinese leaders located at the underground command center known as the Western Hills complex that they had been the victim of an unprovoked American nuclear first strike.

In the nuclear war that followed, China struck several major American cities with retaliatory nuclear attacks from Ju Long-4 missiles launched from new Type 098 missile submarines. The attacks from the nuclear blasts and subsequent radiation plumes would kill some 50 million Americans.

Coinciding with the nuclear conflict, the North Korean military quickly seized the initiative in the chaos that followed the Beijing attack to launch a major land assault and seize all of northeastern China, once known as Manchuria, and which the Koreans believed historically is Korean territory. On the Korean Peninsula, North Korean special operations commandos, among the most deadly and highly trained forces in the world, quickly dispatched the South Korean political leadership after conducting devastating cyberattacks that had crippled the electric power infrastructure of its noncommunist neighbor and rival.

It would be years before the Chinese would discover they had been fooled into a global thermonuclear war by North

Korean information warfare operations in the devastating conflict known as World War III.

The above scenario is fictional but could become reality as the isolated totalitarian state known as the Democratic People's Republic of Korea poses one of the greatest threats in the modern world.

The reality of this North Korean threat can be traced to November 24, 2014. That date will be marked by historians as the beginning of World War C—for World War Cyber. On that day at around 8:30 a.m. Pacific time, cyberattackers working for the North Korean intelligence service the Reconnaissance General Bureau (RGB) fired a new type of shot heard 'round the world. But unlike previous conflicts, this war did not begin with a salvo of precision-guided cruise missiles or long-range bombing runs. The shock and awe was digital and the weapons were keystrokes tapped by RGB cyberwarriors operating secretly from hotels in China and Malaysia on behalf of North Korean dictator Kim Jong Un. Before it would end, Sony Pictures Entertainment, a company owned by Japan's electronics giant Sony, suffered multiple cyberattacks on several electronic fronts. Its computer networks would be pilfered of tens of terabytes of information, including unreleased films. Hardware was destroyed by malicious software planted inside that not only wiped hard drives clean but damaged computer operating systems, leaving the company's employees facing dreaded blue screens of computer death. Perhaps the worst damage was caused by the release of sensitive internal communications hacked by the North Koreans and posted on Pastebin, a common endpoint for hackers to place stolen digital information. The compromised data included lists of salaries paid to actors and Sony executives. The leaked information was quickly seized on by liberal news outlets under headlines decrying gaps in pay between men and women, and whites and nonwhites. In all, 38 million files were stolen and made public in the days following November 24.

The Sony Pictures Entertainment hack highlighted what will be the twenty-first century's predominant form of warfare—nonkinetic computer and information conflict. In the case of Sony, the war was waged by a foreign state against a private company over its production of a movie called *The Interview*, written and produced to mock and denigrate one of the world's worst dictators, Kim Jong Un. Sony's weapon in their own form of entertainment information warfare was humor. North Korea responded with a sophisticated cyberattack made worse by the release of the stolen information from the company, and bolstered with threats to carry out September 11–style terrorist attacks against American movie theaters that dared to show *The Interview*, which had been scheduled for release on Christmas Eve.

The story of North Korea's cyberattack against Sony began months earlier. It was driven by the studio's decision to name the North Korean leader, Kim Jong Un, a ruthless dictator who used large-caliber antiaircraft guns to execute his political opponents. Kim was a third-generation communist dictator from a family dynasty that has kept North Korea an anachronistic totalitarian police state. It is a country where the government routinely must announce that cannibalism is prohibited for citizens starving to death during frequent famines that regularly sweep the mountainous and impoverished Northeast Asian country every decade or so. The most alarming characteristic of North Korea is that it's a nation with an irrational and erratic leader in possession of an arsenal of ten to twenty nuclear weapons—and the missile delivery systems capable of firing those weapons thousands of miles.

Sony Pictures triggered the ire of the Kim regime with the decision of a studio executive to include the actual figure of Kim Jong Un in the script for the comedy. Early versions had referred to the leader as a fictional Kim Il Hwan, only marginally obscuring the actual supreme leader. According to *The Interview* screenwriter Dan Sterling, Kim Jong Un was made the protagonist of what Hollywood calls a "fart movie"—a ribald comedy—by changing Kim Il Hwan to Kim Jong Un. The movie's producers, Seth Rogen and Evan Goldberg, loved the change, according to *Vanity Fair* magazine. The plot follows two journalists, played by Rogen and James Franco, who are granted an interview by Kim Jong Un and are then asked by the CIA to assassinate him. "The CIA would love it if you two could take him out," a CIA character says in the movie. To which the Rogen character responds, "Take him out? Like for drinks?" "No, take him out. . . ."

The film was set for release in October and by June the trailer had been released. North Korea, perhaps the world leader in propaganda superlatives, reacted harshly.

On June 25, 2014, the North Korean Foreign Ministry denounced the film as a "despicable maneuver" by enemies seeking to tarnish the Pyongyang regime's dignity. The statement called Kim "our supreme nerve center" who was being insulted by the United States. "The United States' reckless frenzy of provocation—which is [seeking] to eliminate our supreme nerve center by using a gangster moviemaker as a front—is exploding the surging animosity and rage of our army and people," the statement said, adding that the film is a "blatant act of terrorism" and "an act of war."

"Those who defamed our supreme leadership and committed the hostile acts against [North Korea] can never escape the stern punishment to be meted out according to a law, wherever they might be in the world," the statement said. "If the U.S. administration connives at and patronizes the screening of the film, it will invite a strong and merciless countermeasure."

For its part, North Korea under Kim Jong Un has taken unprecedented steps to threaten the United States, creating videos showing in graphic detail how nuclear missile attacks on the United States would produce mass destruction, including images of mushroom clouds over New York City and the White House. In 2013, North Korean propagandists even managed to obtain film footage of the Hollywood movie *Olympus Has Fallen* that showed a North Korean commando attack on the White House, and used it in a North Korean propaganda video that is part of its over-the-top anti-U.S. propaganda threats.

Within Sony, concerns were raised about North Korean retaliation. Kazuo Hirai, head of Sony Corporation in Tokyo, worried about the film's ending. The final scene shows a missile attacking a helicopter carrying Kim Jong Un, whose head catches fire and explodes. Hirai, according to emails hacked from Sony, voiced concerns about the film disrupting Japan–North Korea relations. The movie received a semi-official U.S. government blessing by the State Department's assistant secretary of state for East Asian and Pacific affairs, Daniel Russel, who was consulted by Sony Corporation of America CEO Michael Lynton, who was concerned the film might produce diplomatic fallout. Robert King, the State Department's special envoy for North Korean human rights issues, also signed off, according to an email made public after the North Korean hack. Writing to Lynton, Bruce Bennett, a RAND Corporation specialist on North Korean affairs, said he had consulted with King and that the threats by North Korea to regard the film as an act of war were hyperventilating rhetoric. "I talked with Amb. King a few minutes ago," Bennett stated in the email. "Their office has apparently decided that this is typical North Korean bullying, likely without follow-up, but you never know with North Korea. Thus, he did not appear worried and clearly wanted to leave any decisions up to Sony." King asked for an advance copy of the film prior to its release "so that they could prepare themselves for the likely onslaught of media questions."

Earlier, Bennett recognized the information warfare value of the movie as a step in the right direction of getting rid of the Kim regime, noting that one likely way to do so would be to kill Kim Jong Un.

As Bennett wrote in the email:

> I also thought a bunch more about the ending. I have to admit that the only resolution I can see to the North Korean nuclear and other threats is for the North Korean regime to eventually go away. In fact, when I have briefed my book on "preparing for the possibility of a North Korean collapse" [September 2013], I have been clear that the assassination of Kim Jong-un is the most likely path to a collapse of the North Korean government. Thus while toning down the ending may reduce the North Korean response, I believe that a story that talks about the removal of the Kim family regime and the creation of a new government by the North Korean people (well, at least the elites) will start some real thinking in South Korea and, I believe, in the North once the DVD leaks into the North (which it almost certainly will). So from a personal perspective, I would personally prefer to leave the ending alone. But that is clearly your call.*

Bennett went on to say that it was ironic for North Korea to be putting out threats against the United States over the film since doing so likely would increase audience viewership. "And while many Americans think of Kim Jong-un as being crazy, the movie's depiction of him as 'crazy as a fox'

---

* For details on a proposed effort to oust the North Korean regime through intelligence operations, see my book *Enemies: How America's Foes Steal Our Vital Secrets—and How We Let It Happen* (New York: Crown Forum, 2006).

(though clearly with the passions of youth) and as being willing to use nuclear weapons may well be a wake-up call to some, though probably less in the United States than in Korea," he stated. As a postscript, Bennett added that the depiction of the CIA plotting to kill the North Korean leader also would be welcomed by Pyongyang as it "allows them to make this kind of extreme 'act of war' statement and appear to many around the world (and especially their people) as having justified outrage." The pressure on Sony from North Korea produced a toned-down ending. After initially resisting changes to the movie, Rogen wrote to Sony Pictures studio chief Amy Pascal on September 25, 2014, that the producers agreed to modify the film to "make it less gory."

"There are currently four burn marks on his face. We will take out three of them, leaving only one," he stated. "We reduce the flaming hair by 50%. The head explosion can't be more obscured than it is because we honestly feel that if it's any more obscured you won't be able to tell its [sic] exploding and the joke won't work. Do you think this will help? Is it enough? If you think this is worth doing, we will dive into it right now and could probably have it done in 24 hrs."

Federal Bureau of Investigation director James Comey disclosed in a speech that the Sony hack probably began in September 2014 when North Korean RGB cyber-intelligence agents carried out phishing email scams against Sony executives. Phishing is the sending of fraudulent emails that appear to be from trusted senders and offer tantalizing places to click online. Once a victim mistakenly clicks on the bogus link, a malicious software package is automatically downloaded, facilitating remote access by the hackers.

The U.S. Computer Emergency Readiness Team, a Department of Homeland Security entity, described the Sony hackers' malware as a Server Message Block Worm Tool. It included five features: a listening implant, lightweight back door, proxy tool, destructive hard drive tool, and destructive target-cleaning tool. The software used a "brute force authentication attack" method—multiple, automated attempts to guess passwords to gain access to remote servers inside the Microsoft Windows operating system used by Sony's networks. Once activated, the malicious software took control and quickly opened the way for the North Koreans to reach administrator-level access to the entire Sony system of networks. Computer administrators, because of their need to monitor, maintain, and repair computer systems, are given carte blanche and thus for two months, North Korean RGB hackers roamed freely, stole everything valuable there was to steal, and readied the destructive attacks that were launched November 24. The data theft was carried out covertly using transfers of data in moderate-sized pieces to avoid setting off intrusion detection software used in Sony networks. The North Koreans were operating from several locations, including the Chilbosan Hotel in Shenyang, northern China, and in Malaysia. According to intelligence sources, the Sony hack was orchestrated by a group known as Unit 121, operating from a hotel in Thailand. Unit 121 also was blamed for the so-called DarkSeoul cyberattacks in 2013, which were traced to North Korean hackers. DarkSeoul cyberattacks were carried out against South Korean banks, television broadcasters, and news outlets and according to forensic analysis were very similar, in terms of malicious software used and attack methodology, to the major Sony hack.

North Korean Internet Protocol addresses have been identified by investigators since 2011, including two specific groups. The first block included 1,024 addresses used since 2010 by Star Joint Venture, an Internet service provider venture between the state-run Korea Posts and Telecommunications Company and Thailand's Loxley Pacific. The addresses were used to handle all official North Korean websites, such as KCNA (Korean Central News Agency, an official organ); Naenara, the official Web portal; the official broadcaster Voice of Korea; and *Rodong Sinmun*, the ruling Workers' Party of Korea daily. They ranged from 175.45.176.0 to 175.45.179.255. A second group of 256 addresses ranged from 210.52.109.0 to 210.52.109.255. The addresses are owned by China Netcom, one of China's largest Internet service providers, and were assigned to Korea Posts and Telecommunications. South Korea's government, which cooperated with the FBI in investigating the Sony cyberattack, linked the 2013 attacks to IP addresses for Korea Post and Telecommunications, which is part of the North Korean Ministry of Post and Telecommunications.

Comey, the FBI director, concluded the North Koreans were "sloppy" in sending messages to its hackers that allowed investigators to trace the activities directly to Pyongyang, despite the use of cutout computer networks designed to mask the origin of the attacks. "It was a mistake by them," Comey said. "It made it very clear who was doing this."

The comments by the FBI chief were somewhat deceptive, as is often the case for senior officials in discussing sensitive U.S. government intelligence operations. By pointing the finger at sloppy North Korean tradecraft, Comey actually was seeking to protect the FBI's actual source for uncovering the North Korea connection to the Sony hack, namely the super-secret cyber spies at the National Security Agency. The NSA had been monitoring North Korean cyber activities directly and through third parties since 2010 in what an internal NSA document described as "Fifth Party Collection," the process of electronically spying on foreign spies. In spy parlance, information gathering is known as collection and in the case of NSA has expanded beyond simply getting information directly from a "second party," like the tapping of underwater cables used by the Russian military and thereby learning their secrets during the Cold War. Third-party collection is electronic spying done on behalf of the United States usually by an ally, such as Britain's electronic signals intelligence agency, GCHQ, which then supplies the data to NSA.

But NSA was able to demonstrate the ultimate state of the art in signals intelligence gathering by clandestinely tapping into foreign intelligence service communications, an extraordinarily difficult operation considering such telecommunications links are usually highly secure, protected with sophisticated and nearly unbreakable encryption, and very difficult to identify in the massive universe of electronic signals. A top-secret NSA memo made public in 2015 identifies fourth-party collection, and provides the first details of what is called fifth-party collection. "Fourth party collection refers to passively or actively obtaining data from some other actor's [computer network exploitation] activity against a target," the memo says. The memo then answered a question posed by an NSA employee on whether the agency had ever achieved the ultradifficult feat of fifth-party collection— spying by obtaining information through spying on spies as they are stealing secrets electronically from targets four layers removed from direct collection.

As an NSA analyst stated in an internal newsletter:

Yes. There was a project that I was working last year with regard to the South Korean CNE [computer network exploitation] program. While we aren't super interested in SK (things changed a bit when they started targeting us a bit more), we were interested in North Korea and SK put a lot of resources against them. At that point our access to NK was next to nothing but we were able to make some inroads to the SK CNE program. We found a few instances where there were NK officials with SK implants on their boxes, so we got on the exfil points, and sucked back the data. That's fourth party. (TS//SI//REL) However, some of the individuals that SK was targeting were also part of the NK CNE program. So I guess that would be the fifth party collect you were talking about. But once that started happening, we ramped up efforts to target NK ourselves (as you don't want to rely on an untrusted actor to do your work for you). But some of the work that was done there was able to help us gain access. (TS//SI//REL) I know of another instance (I will be more vague because I believe there are more compartments involved and parts are probably NF [no foreigners]) where there was an actor we were going against. We realized success because of a 0 day they wrote. We got the 0 day out of passive and were able to re-purpose it. Big win. (TS//SI//REL). But they were all still referred to as fourth party.

Behind all the electronic intelligence jargon was the disclosure of a truly remarkable spying achievement. In nontechnical intelligence terms, the NSA has been able to spy on South Korean intelligence communications—no doubt sent electronically in Korean language and protected against interception by the use of a high level of encryption—that were themselves reporting on the interception of North Korean cyber-intelligence operational information that also was likely encrypted. The ability to do so is a sign of NSA's spying and hacking power. The NSA document was among some of the 1.7 million NSA papers stolen by Edward Snowden.

Another leaked NSA document described this extraordinary capability to spy on the spies as "I drink your milkshake," a line from the 2007 movie *There Will Be Blood,* which was based on Upton Sinclair's novel *Oil!* (1927), about how oil companies drilled and drained oil from prized land by covertly tapping nearby wells. In the film, actor Daniel Day-Lewis tells his adopted son, "If you have a milkshake, and I have a milkshake. And I have a straw, there it is. And my straw reaches across the room and starts to drink your milkshake, I drink your milkshake! I drink it up!"

In the NSA document, the agency's prowess for stealing electronic secrets was so formidable that it was drinking the milkshake of the South Korean spy service as the South Koreans were spying electronically on North Korea. Even more sensitive than the North Korean fifth-party collection is the second reference in the document to the NSA's finding and using a software flaw discovered by another foreign spy service, likely Israel or France, known as a "0 day," or zero-day, exploit. Zero days are extremely valuable hacking tools that result when secret vulnerabilities within software are found that allow for clandestine cyber intrusions. In the electronic spying and hacking world, zero days are the coin of the realm, and nations are known to devote hundreds of technical analysts to scouring the ones and zeros within large software programs to find them. NSA was able to find out that one of America's allies had discovered a valuable zero-day exploit after listening in on the ally's communications. That led in turn to the discovery of the zero day by U.S. analysts and then the use of the security hole in the software by NSA spies, an operation the unidentified NSA analyst called a major U.S. intelligence coup.

The NSA successfully drilled electronically into Chinese and then North Korean networks with the help of South Korean electronic spying operatives. The NSA placed monitoring software inside the North Korean networks, including Unit 121. The NSA then used electronic "beacons" that autonomously mapped out the North's computer networks.

Shortly before the release of *The Interview,* the North Korean hackers, posing as a group called the Guardians of

Peace, threatened terrorist attacks on movie theaters that were planning to show the film on the December 24 release date. The theaters buckled and refused to show it. The film was released instead as streaming online video, first by Netflix and then other streaming services. Many Americans viewed the movie on its opening day as an act of protest against a communist dictatorship seeking to stifle free speech. I was one of them. The film lived up to its reputation as a fart comedy. But watching it provided me with a sense of having taken part in a historic battle—one of the first of the twenty-first century's new-style warfare.

Rogen spoke publicly about the North Korean hack more than a year after the Sony attack. "I made a movie called *The Interview* that almost started a war," Rogen told British talk show host Graham Norton in April 2016. "It was a horrible experience. It's bad to be blamed for almost starting a war. . . . Not fun. Super weird." Sony provided security guards for Rogen and others over concerns North Korean agents would be dispatched in hit teams to kill those involved in the film. North Korea in the past threatened to kill American comedy writers Matt Stone and Trey Parker for their satirical comedy *Team America: World Police,* which included an unflattering portrayal of Kim Jong Un's father, Kim Jong Il.

Despite NSA's penetration of North Korean cyberattack networks, the U.S. government and President Obama mishandled the major attack and sought to minimize its strategic significance. Reflecting his roots as a community organizer steeped in the radical leftist policies that grew out of the 1960s and '70s, Obama deliberately passed up the opportunity to go on the offensive against North Korea. That would have made the United States look strong and powerful and assertive, something Obama had denounced as leading to the Iraq War in 2003. Instead, the president and his advisers refused to describe the attack as an act of information warfare. "No, I don't think it was an act of war," Obama said when asked about the attack. "I think it was an act of cyber vandalism that was very costly, very expensive." The comment was part of the Obama ideology of not seeing threats in warfare terms because doing so would contradict his postmodern ideology of a world void of enemies and sharing common interests.

From the early stages, the FBI also mishandled the Sony hacking case by attempting to minimize the attack. The FBI has frequently made this knee-jerk bureaucratic reaction in the immediate aftermath of unwelcome events involving criminal, intelligence, or cyberattack failures, amid worries that confirming the incidents might reflect poorly on the FBI as an investigative agency. Despite immediate indications detected by NSA shortly after the attack became known that it was carried out by North Koreans—the malware used contained Korean language—and the fact that the obvious goal of the cyberattack was to prevent the release of *The Interview*, the U.S. government mishandled its response by first keeping silent, and naming North Korea only after the hackers threatened September 11–style terror attacks on movie theaters that were to show the film. The threats prompted Sony to capitulate to the dictatorship in Pyongyang.

Instead of immediately exposing the attack for what it was, the U.S. government initially issued vague statements and even denials. "There is no attribution to North Korea at this point," FBI assistant director Joe Demarest, head of the bureau's cyber division, told a security conference on December 9—nearly three weeks after the Sony attack. By that time, however, the NSA had fully linked the attack to Pyongyang, based on its past cyber intrusions into North Korean networks.

Less than a month after Demarest declined to name North Korea, the White House announced it was imposing symbolic economic sanctions against ten North Koreans, including the head of the RGB and three front companies used by North Korea for overseas activities. White House officials who briefed reporters about the action stated that the people and entities named were not involved in the Sony hack. It was meant to send a message. But the message fell on deaf ears. "These entities, which have been previously sanctioned, by sanctioning them again under this authority, and frankly sanctioning them at a time when there is a great deal of international attention being focused on North Korea, will we think further isolate those entities from the international financial system and heighten the concern around the world with potentially doing business with these entities," a senior administration official told reporters in announcing the sanctions. In other words, North Korea would pay no price.

Obama announced on December 19 that the U.S. sanctions were one element of the response and that other actions would be taken "in a place and a time and manner that we choose." The president decried Sony's cancellation of the release of *The Interview* as a dictator imposing censorship in the United States.

A temporary Internet outage in North Korea, where even ordinarily only a limited number of government officials and the elite can access the Internet, was detected in December 2015, setting off speculation that it was a U.S. counterattack. But U.S. officials told me the outage was not related to any U.S. action.

Obama's comments were a bluff and he never followed through on the threat to take further action. North Korea was never punished, other than through the symbolic sanctions that had no impact on any North Korean companies or officials. It was the pattern of inaction and weakness the president followed in dealing with all of America's adversaries, including China, Russia, and Iran.

The damage will be long-lasting. The failure to disclose early on the nature of the attack and players behind it sent a clear message to other would-be cyberattackers—with a relatively low-cost cyberattack, U.S. economic and government policies can be influenced in favor of a foreign government.

After the initial denials, the FBI declared on December 19, 2014, that the North Koreans carried out the attack. No explanation was given for why Demarest had claimed there was no link to Pyongyang. NSA director and U.S. Cyber Command commander Admiral Michael Rogers was categorical about his agency's attribution of the Sony attack. "This was North Korea. Let there be no doubt in anyone's mind," he told Fox Business Network.

Still, the weak Obama administration response prompted many nongovernment cybersecurity experts to question whether North Korea really carried out the Sony cyberattack. Among the skeptics was Jeffrey Carr, who wrote on his blog, Digital Dao, that he did not believe the North Koreans were behind the Sony hack. "As of today, the U.S. government is in the uniquely embarrassing position of being tricked by a hacker crew into charging another foreign government with a crime it didn't commit," Carr stated on January 7, 2015. Carr was convinced a Russian hacker group conducted the Sony attack, despite the evidence, including NSA penetrations of North Korean networks, that Sony was victimized by a state-sponsored North Korean cyberattack.

North Korea's National Defense Commission, the party organ that controls the military, issued a statement calling the American charges groundless and demanding that the United States apologize. The reaction was part of classic North Korean information warfare, which calls for complete denials by high-level government agencies and officials to confuse the enemy about the regime's clandestine operations. According to the North Korean commission:

> It is a common sense that the method of cyber warfare is almost similar worldwide. Different sorts of hacking programs and codes are used in cyberspace.
>
> If somebody used U.S.-made hacking programs and codes and applied their instruction or encoding method, perhaps, the "wise" FBI, too, could not but admit that it would be hard to decisively assert that the attack was done

by the U.S. What is grave is that U.S. President Obama is recklessly making the rumor about "DPRK's cyber-attack on Sony Pictures" a fait accompli while crying out for symmetric counteraction, strict calculation and additionally retaliatory sanctions.

To hammer home its information operation against the Sony film, the commission charged there was clear evidence the Obama administration was "deeply involved in the making of such dishonest reactionary movie." The statement was based on the hacked Sony documents. "It is said that the movie was conceived and produced according to the 'guidelines' of the U.S. authorities who contended that such movies hurting the dignity of the [North Korean] supreme leadership and inciting terrorism against it would be used in an effective way as 'propaganda against North Korea,'" the statement said, noting the leaked emails from Robert King, the State Department special envoy on North Korean human rights. The Pyongyang statement also mentioned the Guardians of Peace, the front group used in the attack. "We do not know who or where they are but we can surely say that they are supporters and sympathizers with [North Korea]. The army and people of [North Korea] who aspire after justice and truth and value conscience have hundreds of millions of supporters and sympathizers, known or unknown, who have turned out in the sacred war against terrorism and the U.S. imperialists, the chieftain of aggression, to accomplish the just cause."

The commission vowed to press ahead with its attacks

beyond Sony. "Nothing is more serious miscalculation than guessing that just a single movie production company is the target of this counteraction. Our target is all the citadels of the U.S. imperialists who earned the bitterest grudge of all Koreans. The army and people of [North Korea] are fully ready to stand in confrontation with the U.S. in all war spaces including cyber warfare space to blow up those citadels." Those targets include the White House and the Pentagon; indeed "the whole U.S. mainland" will be hit by the North Korean military.

Another lesson from the weak American response to the North Korean hack of Sony is that the U.S. government remains ill-prepared to address the most significant twenty-first-century strategic threat—devastating cyberattacks aimed at not just stealing data for economic or military gain, but also influencing foreign and domestic policies of target countries.

In March 2015 in South Korea, I heard firsthand from a North Korean defector who in the past had taken part in training North Korean military hackers. Before defecting to South Korea, Kim Heung-kwang worked as a professor at North Korea's Hamhung University of Computer Technology, a key training facility for the military. Kim warned there is a growing danger from North Korean hackers, who, like those from Iran, are targeting nuclear power plants, transportation networks, electrical utilities, and all major government organizations abroad. "If all of this happens, North Korea is going to destroy the basic units of civil society, and we need to react strongly to prevent this," Kim said, adding that

North Korea's closest allies are Iran and Syria, fellow rogue states united in their opposition to the United States.

Kim disclosed that Unit 121 is the North's leading cyberwarfare organization and is an elite, relatively small unit. "All you need are a few really talented people, geniuses, and you can do a lot of damage," he said. Within Unit 121, a special section is devoted to cyberattacks against North American targets, including both government and private sector networks. The Sony hack exposed vulnerabilities within private sector networks that can be exploited by North Korean cyberwarfare troops. "When you have thousands of people working against the firewalls of Sony, then you can see that it is not so difficult to breach Sony's security," Kim noted. The defector fled North Korea after being arrested on charges of possessing banned videos. He was sent to work in a labor camp for a year and escaped by bribing a North Korean border guard and swimming across the Tumen River into China. He eventually reached South Korea and now heads a group known as North Korea Intellectuals Solidarity, a group devoted to promoting freedom, democratization, and human rights in North Korea.

According to South Korean intelligence sources, which cooperated with the United States in the Sony hacking case, the North Korean Unit 121 of the RGB has its headquarters in a building in a northern part of the capital of Pyongyang. The unit is also called the Cyber Warfare Guidance Bureau. The official in charge, and who ordered the Sony cyber strike, has been identified as RGB chief Kim Yong Chol. "Kim was a four-star general in charge of the Reconnaissance General

Bureau," Director of National Intelligence James Clapper said at a security conference in New York City. "The RGB is the organization responsible with the overseeing [*sic*] attack against Sony." North Korea employs around 1,200 Unit 121 cyberwarfare specialists and a total government hacking force of around 6,000 people.

North Korea is building up its cyberwarfare capabilities with a combination of information and electronic warfare techniques. The capabilities would be used in waging blitzkrieg-style cyber and electronic warfare on the Korean Peninsula as well as conducting long-range attacks on the United States and Japan. North Korea "views cyber capabilities as its answer to a flexible, networked adversary that enjoys near real-time battlefield data among its forces," wrote Jenny Jun, Scott LaFoy, and Ethan Sohn in their January 2016 report for the Center for Strategic and International Studies, "North Korea's Cyber Operations: Strategy and Responses."

"If the [Korean People's Army] cannot conventionally match the technologically advanced weaponry of the United States and ROK, the next best thing is to disrupt the very technology that those weapons systems employ," they said. "Cyber capabilities may not be the key to military victory, but they do seem to offer a means of upsetting North Korea's opponents in peacetime."

The authors, however, missed the essential stance of North Korea today: it is at war with the United States and South Korea, and will continue to wage nonkinetic, information warfare.

The horrific nature of the North Korean regime has become known only in the past several years. A key to exposing the regime was a United Nations special commission on human rights that in February 2014 found the Kim regime had engaged in crimes against humanity, including forced starvation, imprisonment in death camps, torture, rape, and other human rights violations. "I was a judge for thirty-four years and I thought I was beyond tears," Michael Kirby, an Australian who led the inquiry, told me. "Just seeing the huge stress suffered by people who complain about violations of their human rights or about the loss of their children, their loved ones, is rather more searing than even the testimony of a horrible murder."

The danger from North Korea is not theoretical. According to a Defense Intelligence Agency report declassified in 2014, Pyongyang dispatched covert commando units to the United States in the 1990s to prepare for attacks on nuclear power plants and major cities in a conflict. The DIA report was dated September 13, 2004, and revealed that five units of special operations commandos had trained for the U.S. attacks. Mark Sauter, a security adviser to private corporations and longtime North Korea specialist, uncovered the DIA report and warned that it indicated North Korea could undertake September 11–style terrorist attacks inside the United States. "What they've done by the Sony hack is shown they're certainly willing to attack a U.S. corporation," Sauter said. "Now they're threating a physical attack along the lines of 9/11 and it is certainly possible they could have agents inside the United States capable of carrying out terrorist attacks." Sauter noted that North Korean agents in the past committed terrorist attacks and kidnappings around the world, and thus he asked, "Why wouldn't they send agents to the homeland of their biggest enemy?"

By early 2016, North Korean cyberattacks were continuing on South Korea. Cell phones of high-ranking South Korean officials were hacked, including call histories, text messages, and contact lists. The North Koreans were detected attempting to implant malware on the smartphones of "tens" of officials and a fifth of the attempts were said to be successful. The target was secret or sensitive information about strategic plans being formulated in South Korea for responses to North Korean military provocations, such as long-range missile and underground nuclear tests. South Korean intelligence estimates that Pyongyang created networks of up to 60,000 pirated computers around the world into bot networks that are used for cyber operations in 120 countries.

As the Sony hack and other activities of the North Korean regime demonstrate, the United States must engage in offensive information warfare to counter the growing danger of North Korean information warfare.

3

UNITED STATES
Eighty Percent of Success Is Showing Up

*The element of surprise in military operations, which
is psychological warfare translated into field tactics,
is achieved by artifice and stratagem, by secrecy and
rapidity of information, by mystifying and misleading the
enemy. When you strike at the morale of a people or any
army, you strike at the deciding factor, because it is the
strength of their will that determines the length of wars,
the measure of resistance, and the day of final collapse.*
— COLONEL WILLIAM DONOVAN, OFFICE OF
STRATEGIC SERVICES, DECEMBER 12, 1942

The United States today is the strongest and most advanced
military power in the world. Yet America is rapidly losing
the most important war of the twenty-first century: an Information
War that threatens its existence.

That war hit home during the Obama administration,
when the most damaging compromises of classified Amer-

ican secrets occurred. One of the devastating security failures involved a senior official, Secretary of State Hillary
Clinton, who for five years used an unsecure private email
server to send and receive some of the nation's most secret
information—data that very likely was hacked and stolen by
several hostile foreign intelligence services.

Violating security rules from her first day in office as
secretary of state, Clinton ordered a private, nongovernment
email server network to be set up. She used the private email
address hdr22@clintonemail.com for all her official communications. The private system remained out of public view
until the House of Representatives conducted an investigation into the Benghazi terrorist attack in 2012, which had
led to the death of four Americans. In February 2013, the
private email system was uncovered by the State Department
in reviewing documents on the Benghazi attacks and it was
revealed that Clinton had used the private email exclusively
to conduct all her business, both in the United States and
while she traveled to adversary states like China and Russia,
where her communications were almost certainly intercepted
and used in information warfare operations by those states
against the United States.

By the fall of 2016, 30,000 emails between Clinton and
her close aides were released, with an additional 14,900 under
review. Most were found to contain unclassified information.
But an alarming number of the emails were labeled "Top
Secret" and "Secret," information classified because its disclosure would cause grave or serious damage to American
security.

The email scandal that ensued eventually produced an investigation by the FBI that was hampered by the fact that many of the thousands of emails had been destroyed by Clinton aides, along with computer equipment and thirteen BlackBerry handheld devices that were never examined by FBI agents.

In an unusual step, FBI director James Comey, apparently more concerned about embroiling his law enforcement agency in the extreme politics of a presidential campaign, took the unorthodox step of announcing he would recommend that the Justice Department not prosecute Clinton for the use of the illegal server and the compromised secrets found on it. In a public statement on July 5, 2016, Comey noted that the mishandling of classified information, either intentionally or through gross negligence, is a felony. Nonetheless, the FBI director reached the conclusion that "although there is evidence of potential violations of the statutes regarding the handling of classified information, our judgment is that no reasonable prosecutor would bring such a case." Translated into political terms, the FBI chief was giving Clinton, the Democratic presidential nominee, a pass for committing felonies. Comey defended the decision as the correct course of action, but it reeked of a political cover-up in support of the former first lady, former secretary of state, and likely next president of the United States.

Down the street from FBI headquarters in Washington, D.C., Comey's decision not to prosecute Clinton or her close aides immediately was accepted by Obama's attorney general, Loretta Lynch, who only days earlier had sparked widespread controversy for holding a private meeting with Clinton's husband, former president Bill Clinton, aboard an aircraft as she waited to depart the Phoenix airport. The meeting with Clinton on June 27 came nine days before Comey made his announcement. Lynch insisted the conversation with Bill Clinton was limited to talking about grandchildren, social events, travel, and the former president's golf game. Few believed the disinformation since the mere fact of the meeting represented a gross conflict of interest for the attorney general. It perfectly reflected what has been called the Clinton style of corruption—the use of political power and influence for political and financial gain.

Further evidence the email investigation was corrupt surfaced in declassified FBI documents in the case showing that Patrick Kennedy, undersecretary of state for management, sought to pressure the FBI to downgrade its classification of one Clinton email containing counterterrorism secrets from "SECRET/NOFORN" to unclassified. In exchange, Kennedy offered what the document said was a "quid pro quo"—more slots for FBI agents posted to U.S. embassies abroad. According to the report, "in exchange for marking the email unclassified, STATE would reciprocate by allowing the FBI to place more Agents in countries where they are presently forbidden." Both the State Department and FBI denied there was a deal.

Comey's attempt to exonerate Hillary Clinton was incomplete. Despite his recommending against Justice Department prosecution, the FBI director had exposed Clinton's criminal mishandling of classified data. "Although we did not find clear evidence that Secretary Clinton or her colleagues intended to violate laws governing the handling of classified information," he said, "there is evidence that they were extremely careless in their handling of very sensitive, highly classified information." So why wasn't that the gross negligence standard that Comey laid out earlier applied to the crime of mishandling secrets? Comey never explained that contradiction.

A State Department official told me that at least three foreign intelligence services hacked the server, including spies from Russia, China, and Israel.

Clinton would be found to have lied about the server repeatedly, claiming falsely that no classified information was sent or stored on the system and that she did not destroy emails and information systems improperly.

How sensitive were the secrets? The compromises were not disclosed in order to prevent further damage. But they included some of the crown jewels of U.S. government defense, intelligence, and foreign policy information, data that could be a gold mine for America's enemies to use in information warfare operations.

Under pressure from Congress, new details of the FBI probe were made public in a redacted report on the investigation. It revealed the worst: foreign intelligence services likely intercepted Clinton's emails, including those containing secrets, that were sent between 2009 and 2013.

"The FBI did find that hostile foreign actors gained access to the personal email accounts of individuals with whom Clinton was in regular contact, and, in doing so, obtained emails sent to or received by Clinton on her personal account," the report noted.

The secrets found among the emails included information classified above top secret and part of what are called Special Access Programs, or SAPs. This category of classified information is so sensitive the data must be protected with extraordinary secrecy. According to American officials, to protect SAP information from leaking, or to prevent the programs' existence from being known, U.S. government officials are permitted to lie about the programs when questioned about the secret activities. One example of SAP information would be the secret planning by U.S. special operations commandos of the 2011 raid that killed al Qaeda leader Osama bin Laden. Other programs involve protecting secrets about foreign electronics and weapons that would be used in disabling them in a future conflict.

According to the FBI report, Clinton told investigators that she had been briefed by security officials on how to handle the extremely secret SAP information. But she also told agents she "could not recall any specific briefing on how to handle information associated with SAPs," despite her having signed agreements not to disclose SAP information. "In general, Clinton knew SAP information was of great importance and needed to be handled carefully," the report said. However, a large section of the report was blacked out. Immediately after the blacked-out section, the report said Clinton "could not recall a specific process for nominating a target for a drone strike" but said those who would be killed in such unmanned aerial vehicle missile attacks were subject to debate. The reference to drone strikes indicates the likely SAP information she disclosed in her private emails related to secret counterterrorism drone attacks.

The FBI investigation found that hackers from Russia and Ukraine launched cyberattacks against the private server. But investigators could not determine conclusively if the attacks were successful. The bureau described Clinton's unsecure email system as "potentially vulnerable to compromise" and stated that it suffered numerous cyberattacks. One attack succeeded: a remote intrusion by an unidentified hacker who used the hijacked email account of a Clinton staff employee to scan emails and attachments. Additionally, numerous "brute force" cyberattacks targeted the server. Brute-force attacks employ software that makes numerous, rapid log-in attempts in a bid to gain remote access.

The FBI identified a possible Russian hacking connection after the compromise of an AOL account used by Clinton associate Sidney Blumenthal, who was victimized by the Romanian hacker Marcel Lehel Lazar, known as Guccifer. "Lazar disseminated emails and attachments sent between Blumenthal and Clinton to 31 media outlets, including a Russian broadcasting company," the FBI said in a heavily redacted investigative report. "An examination of log files from March 2013 indicated that IP addresses from Russia and Ukraine attempted to scan the server on March 15, 2013, the day after the Blumenthal compromise, and on March 19 and March 21, 2013," the report said. "However, none of these attempts were successful and it could not be determined whether these activities were attributable to Lazar."

The email scandal dogged Clinton throughout her presidential campaign in 2016, a campaign so marked by controversy and scandal that she at one point campaigned for 275 days without holding a single press conference with reporters. She eventually would agree to answer a few questions from reporters traveling with her aboard a campaign plane. Clinton resorted to the denial and dissembling that have characterized her public persona since she was the governor's wife in Arkansas during the 1980s. Her favorite rejoinder was that all the press reporting on her email scandal was nothing but a vast right-wing conspiracy against her.

Asked at one point during the campaign about a continuing congressional inquiry into the email scandal, Clinton dismissed the idea. "The FBI resolved all of this, answered all the questions," she said. "The conspiracy theory machine factory honestly, they never quit. They keep coming back." On deleting emails that are required to be archived under federal laws, Clinton said she was not concerned about whether federal investigators would pursue any violations.

Comey took the sensational step of ordering the Clinton email investigation reopened eleven days before Election Day. The case was reenergized by new evidence indicating classified information may have been transmitted on some 650,000 personal email messages sent by Huma Abedin, Clinton's longtime assistant and vice chair of the presidential campaign. Reopening the criminal probe was a clear sign the FBI had failed to fully investigate the case, or closed it before all the facts surrounding the scandal were uncovered. Two days before the election, Comey again wrote to Congress to say that the FBI had not altered its conclusion after reviewing the emails.

The Clinton security failure was the third major compromise of secrets during the Obama administration and bodes ill for American information warfare capabilities under a possible second Clinton presidential administration. Operational security—the ability to protect information—will be a critical feature in conducting future information warfare and counter-information warfare programs and activities.

The mass disclosure of secrets began in early 2010 when a mentally unstable twenty-three-year-old army sergeant, Bradley Manning, illegally downloaded 400,000 classified documents from an army computer while posted at an intelligence center in Iraq. Manning's stolen secrets were published online by the antisecrecy website WikiLeaks. It was followed three years later by the compromise of even more sensitive information carried out by a delusional National Security Agency contractor named Edward Snowden, who, using his access to secrets as a computer systems maintenance administrator at the agency, stole an estimated 1.7 million documents, containing some of the agency's most sensitive and secret operations used to gather electronic intelligence around the world. Snowden was driven by the false belief, repeated endlessly today by America's enemies, that NSA is engaged in a massive government conspiracy to spy on Americans. Snowden, working at NSA's Kunia facility in Hawaii at the time of the document theft, fled first to Hong Kong, which he mistakenly believed would welcome him and which he falsely believed would be a safe haven because it had a news media independent of Beijing. After surfacing in interviews with news reporters, Snowden eventually fled to Russia and ended up under the protection of the FSB security and intelligence service in Moscow, where he remained as of late 2016, out of reach of U.S. federal prosecutors who have charged him with espionage.

"Whether it was WikiLeaks or Snowden or now the Hillary emails, we have done more to hurt ourselves than the Russians, the Chinese, the terrorists, or anybody else that you want to name," House Armed Services Committee chairman Representative Mac Thornberry, a Texas Republican, told me. "This is serious business when you have top-secret emails on a private server, and then you think it all goes away by saying 'I'm sorry.' The damage to the country is just enormous when you put these compromises together."

In August 2016, FBI agents arrested another insider at NSA who was charged with cyber theft of large amounts of highly classified electronic intelligence information. Harold Thomas Martin III had worked for the same contractor as Snowden and was charged with stealing secret computer code used by NSA to break into foreign computer networks.

The Obama administration's loss of secrets was the culmination of information security failures that would never have occurred years ago, when American leaders understood the need to protect the country from foreign threats.

The United States of America at one time boasted impressive information warfare capabilities. These nonkinetic means of warfare were used effectively in World War II and during the Cold War to defeat America's foes. Unfortunately, today the U.S. government has been rendered incapable of mounting an effective information warfare program, the result of decades of policies that sought to limit this strategic American power. At the same time, America's adversaries worked full speed to apply the same information warfare techniques against the country.

"If the CIA were directed to conduct information warfare today, it would be unable to do so because it no longer has an effective and capable directorate of operations," former CIA operations officer Brad Johnson told me.

How did this happen? The disarming of America ideologically can be traced to liberal politicians who opposed the use of American ideals and values on the world scene as less important than advancing their own political agendas. The politicization of American national security policies, first through Congress and later in Democratic presidential administrations, culminated with the most openly anti-American president in history: Barack Obama, who deliberately worked to transform traditional American institutions and policies through an aggressive liberal leftist political agenda.

A second factor in the failure of American government to develop capabilities and programs for waging information warfare has been the stultifying bureaucratization within the federal government, to the point that federal workers, once regarded as servants to the American people, have turned that concept on its head and created government agencies that have lost both direction and a sense of mission. Government bureaucracy—preserving authority, funding, and turf—has replaced the notion of what Abraham Lincoln called "government of the people, by the people, and for the people." Instead, government under liberal notions has become a power unto itself. The problem of the out-of-control federal bureaucracy is in large measure responsible for the rise of political outsiders like Donald Trump, who in 2016 won the Republican nomination for president over a large field of establishment candidates.*

During World War II, the American government learned nearly from scratch how to conduct information warfare and propaganda operations. It did so through the Office of War Information, which operated from June 1942 until September 1945. During that period the office was tasked with the domestic role of explaining to the American people why the war against Japan and Germany had to be fought, and to counteract strong isolationist sentiment. Producing an array of programs, outlined in an executive order from President Franklin D. Roosevelt, the Office of War Information served as a critical soft-power armament during the global war. Its mandate was to "formulate and carry out, through the use of press, radio, motion picture, and other facilities, information programs designed to facilitate the development of an informed and intelligent understanding, at home and abroad, of the status and progress of the war effort and of the war policies, activities, and aims of the government." The order also coordinated all war information for federal agencies to

---

* For a fuller understanding of this problem, see my book *The Failure Factory* (New York: Crown Forum, 2008).

ensure an accurate and consistent flow of war information to the public and the world at large. The office also worked with American radio broadcasters and motion picture studios. Lastly, the office was given the mandate to "perform such other functions and duties relating to war information as the president may from time to time determine." This vaguely worded passage was president-speak for covert and clandestine activities that would be carried out in connection with the Office of Strategic Services, the secret intelligence and covert action agency and wartime predecessor of today's CIA.

An example of a successful wartime information operation was code-named Operation Annie, carried out in secret by a small group of soldiers from the Psychological Warfare Branch of the U.S. Army's Twelfth Army Group. The soldiers pulled off a very effective deception using radio broadcasts from a residence in Luxembourg, near the German border, which fooled its listeners into believing it was operated by anti-Nazi Germans inside Germany. It was known to German troops and officers who listened as "Zwölf hundert zwölf," the German designation for its frequency of 1212. It provided real and accurate news on the war front and built its credibility. Radio hosts were eight Americans who spoke fluent German, or Germans who were working with the Americans. OSS intelligence reports were used to give an accurate description of Allied bombing and damage, something Nazi-controlled radios were not providing. The radio also broadcast reports about how the station was constantly moving around to avoid detection by German forces. By early 1945, General Dwight Eisenhower, the supreme commander in Europe, ordered the radio to begin providing false reports on rapid advances by Allied troops toward Germany. The reports triggered a panic and prompted German civilians to flee and clog major roads, thus slowing the retreat of the Germany army. Operation Annie would be difficult to pull off today because of liberal opposition to using news media for warfare purposes. But it was an essential effort in World War II.

OSS chief Colonel William "Wild Bill" Donovan led the way in the use of wartime psychological warfare operations that were a key element of the fledgling spy agency. Unlike today's CIA, OSS was a wartime action organization rather than one devoted mainly to gathering intelligence. OSS created the Morale Operations Branch, which was devoted to countering Nazi propaganda and information warfare activities and designed to attack the enemy's will to fight. The unit was based largely on Britain's Political Warfare Executive, which produced open as well as secret propaganda. In a speech on December 12, 1942, Donovan outlined the importance of information warfare. "Since war began, psychological warfare has been used," he said. "You direct your propaganda at the civilian population, at their national emotions, because by doing so you not only involve the leaders, you not only aim at destroying the force of the war machine, but the political or military group who runs that machine." For Donovan, psychological warfare proved crucial to achieving victory in war, and he knew Adolf Hitler was using it effectively. As Donovan put it:

Between wars, the democracies had not prepared in psychological warfare because they had not prepared for war physically or morally. But Hitler did prepare and he changed the kind of political warfare. He said: "The place of the artillery barrage as a preparation for infantry attack will, in the future, be taken by revolutionary propaganda. Its task is to break down the enemy physically before the armies begin to function at all." And under him the Germans developed a deliberate science and strategy of psychological warfare. In this war of machines, the human element is, in the long run, more important than the machines themselves. There must be the will to make the machines, to man the machines, and to pull the trigger. Psychological warfare is directed against that will. Its object is to destroy the morale of the enemy and to support the morale of our allies within enemy and enemy-occupied countries. . . . The ammunition of psychological warfare consists of ideas more powerful than those used by the enemy.

After World War II and during the Cold War, when the enemy shifted from being Nazi Germany to the Soviet Union, CIA covert operations involving information succeeded in preventing communist governments from coming to power in several critical states, such as Italy. CIA operatives were schooled in the black arts of political warfare and the formula was simple: target the three areas that were significant centers of influence: students and youth, labor organizations, and the elites of society, including government officials, media, and other societal leaders. However, the CIA in the decades since has become a politicized organization that is ill-equipped for operating in the Information Age. The agency's liberal culture dates from the 1960s, when the over-zealous anticommunism of Senator Joseph McCarthy drove many liberals in government into the CIA. As a result, CIA covert operations throughout the 1960s and '70s directed from the top floors of the CIA headquarters in McLean, Virginia, were carried out with a significant flaw: CIA limited all its support for foreign political opposition groups and parties to those on the left of the political spectrum. None on the right were supported. Angelo Codevilla, a former professional staff member of the Senate Select Committee on Intelligence, believes these politicized covert action programs of supporting foreign leftists produced "blowback," in intelligence terms, or unintended consequences, that resulted in the election of Barack Obama as president, the most left-wing politician ever to assume the nation's highest office. Obama's grandmother Madelyn Dunham worked as vice president of the Bank of Hawaii, and according to Codevilla the bank had a role in handling bank accounts used by the CIA to funnel money to its covert action programs in support of leftist opposition movements in Asia.

Domestically, the powerful FBI under longtime director J. Edgar Hoover avoided involvement in information warfare. Hoover coveted the FBI's reputation as both a law enforcement agency and a national security agency but strenuously avoided activities that in any way might have undermined its credibility with senior government leaders and the American public. Two exceptions were the FBI's campaign against the Ku Klux Klan, which terrorized blacks and their supporters in the South, and against the Black Nationalist movement of the 1960s and '70s, which had been heavily influenced and in some cases penetrated with agents by the Soviet KGB. This would be the FBI's most damaging political mistake, as the FBI under Hoover would eventually target civil rights leader Martin Luther King Jr. in a campaign of active measures to discredit him. King had the unfortunate distinction of being targeted by both the FBI and the KGB. Files obtained from KGB defector Vasili Mitrokhin reveal that King and his followers were the focus of KGB disinformation and agent infiltration operations in a bid to oust him as a leader of the civil rights movement in favor of more violent and radical black leaders.* An intelligence source told me the KGB had penetrated King's inner circle with Soviet agents, and FBI's counterspies had detected them communicating closely with the KGB. For Moscow, KGB operations against the black nationalist and civil rights movements were an opportunity to conduct information warfare against the main enemy: the United States.

The 1970s saw the further erosion of U.S. information warfare capabilities. The liberal foreign policies of President Jimmy Carter inadvertently led to the Soviet invasion of Afghanistan in 1979—after Carter foolishly announced that the United States needed to shed its "inordinate fear

---

* See Christopher Andrew and Vasili Mitrokhin, *The Sword and the Shield: The Mitrokhin Archive and the Secret History of the KGB* (New York: Basic Books, 1999).

of communism." The assessment within the Kremlin was that Washington would not respond in any serious way to Moscow's military drive to develop an overland bridge to the Middle East by taking over the Southwest Asian state. As a result, Afghanistan became a failed state that would host al Qaeda and spawn the September 11 attacks. Despite years of military support and billions of dollars in American aid, the country continues to provide a safe haven for Islamic terrorists engaged in large-scale opium trafficking that is no doubt contributing to the heroin crisis currently gripping America. Carter's second fiasco was his administration's role in fostering the takeover of Iran, at one time a key Middle East ally of the United States. Carter supported the Shiite radical cleric Ayatollah Khomeini, whom the president falsely viewed as a democratic reformer. The hard-line theocracy that was created in Iran remains today the world's premier state sponsor of terrorism and is on a path to having nuclear weapons in ten years under the nuclear deal concluded by the Obama administration. Equally damaging from a national security standpoint was Carter's wholesale weakening of the CIA under Director Stansfield Turner. It was Turner who recklessly fired hundreds of the agency's most experienced operatives, a devastating blow to its operations capability from which the agency has never fully recovered. Under Turner, the liberal politicization at CIA accelerated.

A recently released 1978 memorandum from Carter administration national security adviser Zbigniew Brzezinski reveals just how hapless Carter and his advisers were in dealing with an expanding Soviet Union that had been aggressively moving to take over significant parts of Africa, using Cuban and East German proxy forces. "I suspect that an impression has developed that the Administration (and you personally) operates very cerebrally, quite unemotionally," Brzezinski wrote, perhaps using the term *cerebral* as code for weak. He continued:

> *In most instances this is an advantage; however, occasionally emotion and even a touch of irrationality can be an asset. Those who wish to take advantage of us ought to fear that, at some point, we might act unpredictably, in anger, and decisively. If they do not feel this way, they will calculate that simply pressing, probing, or delaying will serve their ends. I see this quite clearly in [Israeli prime minister Menachem] Begin's behavior, and I suspect that Brezhnev is beginning to act similarly.*
>
> *This is why I think the time may be right for you to pick some controversial subject on which you will deliberately choose to act with a degree of anger and even roughness, designed to have a shock effect.*

Carter proved incapable of projecting power and strength and instead provoked America's enemies to take advantage of his weakness, a pattern that has been followed under Obama. The intense politicization within government that ultimately produced the current elimination of effective U.S. information warfare capabilities against foreign enemies was on display in 1983 during an incident that pitted the conservative administration of President Ronald Reagan against entrenched liberals in Congress. In March of that year Reagan announced the launch of the Strategic Defense Initiative, a revolutionary missile defense program that would transform the Cold War confrontational nuclear doctrine of mutual assured destruction, or MAD, by which American and Soviet populations were held hostage to the concept of retaliatory nuclear missile and bomber attacks. MAD was once considered to be a cornerstone of stability, but Reagan rejected the MAD doctrine by calling for the creation of strategic missile defenses—high-speed, precision-guided antimissile weapons that could knock out incoming ballistic missiles at various stages of flight, thus neutralizing their strategic threat. The idea meant that the United States would no longer need nuclear weapons to prevent nuclear war. "What if free people could live secure in the knowledge that their security did not rest upon the threat of instant U.S. retaliation to deter a Soviet attack, that we could intercept and destroy strategic ballistic missiles before they reached our own soil or that of our allies?" Secretary of Defense Caspar Weinberger and Secretary of State George Shultz wrote in a March 1989 Pentagon report. SDI, as the program was called, had been dubbed "Star Wars" by critics. But it was an important first step toward realizing the goal of a more secure world. There was one problem, however. For the liberal left elites in government, academia, and think tanks, SDI struck at the heart of an arms control canon, namely the 1972 Anti-Ballistic Missile Treaty between Moscow and Washington. While the Soviets had violated the treaty secretly for decades, and under the treaty maintained a nuclear-tipped antimissile system around Moscow, the United States under Carter committed to remaining defenseless by not building strategic defenses. Thus when SDI was announced, liberal Democrats in Congress vehemently opposed the program.

The Democrats' goal was to stifle what they regarded as a destructive and dangerous conservative policy that would upset strategic nuclear stability. But on the other side of the Atlantic, the Soviet Union in the early 1980s saw SDI as a potentially devastating strategic checkmate to their ability to confront the democratic West with nuclear power. Unknown to most in the West, the Soviets had begun building up strategic defenses of their own while using the ABM Treaty to keep the United States from matching their capabilities. By the mid-1980s, Moscow had an array of programs under way to defeat ballistic missiles, including lasers, particle beam weapons, and the world's only antisatellite system—orbiting bombs that would maneuver close to satellites and explode.

The Soviets wasted no time in waging information war against SDI, including a program of covert measures. On April 22, 1983, a month after Reagan's SDI announcement, the *New York Times* published a letter signed by more than two hundred senior Soviet scientists denouncing the program. Typical of Soviet duplicity, a number of the signatories were closely involved in both traditional and advanced ballistic missile defense programs, a fact unknown to most Americans. Moscow sympathizers, of whom there were many in the West, quickly echoed the Soviet propaganda campaign, taking to the op-ed pages of major newspapers and warning that SDI would doom the coveted arms control negotiations.

Within the Reagan White House, officials were concerned about the Soviet disinformation campaign and tasked CIA director William Casey to formulate a covert information warfare plan to counter it. As part of the approval process, such covert actions had to be approved by Congress, and as part of that process a group of White House and CIA officials traveled to Capitol Hill to brief members of the Senate Select Committee on Intelligence. During the closed-door meeting, one of the senators, liberal Joseph Biden, became so incensed by plans for the secret counter-disinformation plan that he shot back at the witnesses: "You're just doing this to support SDI." Furthermore, according to attendees at the closed hearing, Biden then issued the kind of threat that liberal Democrats had perfected in scuttling unpopular CIA covert action programs. The Delaware Democrat, who would go on to promote his liberal agenda as vice president during the Obama administration, threatened that if the CIA went ahead with the information warfare program against the Soviet anti-SDI operation, the world would read about it on the front page of the *New York Times*. Thus the Soviets were given free rein to go after and discredit the program. The administration was left with few options. The Pentagon, in a March 1985 report on Soviet strategic defenses, noted that "through an intensive, worldwide propaganda campaign, the U.S.S.R. evidently hopes that it can dissuade the United States from pursuing this research program, thereby preserving the possibility of a Soviet monopoly in effective defenses against ballistic missiles—a monopoly that could give the U.S.S.R. the uncontested damage-limiting first-strike capability that it has long sought." Liberal Democrats in Congress became the unwitting tools of Soviet disinformation, blinded by their own political biases.

For the highly partisan liberal Left, conservatives were regarded as a greater threat than America's real foreign enemies. The political opposition from liberals in Congress to the counter-disinformation program sought by the CIA would set the tone for U.S. government information warfare efforts, or more accurately the lack of them, for decades afterward.

During the Cold War, President Ronald Reagan was one of the few American leaders who understood the communist threat and would take steps to hasten its defeat in the Soviet Union.

The date was April 10, 1991. The publication was *Krasnaya Zvezda,* or *Red Star,* the official newspaper of the Soviet Red Army. The author was Major General Gennady Kashuba, head of the USSR Defense Ministry press center. The headline read "How Many Hats Does Mr. Gertz Have?" It was labeled a rejoinder to two articles I had written and published days earlier in the *Washington Times* about a secret visit to recently reunited eastern Germany by Soviet marshal Dmitry Yazov. The Soviet defense minister had traveled to the remnants of the key Soviet satellite nation of East Germany in March 1991, six months after one of the worst police states had been dissolved and unified with West Germany. The Yazov visit coincided with Moscow's role in the clandestine escape of East German dictator Erich Honecker, who had been holed up on a Soviet military base and fled the country and authorities who were seeking to put him on trial for ordering the shooting deaths of some two hundred East Germans killed by border guards as they tried to flee the Stalinist state. At the time of the Yazov visit, Soviet forces in the country numbered 370,000 troops.

The article was a masterpiece of Soviet disinformation—the practice of using false and misleading information to advance strategic and policy objectives. The article accused me of writing "base misinformation . . . couched in the spirit of the 'cold war' times." It claimed that in Britain, if someone were caught lying they would be required to eat their hat. Thus the article asserted that for me, "hats seem to have become a constant dish in his diet."

The real target of the disinformation piece was the second article I had written in the *Times* the same day as the article on the Yazov visit. It was a detailed exposé of Soviet disinformation and what were called "active measures"—covert and overt intelligence and propaganda programs. The information for my article had been provided by a special group within the U.S. Information Agency, at the time the U.S. government's official news and information service, which played a pivotal role in helping win the Cold War.

The group was known as the Active Measures Working Group and was dedicated to exposing Soviet lies and deception. The list of Soviet disinformation operations made public by the group included details on how the KGB intelligence service planted lies and half-truths in Russian and developing-world news outlets that falsely reported the CIA created the AIDS virus and was exporting condoms containing AIDS-infected lubricant to the third world. Other disinformation operations revealed by the group included lies that the CIA had been plotting with separatists to weaken the Soviet Union, and that the CIA was sabotaging the Soviet economy and dividing Soviet leaders. The KGB also spread disinformation that the agency had been arranging the assassinations of world leaders such as France's Charles de Gaulle, China's Chou En-lai, and Egypt's Gamal Abdel Nasser.

As a young news reporter, getting criticized in the official Red Army newspaper was very heady stuff. Rarely does a journalist for a major metropolitan newspaper get singled out for political attack by one of the world's most sophisticated propaganda and disinformation operations. The *Red Star* clipping is now framed in my office. It was a gift from a longtime friend, the late Herb Romerstein, a former communist turned anticommunist who was among the most effective thought leaders on the Active Measures Working Group during the 1980s and '90s in battling the evil empire's disinformation program.

General Kashuba's attempt to smear me proved ineffective and ill-fated. The last laugh would be mine eight months after the *Red Star* article appeared, when the massive disinformation operation of the KGB and Red Army itself were relegated to the ash heap of history on December 26, 1991, the day the Soviet Union was dissolved.

The Active Measure Working Group was one of the few successful information operations by the U.S. government since the end of World War II. It was created—despite opposition from the Left—after KGB disinformation operations began expanding to target key administration officials. The Reagan administration took action against KGB disinformation that was relentless, sophisticated, and inflicted serious damage on the image of America around the world. As mentioned, the covert information warfare emanating from Moscow included the planting of foreign press stories by the KGB. But the KGB took the activities to a new level in spreading forged U.S. government documents that aimed to discredit senior officials, such as the United States ambassador to the United Nations Jeane Kirkpatrick. In 1983, an Indian newspaper published a report, based on a forged Soviet KGB document that was purportedly a speech by Kirkpatrick discussing a plan to divide up India. Earlier, in 1980, the Soviets circulated a forged presidential review memorandum on Africa claiming the U.S. administration had adopted racist policies. And in 1986 the Soviets spread a forged speech by defense secretary Caspar Weinberger falsely claiming the United States Strategic Defense Initiative was part of American plans for a protracted nuclear war and would be used as part of offensive nuclear warfare to prevent counterattacks.

The interagency Active Measures Working Group was staffed by a small group of dedicated officials and proved to be one of the most important postwar government programs on the information warfare front and is a model for information warfare programs in the twenty-first century. "The working group also changed the way the United States and Soviet Union viewed disinformation," states a National Defense University study. "With constant prodding from the group, the majority position in the U.S. national security bureaucracy moved from believing that Soviet disinformation was inconsequential to believing it was deleterious to U.S. interests—and on occasion could mean the difference in which side prevailed in closely contested foreign policy issues." The report noted the applicability of the working group to the Information Age. "In an increasingly connected age, America will need to protect its public reputation from those who would malign it to weaken our national security," Dennis C. Blair, the former director of national intelligence, and James R. Locher III, a former Pentagon assistant secretary for special operations and low-intensity conflict, wrote in a foreword to the study.

The working group's origins were traced to 1983, when a pro-Soviet newspaper in India, *Patriot*, published several stories that had been planted by the KGB claiming the U.S. military secretly had developed the deadly AIDS virus and released it as a weapon. The report also said the virus had been genetically designed to afflict Africans. The disinformation spread quickly throughout the undeveloped world and eventually was picked up and reported by the official Soviet cultural weekly *Literaturnaya Gazeta*. By 1987 the state-sponsored, anti-U.S. libel had appeared more than forty times in Soviet-controlled news outlets and had reached eighty countries, in thirty different languages. At the time, the virus was not understood and the disease was terrifying. It was an especially damaging piece of disinformation that undermined America in the eyes of millions of people in the developing world.

The working group toiled in relative obscurity until October 30, 1987. During a meeting that day between Secretary of State George Shultz and the new Soviet leader, Mikhail Gorbachev, the Soviet leader held up a copy of a report titled "Soviet Influence Activities: A Report on Active Measures and Propaganda, 1986–1987." He charged the report was part of American efforts at "nourishing hatred" of the Soviet Union. In reality, the report was a carefully documented exposé of damaging KGB disinformation operations against the United States, including the AIDS-made-in-America falsehood. Shultz stood his ground in the showdown, telling Gorbachev the report told the true story about the lies Moscow was spreading about the United States. He noted that the disinformation was undermining Gorbachev's glasnost, or opening-up, policy. For the team operating out of the State Department, denunciation of the report was tremendous confirmation that the working group had impacted the highest levels of the Soviet leadership and, more important, its self-declared sword and shield, the KGB.

A strategic victory was gained beyond the actual countering of Soviet information warfare. The working group helped the U.S. government for the first time in decades realize and understand that foreign enemies were conducting information warfare operations, something that it had almost universally ignored or dismissed until then. Since the Office of War Information went out of business forty years earlier, the American government had been left defenseless against this ideological assault posed by communist and authoritarian regimes of past and present. How important were these activities? Colonel Rolf Wagenbreth, director of Department X of the East German foreign intelligence service, would reveal later that his KGB proxy service relished the operations: "Our friends in Moscow call it 'dezinformatsiya.' Our enemies in America call it 'active measures,' and I, dear friends, call it 'my favorite pastime.'"

One reason U.S. government efforts to counter Soviet disinformation atrophied significantly prior to the 1980s was bureaucratic backlash within the CIA to James Jesus Angleton, the master counterspy who ran afoul of agency higher-ups in a hunt for KGB moles. After Angleton's retirement, the agency halted all training of officers and analysts in strategic deception. Liberal intelligence bureaucrats would come to regard all counterintelligence under the rubric of "sickthink." A policy that lasted until the discovery in the early 1990s that all its recruited agents in Russia had been sold out by a traitor inside the CIA, Aldrich Ames, a drunk who used his access to CIA counterintelligence files to get money from the KGB. More Soviet penetration agents would be uncovered, but CIA counterintelligence today remains a strategic vulnerability for the United States, since the view from abroad is that the agency is ripe for penetration by spies.

Counterintelligence became a priority for the Reagan administration under Kenneth E. deGraffenreid, a former Senate Select Committee on Intelligence staffer who became White House National Security Council staff intelligence director. Under deGraffenreid's leadership, the U.S. government sharply changed course in the 1980s and the Active Measures Working Group proved to be one of its more significant information warfare tools. DeGraffenreid helped draft one of Reagan's first directives as president, National Security Study Directive No. 2, on "Detecting and Countering the Foreign Intelligence Threat to the United States." The top-secret directive, since made public, stated that foreign spying posed a significant threat and added: "Moreover, collection is not the only threat; Soviet 'active measures' include subversion, disinformation and other clandestine activities inimical to U.S. interests." Presidential-level attention thus set the tone for the rest of the government bureaucracy, which had continued to resist security reforms. Indeed, many of the reforms were pushed through despite fierce opposition from the bureaucrats. An example was Admiral Bobby Ray Inman, who became deputy director of national intelligence as part of a deal in Congress to confirm Bill Casey, a close Reagan adviser, as CIA chief. After the directive was signed, Inman clashed with White House national security adviser Bill Clark in opposing the directive, threatening to resign unless it was reversed. Clark, a former judge, refused to be bullied and called Inman's bluff. He told Inman to see his secretary in the reception area and draft his resignation letter. The incident highlighted how much the intelligence bureaucracy was opposed to President Reagan's policies.

"The Active Measures Working Group was a significant White House–driven example of all-too-rare interagency cooperation that exposed Soviet disinformation and influence operations for the strategic threat that they posed," deGraffenreid told me. "And for the first time in decades it energized government to begin doing something about it."

The working group is a model for urgently needed efforts today to conduct similar activities and programs against foreign adversaries, especially the Islamic threat, deGraffenreid added. "The Islamists went to school on the Soviets for their own active measures, which is why they use it today and why they're good at information warfare," he said.

The Active Measures Working Group and many of the policies under Reagan helped steer the government in a positive direction during the eight years of his administration. Ten years after Reagan left office, however, in 1999, one of the most damaging government reforms in the field of U.S. information warfare capabilities took place. The agency that hosted the Active Measures Working Group, USIA, was disbanded and its functions placed within the State Department, an agency that was and remains ill-suited to conducting aggressive public diplomacy and, more important, information warfare. USIA was set up in the early days of the Cold War and at its peak was funded with more than $2 billion annually, providing vitally important information about the American ideals of democracy, freedom, and free markets to millions of people around the world in about 150 different nations. USIA created libraries in foreign capitals around the world that were extremely valuable resources for people in countries seeking to know and understand America. A Chinese-born American university professor told me the USIA was a godsend because it was a source for truthful information that helped counteract the lies and deception of the communist regime in China. Russian and Eastern European dissidents, too, have praised

USIA and American radio broadcasts for helping to bring down the Soviet empire.

Formally, USIA had been given the simple task of informing and influencing foreign publics about American interests. During the Cold War, the agency's easiest task was highlighting the differences between free societies and the repressive Soviet Bloc while working to spread America's message. The agency became the unfortunate victim of shortsighted cost cutting by Congress, specifically, Senate Foreign Relations Committee chairman Jesse Helms, a North Carolina Republican. After becoming committee chairman, Helms, a staunch conservative and one of the most pro-American lawmakers to serve in Congress, set his sights on eliminating three State Department–controlled agencies: USIA, the Agency for International Development, and the liberal-dominated Arms Control and Disarmament Agency. Of the three, Helms was particularly focused on eliminating the arms control agency, which had been an aggressive promoter of liberal arms control policies and agreements such as the 1972 Anti-Ballistic Missile Treaty. The senator believed arms agreements more often than not ended up limiting the United States while ignoring systematic violations by the Soviet Union, in particular. In 1997, then–secretary of state Madeleine Albright bargained with Helms to allow the State Department to pay $2 billion in unpaid American government dues owed to the United Nations that had been held up by Congress in protest of anti-Americanism at the international organization.

The lights would go out on USIA on October 1, 1999, ending the semi-independence that had provided it with sufficient credibility in producing broadcasts, written publications, and other media that did not come off as self-serving propaganda. "By keeping a relative distance from the State Department's diplomats, though housed in State's embassies abroad, [USIA] put across a view of the United States that was closer to what foreigners who visited here recognized as the real thing," RAND Corporation analyst Robert E. Hunter wrote on the day the agency went out of existence. "It thus got a hearing for U.S. policy and actions that many a diplomat, tied to the prevailing party line, could not achieve."

USIA's broadcast arms were transferred to a new entity called the Broadcasting Board of Governors and its radio outlets—the flagship Voice of America (VOA), Radio Free Europe/Radio Liberty, and several others. Since then the radio's capabilities have bordered on completely ineffective, mired by poor leadership and a lack of direction. According to some officials within the staff, the radio networks were penetrated by foreign intelligence service personnel and sympathizers of the foreign governments the radios were seeking to influence. In 2014, VOA scrapped several significant broadcast operations into China by ending all shortwave radio broadcasting. The move resulted in limiting the reach of VOA broadcasts to millions of Chinese and others in Asia who do not have Internet access and rely on shortwave radio for reliable news and information. The cuts were made at the same time Chinese and Russian state-run propaganda outlets were given unprecedented access to U.S. markets, including China Central Television, which is the Beijing government's official television broadcast outlet. CCTV can be found on most American cable service providers, yet few American cable outlets can be freely viewed in China. The state-run Russian propaganda television outlet Russia Today, or RT, also broadcasts widely in the United States and Europe, with no opposition from governments or demands that Western free media outlets be allowed greater broadcast access as reciprocity for their presence.

In January 2016, the Broadcasting Board of Governors recognized that it was losing the information war to countries like Russia and China and did not have enough money to do its job properly. "There's no question we're badly underfunded and don't have enough money to compete with our adversaries," Jeff Shell, chairman of the Broadcasting Board of Governors, told the *Washington Times*. With an annual radio budget of around $730 million, Shell said, the U.S. radios are funded with a small fraction of what America's adversaries are spending on propaganda and broadcasts, including modern and far-reaching satellite television operations like RT, CCTV, and Qatar-based Al Jazeera. "If we have limited taxpayer funds, we should be much more focused on influencing people than rough audience numbers," Shell said. "We have to make both regional and technological choices. We'd love to be on FM and on TV and all over the world, but we've decided in some countries that it's more important to reach young people in the digital realm." According to Shell, the major challenges come from Russia's new nationalistic media, China's challenge through cyber technology, and violent Islamic extremists using online outlets to spread propaganda. Official U.S. broadcasting, Shell says, seeks to influence people to feel better about America. "Nobody disagrees that we need to be fighting the information war and that winning hearts and minds is very important in this world where we have lots of different challenges to this country," he said.

Yet the U.S. government's most senior official in charge of public diplomacy revealed in 2014 that the United States is not waging a war of ideas in the battle against Islamic terrorists. Rick Stengel, a former *Time* magazine reporter and the Obama administration's undersecretary of state for public diplomacy, revealed the lack of an information warfare capability during a speech when he stated the administration would not wage a war of ideas against the Islamic State. "I would say that there is no battle of ideas with ISIL," he said, using another name for the Islamic State. "ISIL is bereft of ideas, they're bankrupt of ideas. It's not an organization that is animated by ideas. It's a criminal, savage, barbaric organization—I feel like we won that battle already." The statement is one of the clearest examples of the surrender by the Obama administration in the war of ideas, and why America's enemies continue to advance with deadly consequences.

The State Department's effort to combat Islamic ideology has been a failure since the September 11, 2001, terrorist attacks. Since the administration of George W. Bush and the 9/11 attacks, I became convinced that the ideology of Islamism must be confronted, that this was the key to defeating a deadly enemy. Unless the ideology was attacked and defeated there could be no victory and the United States was doomed to endless war. In response, I developed a policy proposal that was presented in briefings at the State Department and Pentagon for two senior officials. It was a concrete plan of action for countering the deadly ideology of al Qaeda. The first meeting on the plan was held with Douglas Feith, the undersecretary of defense for policy, who was told one solution to counteracting Islamic terrorism would be to develop a network of interreligious, faith-based, nongovernmental organizations that could advocate publicly for nonviolent and noncoercive means to practice religion and promote the concept of toleration among all faiths. The strategic goal would be to work with Muslims in reforming the tenets of Islam so that groups like al Qaeda (and today, the Islamic State) could be theologically declared un-Islamic. While difficult, the prospect of triggering a nonviolent reformation of Islam is not impossible.

Under my plan, a network of academic and nongovernmental organization centers would be set up, staffed, and funded around the world to study and develop critiques and counterproposals to the destructive tenets of radical Islam. Feith lamented that while he liked the plan, resistance was likely from Congress, where he had been unable to get support for Pentagon funding of programs to counter radical madrassas in Pakistan that were—and remain—a major ideological breeding ground for Islamic extremists. A second briefing was held at the State Department for Karen Hughes, the Bush administration's undersecretary of state for public diplomacy. Hughes listened politely to the ideological warfare counterterrorism proposal but did nothing to implement it.

The main State Department entity initially charged with using information operations to counter foreign Islamic terrorism was the Center for Strategic Counterterrorism Communications. The center began operating in 2010 and was formalized under a presidential order signed by Obama in September 2011. The order was remarkable for the fact that no mention in the document was made of the word *Islam*, or of *Islamic*—the source of the terrorists' ideology. Instead, the directive called for "developing expertise on implementing highly focused social media campaigns." Launched under Secretary of State Hillary Clinton, the center failed to counter al Qaeda's strategic propaganda, which early on consisted of poor-quality videos and faxed manifestos. The center would become the butt of jokes that its mission was to become an American Twitter troll to out-tweet the Islamists, who quickly were able to master highly effective and religious-based propaganda and social media campaigns to recruit terrorists and propagandize Muslims.

The Center for Strategic Counterterrorism Communications focused on operating as a social media troll, and its poor management and operations would produce one of the worst outcomes for overall U.S. government counter-ideology programs. By the end of 2015, a panel of nongovernment experts concluded that the center's efforts were so ineffective and poorly executed that *the U.S. government should not be engaged in counterpropaganda programs at all*. The panel, made up of Silicon Valley tech experts, believed that the task of countering Muslim extremists was too difficult for the U.S. government because the propaganda efforts lacked credibility, and that therefore, rather than try to conduct credible information warfare operations, the government simply should not engage in counter-ideology programs. It was another major setback for American information warfare efforts against terrorism.

Without American leadership, the government decided instead to farm out its counter-ideology effort to foreign Muslim nations, including those that promote Islamist ideologies. It was a damning indictment and a complete abdication of American leadership for the single most important element in the entire enterprise—military, diplomatic, intelligence— targeting Islamist terrorism. Without defeating the Islamist ideology of the Islamic State and other terrorist groups, there will be no way to ultimately win what has shaped up to be a very ineffective "war" against the extremists.

The panel of experts' report was kept secret to avoid making the president and his national security team look bad, including Clinton, who was in charge of the department when the failed center was first created. A U.S. official familiar with the report told the *Washington Post* the experts "had serious questions about whether the U.S. government should be involved in overt messaging at all." The problem was highlighted in testimony to Congress by Department of Homeland Security secretary Jeh Johnson, who suggested that the U.S. government had given up in the war of ideas because government-produced anti-jihad messaging, "just given the nature of it, would not be very credible." He did not explain why the government lacked credibility. But the comment was a clear indication the Obama administration was not prepared to even attempt building a credible countermessaging group like the Cold War–era Active Measures Working Group. The director of the center, Rashad Hussain, a Muslim American, was transferred to a position at the Justice Department. Hussain had previously been appointed by Obama to be a special envoy to the Organization of the Islamic Conference.

Following the critical report, the center rebranded itself in early 2016 as a new Global Engagement Center, also located at the State Department but continuing the policy of farming out counter-ideology efforts to Muslim states. The new center was headed by former Navy SEAL Michael Lumpkin, who was transferred from the Pentagon, where he had been assistant defense secretary for special operations and low-intensity conflict. Lumpkin sought to improve the program by bringing in specialists in information technology, along with officials from the intelligence community, Pentagon, and State Department. "It's an effects-based organization," Lumpkin told me, referring to the Global Engagement Center. "This isn't your traditional diplomatic endeavor, where I'm trying to negotiate a treaty with violent extremist groups. At its core, what we're trying to do is prevent individuals from turning to violence. Whether it's traveling to the physical battlefield or committing individual acts of terror around the world, we're trying to change the behavior of a specific audience. So, what we had to do is build an effects-based structure that is agile and can yield the results that we're looking for."

The battle space for the center is social media, Twitter and Facebook being the largest and a major component of

Islamic State propaganda. The Global Engagement Center does about 90 percent of its thematic campaigns in Arabic and only a small portion in English. The Islamic State similarly promotes only about 3 percent of its content in English, the rest in Arabic. For Syria, satellite television is another major vehicle for the center's work. The goal is to expose the true nature of the Islamic State, perhaps the most violent terrorist group to emerge in at least a century. That is carried out through thematic campaigns of targeted emails and social media postings, as well as videos. From a data analytics perspective, the Global Engagement Center, as the Chinese have done, is developing ways of technically skewing search engine results so that Islamic State–origin or sympathetic content appears on page 35 of the search results. The search engine optimization would be an effective counter since most people end their search after a single page or the first few pages of results and rarely go beyond ten pages. Another tactic by the center is using so-called lawfare tools, such as seeking enforcement of terms of service agreements software companies impose on their customers, and identifying Islamic State recruiters and propagandists who violate social media and other terms and use it as leverage against them.

Data analytics also are being used to target audiences that the center believes are vulnerable to the Islamic State's messages. The center then develops countermessages honed through focus group testing that provide key influence language that is likely to resonate with specific groups. The center has few metrics that provide feedback on whether the programs are working. However, intelligence agencies reported a sharp decline in IS's foreign fighter recruitment numbers. Another, more ominous sign of the center's effectiveness is death threats issued against the center and its people by the Islamic State. The Global Engagement Center set itself the goal of focusing on countering the Islamic State messaging and propaganda through an innovative and agile organization better focused on a more modern information warfare threat posed by IS.

The center also is trying to tap into Silicon Valley and other nongovernment partners and has set as another goal the creation of a network to defeat a network. It is organized into a content office that produces information for use in campaigns targeting various foreign audiences. Another office works on analytics, using big data to identify those involved in influencing foreign audiences and then working to influence them. A third section is called the network engagement office, which orchestrates various U.S. government agencies in the messaging campaigns. The budget has been increased from $5.6 million in 2015 to $15.8 million in 2016 and is slated to reach between $19 million and $21 million in 2017, far short of the $2 billion once allocated to USIA. Located within the main State Department building not far from the iconic Lincoln Memorial in Washington, the center has set as a major target the blocking of Islamic State recruitment efforts. The overall goal is to starve terrorist organizations of recruits and use military operations to finish off the rest. Strategic messaging will try to break the brand of the Islamic State by revealing its true nature and its use of brutal executions and mass-murder videos of its captured opponents. It has no plans to engage in Twitter warfare with the hard-core Islamic terrorists. For the hard core, the only recourse is to take them out militarily.

But, as done with its predecessor, the politically correct constraints imposed on the center that prevent it from engaging in debates on the nature of Islam signal that the program is destined to fail. The center is bound by the Obama administration's prohibition against addressing Islam and instead has farmed out the responsibility for countering Islamic radicalization to foreign states. It is based on the false notion that the Constitution's establishment clause prohibiting state religion applies to all government counterterrorism efforts.

The U.S. government's loss of information warfare capabilities resulted in the failure to wage ideological warfare against the al Qaeda terrorist organization. Systematically killing off al Qaeda senior leaders in drone strikes was a key factor contributing to the creation of the ultraviolent al Qaeda offshoot known as the Islamic State, a group that has usurped al Qaeda's role as the leading Islamic terrorist organization and is expanding the nature of the threat from an underground group waging low-level warfare to an aspirational nation-state controlling territory and people. After the Islamic State took over large portions of Iraq and Syria in 2015, Obama announced a new strategy for countering the group, a strategy that again was doomed from the start by its failure to understand the nature of Islamist ideology. This is a direct result of the liberal left political agenda, which prevents successful information warfare against a host of enemies.

4

CHINA
The Panda That Eats, Shoots, and Leaves

As cyber technology continues to develop,
cyber warfare has quietly begun.
—Huang Hanwen, Lu Tongshan, Zhao
Yanbin, and Liu Zhengquan, "Aerospace
Electronic Warfare," December 1, 2012

The year is 2028. It is August and the weather is hot. People's Liberation Army (PLA) colonel Sun Kangzhou and three highly trained special operations commandos from the Chengdu military region in southern China are sitting in two vehicles outside a Walmart Supercenter in rural Pennsylvania about 115 miles northeast of Pittsburgh. Dressed in jeans, T-shirts, and work boots, the men appear to be just like any construction workers. In fact, Colonel Sun and his men are members of the elite Falcon special forces team. One of the vehicles is a heavy-duty pickup truck with a trailer carrying a large backhoe. The other is a nondescript blue sedan. The commandos' target today is not a military base but something much more strategic.

It has been two weeks since the deadly military confrontation between a Chinese guided-missile destroyer and a U.S. Navy P-8 maritime patrol aircraft thousands of miles away in the South China Sea. The 500-foot-long Luyang II missile warship *Yinchuan* made a fatal error by firing one of its HHQ-9 long-range surface-to-air missiles at the P-8 as it flew some seventy-seven miles away. The militarized Boeing 737 had been conducting a routine electronic reconnaissance mission over the sea, something the Chinese communist government in Beijing routinely denounces as a gross violation of sovereignty. The Chinese missile was tracked by the P-8's sensors after a radar alarm signal went off, warning of the incoming attack. The advance sensor warning allowed the P-8 pilot to maneuver the jet out of range of the missile. The crew watched it fall into the sea. Fearing a second missile launch, the pilot ordered the crew to fire back. The aircraft bay doors opened and an antiship cruise missile, appropriately named SLAM-ER, for Standoff Land Attack Missile-Expanded Response, took off. Minutes later, the missile struck the ship, sinking the vessel and killing most of the crew.

The South China Sea incident, as the military encounter was called, was just the kind of military miscalculation senior American military leaders feared would take place for years, as China's military forces over the years had built up military forces on disputed islands and gradually claimed the entire strategic waterway as its maritime territory.

Following the South China Sea incident, U.S.-China tensions reached a boiling point with threats and counterthreats, including official Chinese government promises of retaliation. In Washington, phone calls to Chinese political leaders went unanswered. Beijing streets were filled with thousands of protesters in what were carefully orchestrated government-run demonstrations denouncing America. The demonstrators were demanding payback for sinking the warship. Tensions were the highest in history and threatened to end the peaceful period since the two major trading partners shelved their ideological differences beginning in the 1980s.

Colonel Sun and his team are now striking back in ways the United States would never suspect. The sabotage mission they have embarked on is unlike any conducted before and is one that China's military over the past two decades has been secretly training to carry out: an information warfare attack on the American electrical power grid.

Chinese military intelligence hackers, after decades of covert cyber intrusions into American industrial control computer networks, have produced a detailed map of the United States' most critical infrastructure—the electrical power grid stretching from the Atlantic to the Pacific and north and south between Canada and Mexico.

Unbeknownst to the FBI, CIA, or National Security Agency, the Chinese have discovered a strategic vulnerability in the grid near the commandos' location. The discovery was made by China's Unit 61398, the famed hacker group targeted in a U.S. federal grand jury indictment more than a decade earlier, which named five of the unit's PLA officers. The officers and their supporters had laughed off the Ameri-

cans' legal action as just another ineffective measure by what
Beijing believed had become the weakened "paper tiger" that
was the United States.

The raid is code-named Operation Duanlu—Operation
Short-Circuit—and was approved by the Communist Party of
China Central Military Commission a day earlier. The commission is the ultimate power in China, operating under the
principle espoused by People's Republic of China founder Mao
Zedong, who understood that political power grows from the
barrel of a gun.

The two commandos in the truck drive off to a remote
stretch of highway several miles away to a point that was previously identified near a large hardwood tree that has grown
precariously close to a key local power line. The truck drives
by the tree, whose roots have been weakened on the side
away from the power lines by the commandos weeks earlier.
The backhoe arm pushes the tree over and into the power
lines, disrupting the flow of electricity and shutting down
power throughout the area.

At precisely the same time as the tree strikes the power
lines, Colonel Sun sits in the car, boots up a laptop computer,
and with a few keystrokes activates malicious software that
has been planted inside the network of a nearby electrical
substation. The substation is one of the most modern power
centers and is linked to the national grid through "smart
grid" technology designed to better automate and operate
the U.S. electrical infrastructure. The smart grid technology,
however, has been compromised years earlier during a naïve
U.S. Energy Department program to cooperate with China

on advanced electrical power transmission technology. The Chinese cooperated, and they also stole details of the new U.S. grid system and provided them to Chinese military intelligence.

Once in control of the substation's network, Colonel Sun sets in motion a cascading electrical power failure facilitated by cyberattacks but most important carried out in ways that prevent even the supersecret National Security Agency, America's premier cyber-intelligence agency, from identifying the Chinese cyberattackers and linking them to Beijing. The agency never recovered from the damage to its capabilities caused years earlier by a renegade contractor whose charges of illegal domestic spying led to government restrictions on its activities that ultimately prevent the agency from catching the Chinese before the electrical infrastructure cyberattack. For political leaders, the devastating power outage is caused by a tree in Pennsylvania, leading to a cascading power outage around the nation.

The Chinese conducted the perfect covert cyberattack, which cripples the United States, throwing scores of millions of Americans into pre-electricity darkness for months. Millions of deaths will ensue before Washington learns of the Chinese military role and, rather than fight back, makes a humiliating surrender to all Beijing's demands—withdrawal of all U.S. military forces from Asia to areas no farther west than Hawaii, and an end to all military relationships with nations in Asia.

• • •

The above scenario is fictional. Yet the devastation a future information warfare attack would have on critical infrastructures in the United States is a real and growing danger.

No other nation today poses a greater danger to American national security than China, a state engaged in an unprecedented campaign of information warfare using both massive cyberattacks and influence operations aimed at diminishing what Beijing regards as its most important strategic enemy. Yet American leaders remain lost in a Cold War political gambit that once saw China as covert ally against the Soviet Union. Today the Soviet Union is gone but China remains a nuclear-armed communist dictatorship on the march.

From an information warfare stance, China today has emerged as one of the most powerful and capable threats facing the United States. By May 2016 American intelligence agencies had made a startling discovery: Chinese cyber-intelligence services had developed technology and network penetration skills allowing them to control the results of Internet searches conducted on Google's world-famous search engine.

By controlling one of the most significant Information Age technologies used in refining and searching the massive ocean of data on the Internet, the Chinese are now able to control and influence what millions of users in China see when they search using Google. Thus a search for the name *Tiananmen*—the main square in Beijing, where Chinese troops murdered unarmed prodemocracy protesters in June 1989—can be spoofed by Chinese information warriors into returning results in which the first several pages make no reference to the massacre. The breakthrough is similar to the kind of totalitarian control outlined in George Orwell's novel *Nineteen Eighty-Four* with the creation of a fictional language called Newspeak, which was used to serve the total dominance of the state.

Technically, what China did was a major breakthrough in search engine optimization—the art and science of making sites appear higher or lower in search listings. The feat requires a high degree of technical skill to pull off and would require learning the secret algorithms—self-contained, step-by-step computer search operations—used by Google. The intelligence suggests that Chinese cyberwarfare researchers had made a quantum leap in capability by actually gaining access to Google secrets and machines and adjusting the algorithms to make sure searches are produced according to Chinese information warfare goals.

Those goals are to promote continued rule by the Communist Party of China and to attack and defeat China's main enemy: the United States of America. Thus Chinese information warriors can continue the lies and deception that China poses no threat, is a peaceful country, does not seek to take over surrounding waterways, and does not abuse human rights, and that its large-scale military buildup is for purely defensive purposes.

The dominant battle space for Chinese information warfare programs is the Internet, using a combination of covert and overt means. The most visible means of attack can be seen in Chinese media that is used to control the population domestically, and to attack the United States, Japan, and other declared enemies through an international network of state-controlled propaganda outlets, both print and digital, that have proved highly effective in influencing foreign audiences. One of the flagship party mouthpieces is *China Daily,* an English-language newspaper with a global circulation of 900,000 and an estimated 43 million readers online. China Central Television, known as CCTV, operates a twenty-four-hour cable news outlet as well to support its information warfare campaigns.

"The People's Republic of China has studied the U.S. approach to information warfare from the Cold War and has successfully navigated itself into a position of 'respectability' compared to their brothers from Russia and their ham-fisted 'Russia Today' (RT)," said retired navy captain James Fanell, a former Pacific Fleet intelligence director who specializes in Chinese affairs. Fanell compares Chinese information warfare targeting the United States and the inability to recognize the danger to a frog being slowly boiled alive. "The heat in the pool just keeps going up one degree at a time," he says.

Chinese information warfare is being developed within the Communist Party of China's Central Military Commission, the highest-ranking military body in the nation. One of the most visible uses of information operations can be seen in China's systematic approach to acquiring territory around the periphery of the country, specifically the waters stretching from the Pacific northeast southward through the South China Sea and Indian Ocean.

China's aggression in the South China Sea, the strategic waters joining the Pacific and Indian Oceans, is among the more visible examples of this new strategic information warfare. The effort remained at low levels for years but emerged as a major policy issue for the United States around 2011. China carefully avoided provoking a U.S. reaction and decided to carry out its island building at the lowest profile possible. Before long, it had built up some 3,200 acres of islands, through dredging the seafloor and using the sand to produce above-water islands that had once been coral reefs. The Chinese were able to deceive the world into believing that the waters were historically theirs and that any other countries' claims to the sea as international waters were false. Beijing also announced, significantly, that any attempt to counter these claims posed a threat to China's central national interests—language widely viewed as a basis for going to war to defend those interests.

Behind the campaign was a sophisticated combination of information warfare and Chinese deception operations that lulled the United States into first ignoring the problem and later halfheartedly attempting, through public statements, to prevent military weapons and facilities from being added. But it was too late. By 2016, China had finished building a series of military bases in the South China Sea, first on Woody Island in the Paracels, in the northern part of the sea, then on three separate maritime outposts in the Spratly Islands in the southern part; it also revealed plans for a major base on Scarborough Shoal, a fifty-eight-square-mile shoal that is strategically located some 120 miles west of the Philippines—where

U.S. warships and warplanes are deployed at Subic Bay as part of an enhanced U.S.–Philippines defense agreement.

China launched an aggressive information and cyberwarfare operation against regional states beginning around 2010, using military cyberwarfare units located in the Chengdu military region under a code-named Unit 78020. No government was spared in the attacks that involved cyber strikes against computer networks in Cambodia, Indonesia, Laos, Malaysia, Myanmar, Nepal, the Philippines, Singapore, Thailand, and Vietnam. "We assess Unit 78020's focus is the disputed, resource-rich South China Sea, where China's increasingly aggressive assertion of its territorial claims has been accompanied by high-tempo intelligence gathering," states a report by the cybersecurity firm ThreatConnect. "The strategic implications for the United States include not only military alliances and security partnerships in the region, but also risks to a major artery of international commerce through which trillions of dollars in global trade traverse annually." According to the report, "Dominating the South China Sea is a key step for Beijing in achieving regional hegemony." Additionally, the other claimants to the sea, notably Vietnam and Philippines, are weaker and lack the security guarantees from the United States that have helped temper similar tensions with Japan in the East China Sea.

The information warfare campaign focused on all the governments of Southeast Asia, including the headquarters of the ten-nation Association of Southeast Asian Nations and private and public energy organizations. The goal was data theft, to gain valuable commercial information and foreign government secrets that could be given to Chinese companies or used in negotiations. For the longer term, Chinese military hackers were gaining strategic access to target government computer networks that could be attacked and shut down in a crisis or conflict, or used to spread disinformation internally to confuse and weaken the enemy. For the South China Sea campaign, the Chinese used an extensive network of hundreds of Internet Protocol addresses that in some cases were used for only an hour before being abandoned—all in line with a methodology designed to avoid detection by cybersecurity services, both government and private. The operation was first detected in September 2010 and continued at the time the ThreatConnect report was published in August 2015. The domain used for the attacks by the Chinese, known as "greensky27.vcip.net," included 1,236 IP addresses spanning twenty-six cities in eight nations.

Through these information warfare activities China incrementally gained control over the South China Sea and employed multiple pillars of national power with the larger goal of influencing and ultimately exercising control over the entire region. The shadow information war is typical of the kinds of activities China engages in not just in Southeast and Northeast Asia but globally as part of its drive for world acceptance and domination.

As ThreatConnect states:

All of China's activities in the South China Sea, whether military, diplomatic, or economic, have been long supported by a well-resourced covert signals intelligence and digital exploitation unit that maintained deep access within China's Southeast Asian neighbors' public and private sector enterprises. . . . What is really at hand is a broader national objective of physically intruding into the 1.4 million square miles that make up the South China Sea. It is likely that China does not view this behavior as criminal in nature, insofar as it cannot be stealing if you already consider something to be yours. But the targets of this activity most certainly do not share that view. This aggressiveness clearly comes at an expense to China's reputation regionally and internationally as credible proof of these operations continues to mount.

What made the ThreatConnect report so compelling was its detailed analysis of one of the players involved in the campaign. A PLA officer code-named GreenSky27 was exposed as Ge Xing, a cyber operative with an extensive public persona on Chinese social media sites dating to 2004. Ge posted photos of himself within the compound located in Kunming, in Yunnan Province, China, which borders Myanmar, Laos, and Vietnam and is the center of information warfare operations against South China Sea states. Ge was shown biking and holding an infant and posting about his "beloved Party school" in Kunming where he attended courses as part of his career as a PLA officer. He also attended the PLA International Studies University in 2014 and published several academic papers for Unit 78020, including "Analysis of Post-War Thailand's Political Democratization Characteristics and Factors" and "Examination of Trends in Thailand's

Southern Muslim Separatist Movement." Ge was born in 1980 and graduated from Yunnan University in 2008. GPS routes used in Ge's various bike rides in Kunming also were posted. Technical analysis of Ge's online activities in the Unit 78020 hacking operations included his links to the cyberattacks, which showed a decline in malicious hacking activities during his travel and vacations and a corresponding decline in his social media postings during the same absences. There was even a gap in his Unit 78020 cyber operations when Ge's child was born. The infrastructure used in the South China Sea cyberattacks also ceased operating during Ge's visits to his ancestral memorial, and during two vacation trips in the summer of 2014.

In May 2014, after the Justice Department indicted five PLA hackers belonging to another cyberwarfare unit, Shanghai-based Unit 61398, the South China Sea cyberattack operations showed a dramatic drop-off in activity. The high-profile indictments targeted military hackers who stole valuable information from major companies in Pennsylvania, including Westinghouse and Alcoa.

The PLA indictments were largely symbolic since the Justice Department has no real prospect of ever prosecuting the Unit 61398 hackers. But the indictment was the first time the U.S. government had taken off the veil of secrecy surrounding Chinese cyberattacks against the United States. The PLA hackers were identified as Wang Dong, Sun Kailiang, Wen Xinyu, Huang Zhenyu, and Gu Chunhui and their activities outlined in the fifty-six-page indictment. The group was part of the Third Department of the General Staff, also known as

3PLA, and its Unit 61398. The FBI went so far as to draw up wanted posters for the five.

Since 2006 the hackers had used sophisticated technology and traditional fake emails to fool targeted Americans with access to corporate secrets into providing break-in points to company networks. They then methodically stole key commercial secrets, such as technical design details for Westinghouse nuclear reactors and solar panel technology. Internal communications containing valuable economic data were also stolen and provided by the PLA to Chinese state-run competitors.

The companies hit in the cyberattacks included Westinghouse Electric; SolarWorld AG; United States Steel; Allegheny Technologies; the United Steel, Paper and Forestry, Rubber, Manufacturing, Energy, Allied Industrial, and Service Workers International Union; and Alcoa.

The indictment "will scare the PLA hackers, at least for a few months, while they try to find out how they were detected," said Michael Pillsbury, the Pentagon consultant and specialist on China. "Much stronger medicine will be needed next time," added Pillsbury, a senior fellow at the Hudson Institute.

The Justice Department prosecutor in the case explained later that the indictment came out of Chinese government demands for proof of U.S. government charges of widespread Chinese cyberattacks. John Carlin, assistant attorney general for national security, told a security conference in Colorado that after years of ignoring or playing down the Chinese cyber threat, the government was seeking to deal with Beijing's nefarious data theft and network penetrations the way it dealt with terrorism after the September 11 terrorist attacks. "We heard directly from the Chinese, who said, 'If you have evidence, hard evidence that we're committing this type of activity that you can prove in court, show us.' So we did," Carlin said, adding that the indictment was a first step in what he called a multipronged strategic approach that set up a "red line" for the Chinese that was designed to dissuade future attacks. Carlin threatened further action, despite the White House's general lack of interest in effective countermeasures. "We will continue to increase the cost of committing this type of activity on American soil where it is occurring, where they are taking the information, until it stops, and we need to maintain that commitment," he said.

The commitment was not maintained. And one of the most damaging Chinese cyberattacks against the United States would follow shortly: the theft of federal employee records in the Office of Personnel Management (OPM). That took place after an earlier private sector cyber strike against millions of medical records held by the major health-care provider Anthem.

On June 4, 2015, the OPM posted a message to the 2.7 million federal employees on its website revealing that in April 2015 the agency detected a cyber intrusion on its networks affecting some 4 million current and former federal workers. Within weeks of that disclosure OPM released further news that the cyberattack was far more damaging than originally assessed. Instead of the initial 4 million people involved in the data theft, the total had increased to 21.5 million. Worse, the agency delicately announced that among those millions of stolen records was "an incident" affecting background investigation records, among some of the most sensitive information in the government's possession used in determining eligibility for access to classified information. "OPM has determined that the types of information in these records include identification details such as Social Security Numbers; residency and educational history; employment history; information about immediate family and other personal and business acquaintances; health, criminal and financial history; and other details," the agency said. "Some records also include findings from interviews conducted by background investigators and fingerprints. Usernames and passwords that background investigation applicants used to fill out their background investigation forms were also stolen."

It was a security disaster for the millions who held security clearances and were now vulnerable to Chinese intelligence targeting, recruitment, and neutralization. A senior U.S. intelligence official briefed on the classified details of the OPM told me that the early technical intelligence analysis of the data theft revealed that it was part of a PLA military hacking operation. "It is fair to say this is a Chinese PLA cyberattack," said the official, adding that the conclusion was based on an analysis of the software operating methods used to gain access to the government network.

Intelligence officials believe the source behind the attack is the PLA's Unit 61398 and that it was carried out in retaliation for the May 1 indictment of the five hackers. Months before the OPM hacking was discovered, Chinese hackers also carried out one of the largest data thefts of a health-care provider in history, targeting Anthem and stealing an estimated 80 million records. The breach, made public in February 2015, included names, birthdates, Social Security numbers, medical identification data, street and email addresses, and employee data, including income, the company announced.

A staff report by the House Committee on Oversight and Government Reform concluded the data breach could have been prevented had government officials heeded numerous warnings about the danger of cyberattacks.

Cyberattacks against the State Department, White House, and Nuclear Regulatory Commission and other compromises pale in comparison to the damage done by the OPM attack.

"As a result, tens of millions of federal employees and their families paid the price," the report said. "Indeed, the damage done to the Intelligence Community will never be truly known. Due to the data breach at OPM, adversaries are in possession of some of the most intimate and embarrassing details of the lives of individuals who our country trusts to protect national security and its secrets."

The Department of Homeland Security (DHS) and its National Cybersecurity and Communications Integration Center revealed in an internal bulletin that the OPM and Anthem hackings were just the tip of the iceberg in a major Chinese data collection operation that stretched from July 2014 to June 2015. Sticking to the White House policy of not naming China as the culprit, to avoid upsetting Beijing, the DHS bulletin outlined the major theft of what is called personally identifiable information (PII). It stated that the U.S. Computer Emergency Readiness Team had outlined the details of the attacks. "US-CERT is aware of approximately nine major security incidents in which PII was stolen from private sector companies, U.S. government agencies, and a cleared defense contractor," the bulletin stated. "The cyber threat actors involved in each of these incidents demonstrated a well-planned campaign and high level of sophistication."

The Chinese stole the records in what the commander of the U.S. Cyber Command, Admiral Mike Rogers, described as big data mining for use in future cyberattacks, and for counterintelligence purposes—the identification of American intelligence officers operating undercover overseas. Once identified, the American spies can be co-opted and neutralized, or worse, fooled into reporting back deliberately provided false information—all in support of the Beijing information warfare campaigns. William Evanina, a senior counterintelligence official within the Office of the Director of National Intelligence, warned that big data mining could disclose "who is an intelligence officer, who travels where, when, who's got financial difficulties, who's got medical issues, [to] put together a common picture." Asked by the *Los Angeles Times* if foreign adversaries have used data to glean information on U.S. intelligence operatives, Evanina bluntly replied, "Absolutely."

The threat was not theoretical. In the months after the OPM breach, several former intelligence officials began receiving threatening telephone calls that authorities believe stemmed from the compromised information obtained from OPM background investigation data hacked by the Chinese.

The response by the Obama administration to the Chinese hacking was to ignore it, despite appeals from both national security officials and private security experts that immense damage was being done to American interests and that something needed to be done to stop the attacks.

The White House, however, under Obama had adopted a see-no-evil approach to Chinese hacking that would endure throughout his administration and border on criminal neglect. On several occasions, Obama and his key White House aides were presented with proposals for proactive measures against the Chinese designed to send an unmistakable signal to Beijing that the cyberattacks would not be tolerated. Intelligence officials revealed to me that beginning in August 2011, a series of policy options were drawn up over three months. They included options for conducting counter-cyberattacks against Chinese targets and economic sanctions against key Chinese officials and agencies involved in the cyberattacks. The president rejected all the options as too disruptive of U.S.-China economic relations. Obama never explained why he refused to take action against China, but he clearly rejected anything that might make the United States appear as a world leader and power.

The White House seemed more concerned that U.S. offensive cyberattacks might upset relations with a major trading partner that was holding $1.2 trillion in U.S. Treasury debt. The secret plans were proposed by civilian and military officials who were part of the White House Interagency Policy Committee. The committee is made up of representatives from the Pentagon, intelligence community, law enforcement, homeland security, and foreign affairs agencies.

By the summer of 2015, the group of sixteen U.S. intelligence agencies—including the CIA, DIA, and NSA—that make up what is called the intelligence community weighed in on the growing threat of strategic cyberattacks against the United States. In their top-secret National Intelligence Estimate, the consensus was that as long as the continued policy of not responding remained in place, the United States would continue to be victimized by increasingly damaging cyberattacks on both government and private sector networks. A strong reaction was essential.

The intelligence assessment was produced as the president and his advisers debated what to do to China in response to the OPM and other hacks. The assessment was reflected in comments made by Obama and other officials weeks before the assessment was disclosed. The president said at a summit meeting of world leaders on June 8, 2015, that he expected additional cyberattacks like the OPM hacking to continue. "We have known for a long time that there are significant vulnerabilities and that these vulnerabilities are going to accelerate as time goes by, both in systems within government and within the private sector," the president said while refusing to publicly blame China for the attacks. A week earlier, Admiral Rogers warned that the increase in state-sponsored cyberattacks was due in part to the perception by the attackers that "there's not a significant price to pay" for conducting large-scale cyber intrusions and stealing large quantities of private information.

Retired army lieutenant general and former DIA director Michael Flynn has criticized the failure to understand Information Age threats and respond to them forcefully. "Until we redefine warfare in the age of information, we will continue to be viciously and dangerously attacked with no consequences for those attackers," he told me. "The extraordinary intellectual theft ongoing across the U.S.'s cyber-critical infrastructure has the potential to shut down massive components of our nation's capabilities, such as health care, energy, and communications systems. This alone should scare the heck out of everyone." James Lewis, a cybersecurity expert at the Center for Strategic and International Studies, agreed. "Unless we punch back, we will continue to get hit," Lewis said, suggesting that among the responses would be leaking details of a Chinese Communist Party leader's bank account. "We're all coming to the same place—that a defensive orientation doesn't work," he said.

Chinese cyberattacks have been massive and have inflicted extreme damage to U.S. national security. A sample of the internal U.S. government assessment of the toll became public in some of the 1.7 million highly classified documents stolen from the NSA by Edward Snowden. An NSA graphic on Chinese theft of government and private sector secrets, labeled "secret," bore the headline "Chinese Exfiltrate Sensitive Military Technology." The cyber-spying operation was code-named "BYZANTINE HADES" and the NSA concluded that it resulted in "serious damage to [Defense Department] interests." The statistics were nothing short of alarming. Under "resources" used in the operation, the agency found at least 30,000 incidents, of which more than 500 were "significant intrusions of DoD systems." At least 1,600 network computers were penetrated; at least 60,000 user accounts were compromised; and the attacks cost more than $100 million to assess damage and rebuild compromised networks.

The damage included some of the most strategically important information, such as air refueling schedules for the U.S. Pacific Command. Knowing the schedules is critical information that allows an enemy to learn the range of military aircraft. The information would assist the Chinese military in targeting enemy warplanes and transports with increasingly sophisticated air defenses. The compromise involved the details of how the command moves jet fighters, such as the frontline F-22 fighter, over long distances by following the jets with aerial refueling tankers. The missions are known as Coronet missions. A Coronet refueling operation is a delicate and complex aerial ballet requiring the traveling jets to meet tanker aircraft at precise coordinates and altitudes at exact times. The jet fighters also are required to conduct air-to-air refueling several times during the long flights. Knowing Coronet details would allow China's growing fleet of sophisticated aircraft to conduct similar maneuvers.

Additional data theft involved the compromise of 33,000 general and field-grade officer records from the U.S. Air Force; more than 300,000 user identifications and passwords for the U.S. Navy; and navy missile navigation and tracking systems information and navy nuclear submarine and anti-aircraft missile designs. Export-controlled sensitive technology information taken by the Chinese included data limited under the U.S. International Traffic and Arms Restriction regulations and defense contractor research and development. Activity included defense industrial espionage against some of the military's most advanced systems, including the B-2 bomber, F-22 and F-35 fighter aircraft, the space-based laser, and others. The NSA estimates that the amount of data stolen by Chinese cyber spies amounts to an extraordinary fifty terabytes of data—the equivalent of five times all the information contained in the nearly 161 million books and other printed materials held by the Library of Congress.

On the positive side, the Snowden documents disclosed that despite the damaging attacks, NSA in the past has succeeded in disrupting Chinese cyberattacks. The method was outlined in a PowerPoint slide revealing how NSA cyber spying "discovers adversary tools" used for cyberattacks as they are being developed. The malware tools are then studied and a "tailored countermeasure [is] developed and deployed" so that when the Chinese begin the cyberattack, NSA's "SIGINT [signals intelligence] discovers adversary intentions" and blocks the attacks. Unfortunately, the Snowden betrayal revealed to the Chinese just how proficient NSA was in gaining access to Chinese computer networks, a capability that was effective only so long as it remained secret.

Stefan Halper, editor of the Pentagon study on China's Three Warfares, says the Chinese are using cyber along with information operations in the South China Sea and else-where. Information warfare is "a natural inheritor to party deliberations which took place as early as 1923 when they started talking first about information warfare and is built into Chinese strategic thinking."

Chinese media have been conducting media warfare for the past decade but have been ignored completely in that respect by the U.S. government. On October 30, 2013, an official publication of the Communist Party of China published a chilling reminder of the true nature of the People's Republic. The *Global Times* newspaper disclosed in minute detail how China's People's Liberation Army developed plans for nu-clear missile attacks on the western United States. The news-paper is no ordinary publication, like the scores of officially sanctioned news outlets produced in China. *Global Times* is a tightly controlled organ of the Chinese Communist Party and a subsidiary of its flagship *People's Daily* newspaper. Nothing published in *Global Times* is produced by chance or accident. Any editors and writers who slip up in even the slightest way by publishing unsanctioned content find them-selves behind bars.

The headline in bold Chinese characters did not signal what was coming in the article. "China Has Undersea Stra-tegic Nuclear Deterrent Against United States for the First Time" was not news to those who have watched the PLA develop its conventional and strategic nuclear forces over the past two decades. But at the top of the seven-thousand-word

article the authors disclosed that China's long-range Ju
Lang–2, or Giant Wave–2, missiles would rain death and
destruction on the United States. Imposed over a map of the
western United States, a red shaded area from Seattle south
to San Francisco Bay revealed the destruction of a nuclear
strike, with additional shaded areas stretching from Montana
south to Las Vegas and Los Angeles and narrowing eastward
to a point at Chicago. The caption read "Speculated Overall
Destructive Effect Assessment of China's Intercontinental
Nuclear Missiles Hitting Seattle" in phases of three days, a
week, and a month after the blast.

"In general, after a nuclear missile strikes a city, the radioactive dust produced by 20 warheads will be spread by
the wind, forming a contaminated area for thousands of
kilometers," the publication said. "Based on the actual level
of China's one million tons TNT equivalent small nuclear
warhead technology, the 12 JL-2 nuclear missiles carried by
one Type 094 nuclear submarine could cause the destruction
of 5 million to 12 million people, forming a very clear deterrent effect." The report added that to increase the casualties
in the sparsely populated U.S. Midwest, the proposed strikes
would be designed to spread radiation using west to east
winds, and stated: "So to increase the destructive effect, the
main soft targets for nuclear destruction in the United States
will be the main cities on the west coast, such as Seattle, Los
Angeles, San Francisco, and San Diego." As if to indicate the
Chinese military believes the death of millions of Americans
in a nuclear missile attack is more than theoretical, a second
graphic of the Los Angeles area included five black circles

representing blast zones over the heart of the city. "The picture shows the overall destructive effect assessment of an intercontinental missile strike against Los Angeles," the caption noted dryly.

The article is classic Chinese information warfare—the use of nonkinetic, information-based programs and activities as surrogates for military conflict to achieve strategic objectives, an approach generally outlined centuries ago by famed strategist Sun Tzu. It was Sun Tzu who declared that the acme of skill is defeating your enemy without firing a shot. His is the guiding thought behind China's aggressive information warfare today.

As Jake Bebber, a U.S. Cyber Command military officer, put it, the threat from China and its strategy of seeking the destruction of the United States have been misunderstood by the U.S. government and military. "China seeks to win without fighting, so the real danger is not that America will find itself in a war with China, but that America will find itself the loser without a shot being fired," he wrote in a report for the Center for International Maritime Security.

These types of information warfare activities, along with cyberattacks, influence operations, and the buying of former American officials and military officers who can spout China's key information warfare themes, have reached unprecedented levels. And the programs have accelerated under the hard-line Marxist-Leninist policies of current supreme leader and party general secretary Xi Jinping.

While China today remains ruled by a nuclear-armed communist dictatorship, many Americans have been beguiled by successive reformist regimes in China that emerged after the madness of the Cultural Revolution in the 1970s and ouster of radical Maoists. Communism in China remains unfamiliar and to some even nonexistent. After I took part in a debate in New York City in 2007 on the threat posed by China, I was astounded by businessman James McGregor, an adviser to both the U.S. and Chinese governments, who told me after doing business in China for twenty years he had never met a communist. The ruling party boasts 88.6 million members and controls or influences most domestic businesses.

The roots of Chinese information warfare can be found in the writings of ancient strategists. Sun Tzu is well known and his precepts mainly focus on the use of covert intelligence operations to win wars. "Warfare is the way of deception," he wrote. "Thus although you are capable, display incapability to them." But another less well-known Chinese philosopher, Tai Kung, provides a larger strategic perspective on China's information warfare activities today. In a series of revolutionary military strategies called the Six Secret Teachings, which were passed down through the centuries verbally and eventually in writings, Tai Kung introduced the concept of "total warfare"—the use of all available means to achieve victory, including feigning and dissembling to deceive the enemy and allay suspicions, along with bribing and sending gifts to enemies as a way to foster disloyalties among foreign officials and create chaos in their ranks. Tai Kung also advocated covert action as a way of inducing extravagance and wastefulness in the enemy by providing the tools for the enemy's self-destruction. China operates under the concept that utmost secrecy is required in preparation for warfare and that once the battle begins, warfare must be unrestricted by any constraints.* These concepts directly apply to the element of Chinese information warfare currently used by the rulers in the People's Republic of China.

Based on these ancient principles, China has been developing its information warfare programs in earnest since the early 2000s, and despite its penchant for utmost secrecy, military writings obtained by the CIA and Pentagon have revealed the underpinnings of this new strategy. Shen Weiguang, one of China's leading military theorists on information warfare, stated in his 2000 book, *World War, the Third World War—Total Information Warfare,* that warfare in the twenty-first century will shift from traditional mechanized warfare to information-based conflict, the new "leading form of war." In a society dominated by information, Shen, a former People's Liberation Army officer, writes, control is the prime objective and controlling the information domain will be the key to victory. "Whoever controls information society will have the opportunity to dominate the world and even the universe," he warns.

Shen makes the dubious assertion that information warfare will be a bloodless, nonviolent war carried out in the domain of information systems and that it will ultimately replace traditional armed conflict. Echoing Sun Tzu, he states:

---

* Ralph Sawyer, *The Seven Military Classics of Ancient China* (New York: Basic Books, 2007).

"Because one can win an information war without fighting, it is thousands of times more efficient than armed aggression." He called on China to rapidly learn this new form of warfare because China's communist system is "locked in a fierce conflict with the capitalist system."

For the Chinese, information warfare encompasses six aspects: obtaining information by various means, analyzing and verifying information, protecting information from attack or theft, utilizing information fully for military objectives, denying the enemy the ability to gather information, and managing information through electronic means to ensure its use. Its essence is to defeat enemy forces without fighting or with as little fighting as possible. China's plan for information warfare includes both wartime and peacetime variants. For periods of peace, China will wage economic information war, to weaken a country's economy by cutting off the source of information. Cultural information war, psychological war, and Internet war also will be employed in both peacetime and times of conflict. According to Shen, here's what the United States will face from China's military during a future conflict: "Strategically the objective of information war is to destroy the enemy's political, economic, and military information infrastructures, perhaps even the information infrastructure of the whole society. This includes destroying and paralyzing the enemy's military, financial, telecommunications, electronic, and power systems as well as computer networks. Moreover, psychological war and strategic deception would be employed to undermine morale among enemy forces and in the civilian population and weaken confidence in the government in hopes of stripping the enemy of its ability to go to war."

Shen concludes:

Not for a single day have the imperialists given up their desire to destroy socialism. Instead they have adopted all sorts of strategies and taken all kinds of actions to achieve that goal. Peaceful evolution is precisely the product of the failure of the imperialists' armed suffocation strategy and global containment strategy, a shift from "hard confrontation" to "soft confrontation," from "armed conquest" to "victory through peace," an effort to use peaceful methods to achieve objectives unattainable by military means, an attempt to change the face of socialist nations and turn them into the appendages of the capitalist world.

Many of the concepts and theories put forth in 2000 by Shen have been implemented by the Chinese leadership, including the shift within its armed forces from a traditional, ground-force-oriented military to what Beijing calls an "informationized" one.

In 2012 China's National Defense University produced a revealing internal study that includes the first details on information warfare programs and operations being developed by PLA forces for use in both peacetime and wartime.

The offensive information missions will seek to destroy American high-technology networks and systems, including satellites and their ground stations "so as to strip away and weaken the enemy's information collection, dissemination, and processing capabilities," according to a chapter of the report that I obtained. In the next war the Chinese will be using electronic, cyber, and military influence operations for attacks against military computer systems and networks, and specifically against air defenses and for jamming American precision-guided munitions and the GPS satellites that guide them. American antimissile systems also have been made a priority target of Chinese electronic warfare attacks as a way to assist "the penetration of our conventional missiles." By electronically disrupting U.S. missile defenses, Chinese warfighters plan to increase the ability of their large and diverse missile forces to reach and destroy regional targets.

For network attacks, special computer programs and viruses will be used in the attacks to "weaken, sabotage, or destroy enemy computer network systems or to degrade their operating effectiveness." Chinese cyberwarriors plan to exploit what the report called "loopholes and weak links in the enemy network operating system, network protocols, applications software, and management operation." The operations will require Chinese hackers to conduct forced or secret entry into American networks by penetrating security protection measures such as firewalls, gateways, and encryption authentication measures. Once network security is broken, follow-on attacks using "deception and disruption" will take place.

The report provides the first official Chinese evidence that its military forces are developing extremely powerful weapons for what were described as special information warfare attacks. "These weapons can effectively destroy electronic targets, and have become a new means with the highest lethality in information attacks," the report said. "They mainly include directed energy weapons, kinetic energy weapons, incapacitating weapons, and plasma weapons. . . . They mainly include laser weapons, high-power microwave weapons, EM-pulse [electromagnetic pulse] bombs, and particle-beam weapons."

Psychological information warfare attacks by the Chinese military will combine "soft strike" with "hard destruction" means to inflict "enormous shock to the enemy in psychological respects, keep the enemy in a state of fear for a long period, and thus achieve the goal of victory without fighting."

According to the report:

The important means for executing psychological attack against the enemy include the following: first is to organize and conduct public opinion propaganda. No matter whether before a war or during war, it is always necessary to fully exploit carriers such as leaflets, photos, radio and TV, computer networks, multimedia newspapers & magazines, and the Internet, and adopt modes such as sea floats, air projection, and battlefield front-line propaganda directed to the enemy, to carry out psychological deterrence and psychological inducement of the enemy, so as to shake the enemy troops' morale, disintegrate the enemy morale, break up the hostile forces, and win over the enemy people's support. Second is to apply psychological warfare (PSYWAR) weapons to execute psy-

chological attacks against the enemy. This can apply special-
ized PSYWAR weapons such as noise simulators, electronic
whistlers, thought-control weapons, and virtual reality [VR]
means to attack and deter the enemy, generate psychological
fear or various hallucinations in the enemy military and ci-
vilians, and thus shake their will to wage war and degrade
the enemy's operational capability.

Among the exotic Chinese information weapons are holographic projectors and laser-glaring arms that can present large unusual images in the skies above enemy forces that would simulate hallucinations among troops on the ground. Traditional propaganda also will be used, including "public opinion propaganda and PSYWAR weapons to execute psychological attacks against the enemy, so as to disrupt the enemy command decision making, disintegrate the enemy troop morale, and shake the enemy's will to wage war."

All the operations would require military forces to use speed, surprise, and utmost secrecy. Also, Chinese troops are being ideologically hardened against enemy psychological warfare operations and U.S. EMP weapons.*

The response of American leaders to the unprecedented published threat to inflict nuclear annihilation on the United States was equally chilling. Under the liberal left policies of

---

* Thanks to Michael Pillsbury, senior fellow and director for Chinese Strategy at the Hudson Institute, for translating Chapter 7 of the report, "Introduction to Joint Campaign Information Operations," Beijing, National Defense University Press, June 2012. (Military internal distribution only.)

President Barack Obama, every element of the U.S. government was ordered to silence all public criticism of China.
Government spokesmen were prohibited from saying anything about the Chinese threat. The American response to a
state-run Communist Party newspaper's outlining of plans
to kill up to 12 million Americans was silence. It would be
another seventeen days before I posed a question about the
Global Times report to Chief of Naval Operations Admiral
Jonathan Greenert during a conference at the Reagan Presidential Library in Simi Valley, California. Greenert, among
the more dovish navy chiefs in recent years, had been politicized under the Obama administration into not highlighting
any threat posed by China. In response to my question,
he astoundingly dismissed China's submarine-launched nuclear attack threat as "a deterrent" that lacked credibility.
The four-star admiral instead suggested that U.S. attack submarine forces were capable enough to prevent such attacks.
"For a submarine-launched ballistic missile to be effective it
has to be accurate, and you have to be stealthy, and survivable
and I'll leave it at that," Greenert said, adding that American
nuclear-armed missile submarines remain a powerful deterrent despite an aging U.S. nuclear arsenal and the urgent need
to upgrade those forces, including new missile submarines, in
the face of eight years of sharp defense spending cuts under
Obama.

Several weeks before the *Global Times* article boasting
of the deaths of millions of Americans, Xi Jinping, China's
supreme leader, spoke to a gathering of party propaganda
officials tasked with waging what he termed "public opinion

struggle," the Marxist concept of using all means to wage information warfare. The secret speech was reproduced in *China Digital Times,* an uncensored aggregator of news and information on China. It was significant for revealing the true and secret objectives behind the current leadership of China's efforts to master the power of the Information Age. Bemoaning how the Communist Party is besieged by hostile Western forces promoting values such as freedom and democracy, Xi issued an urgent appeal for cadres to step up the use of information warfare to defeat the United States and its democratic allies. The Chinese leader first made clear that the Chinese communist system—socialism with Chinese characteristics—is threatened by the West, along with the Communist Party itself. "The disintegration of a regime often starts from the ideological area, political unrest and regime change may perhaps occur in a night, but ideological evolution is a long-term process," Xi proclaimed. "If the ideological defenses are breached, other defenses become very difficult to hold.... Communist Party members should fight and struggle for their beliefs, and contribute all their energies or even their lives." The comments provide a clue to a future U.S. information warfare program against China.

The speech was an ideological call to arms, an appeal to step up information warfare against the West, an enemy Xi sees as posing an existential threat to party rule and what he has called the China Dream—the objective of diminishing all opposition to the Chinese communist system and leading to world domination by China, economically, politically, and militarily. This is the Chinese supremacist view of a world dominated by a Communist Party whose current leaders are the heirs of totalitarians behind the deaths of 65 million Chinese since coming to power in 1949, and who have never acknowledged that carnage or been held accountable for the atrocities committed under what has been called Marxism–Leninism–Mao Zedong thought, the official state ideology.

In December 2015, Xi completed a major reformation of the Communist Party–led People's Liberation Army and its massive intelligence system with an eye to projecting power—both military and informational—around the world. The revamping of the military command structure has increased the danger posed by China's cyberwarfare capabilities, which were folded into a new military entity called the Strategic Support Force and given greater prominence within China's overall military forces. The Strategic Support Force, including intelligence, cyberwarfare, and information warfare units, was elevated to an equal footing with China's other military services, the army, navy, air force, and strategic rocket forces that operate both nuclear and conventional missiles.

China's main cyberwarfare capabilities were developed and are mainly carried out by one key unit within the all-powerful military, the Third Department of the General Staff, also known as 3PLA. American intelligence agencies estimate 3PLA has as many as 100,000 cyberwarfare troops—hackers and electronic intelligence-gathering specialists—under its control. They include highly trained people who specialize in conducting network attacks, information technology, code

breaking, and foreign languages. The new force also includes
the Fourth Department, China's separate military electronic
intelligence and electronic warfare service, and the more
traditional military intelligence service devoted to human
spying known as 2PLA.

Despite its secrecy, Xi made a revealing call for greater
military information warfare efforts in the late summer of
2014. In a little-noticed report on China National Television,
the Web version of state-run China Central Television, the
Chinese leader announced at a meeting of the Communist
Party Politburo on August 1, 2015, that China must adopt a
new information warfare strategy as part of greater military
innovation. "Xi Jinping encouraged the army to change fixed
mindsets on mechanized warfare and create a concept of information warfare, as the country faces escalating tensions
on intelligence issues with other countries," the English-
language CCTV broadcast announced. According to Xi,
the PLA needs to "counter nontraditional security threats,
including economic threats." The disclosure went unreported
in Western news media but confirmed the growing danger
posed by China.

For China, these events—the call to revamp information warfare against the West and reorganize the PLA into
a high-tech power projection force—represent the ultimate
repudiation of several decades of U.S. policies of conciliation
toward China, which were the hallmark of successive U.S.
administrations since the 1970s. That was when President
Richard Nixon's national security adviser Henry Kissinger

introduced the Cold War policy of playing the China card against the Soviet Union. Since then, Kissinger and others of his ilk have dominated U.S. policy toward China, which has been characterized as unfettered engagement, regardless of Chinese threats, be they support for enemy states, theft of American nuclear secrets, or the spread of nuclear weapons around the world.

The height of the appeasement of China occurred during the administration of President George H. W. Bush, when National Security Adviser Brent Scowcroft secretly traveled to China in July 1989 weeks after Chinese tanks crushed unarmed prodemocracy protesters in Tiananmen Square. Scowcroft and Deputy Secretary of State Lawrence Eagleburger were shown in photographs toasting Chinese leaders by candlelight during the visit. The message was unmistakable: despite curbing high-level contacts with China over the Tiananmen massacre, the U.S. government would continue business as usual with leaders who had been widely denounced as the Butchers of Beijing. The argument of the appeasers of China in the United States, who dominate not only the upper echelons of American government policy making and the halls of academia but the ranks of senior military and intelligence officials as well, is that by adopting conciliatory policies toward Beijing, the United States will foster the evolution of a free and democratic China. Instead the United States has become the target of Chinese hostility and venom and nonkinetic information warfare designed to destroy the nation.

As Grant Newsham and Kerry Gershaneck, two former

U.S. policy makers, put it, the accommodationist approach has been a disaster. Their evidence was China's covert, information-warfare-based program to take over the South China Sea without firing a shot. As they stated in the *National Interest*:

> The United States' approach to dealing with China from the Nixon-Kissinger era onwards resembles a forty-five-year science experiment—an experiment that has failed. In fact, the PRC's relentless effort to create what might cheekily be called a "Greater South China Sea Co-Prosperity Sphere" belies any notion this view was ever correct. China's island-building expansion across the South China Sea is just the latest evidence that most of the "experts" got China wrong.

These wrongheaded policies were not limited to the policy makers, in Republican as well as Democratic administrations, who worshipped at the altar of what they regarded as the great China economic miracle, which for decades appeared to produce a workable Marxist-Leninist economic system. Successive military leaders at the United States Pacific Command, based in Hawaii and charged with keeping the peace in the Asia Pacific, swooned at the prospect of regular meetings and exchanges with Chinese military leaders who were keen to deceive what they must have regarded as hapless Americans into believing that such high-level visits and other military exchanges could "build trust" between the two militaries. The U.S. military leaders have been badly mistaken. In the Chinese system, any Chinese military leader even perceived as having a trusting and friendly demeanor toward the American military would be prosecuted for party disloyalty or treason.

Typical of the U.S. military's self-delusional approach to China was Admiral Samuel Locklear, an ambitious four-star officer. Locklear, in an apparent bid to curry favor with his superiors in Washington, adopted conciliatory postures toward China that sought to play down or ignore dangerous Chinese activities and behaviors. As an example, Locklear suggested in 2013 that China's growing military capabilities were less of a concern than claims that climate change, based on dubious scientific claims about global warming, will eventually produce disastrous rising sea levels. Climate change was a key policy of the liberal left Obama administration, and Locklear's suggestion is an example of how politicized the U.S. military, and the navy in particular, had become under Obama.

According to a senior navy officer, it was Locklear's failure while head of Pacific Command from 2012 to 2015 to assert the U.S. Navy's rights of free navigation in the South China Sea that historians will mark as a failing that facilitated the growth of Chinese military dominance in Asia.

Lured by the prospect of improved relations with the People's Liberation Army and hesitant to take any actions that would upset Chinese generals, Locklear failed to press political leaders in the administration to approve any U.S. Navy freedom-of-navigation operations in the South China Sea beginning in 2012. Prior to that, such operations were regularly carried out. However, approval of naval passage operations was put off by political appointees who wanted to avoid upsetting the Chinese government, which opposed the operations as encroachment on its claimed maritime territory. The failure to maintain free and open seas with warship passes within twelve nautical miles of disputed islands, reefs, and shoals turned out to be a major strategic mistake. China's military interpreted the lack of naval operations or aircraft overflights near the disputed islands claimed by China, Vietnam, Philippines, and other regional states as a green light to move ahead with an aggressive program of dredging and building up the islands—to solidify its claim to own most of the entire sea. The South China Sea is a vital strategic waterway used annually by ships that move $5.3 trillion in goods, including $1.7 trillion in trade bound for the United States. The island-building campaign is part of the key objective of Beijing of driving its main enemy out of the region and gaining complete control over it.

Another significant shortcoming of the dominant establishment China specialists in and out of government is the failure to understand the emergence and dominance within China of a hard-line, anti-American Chinese military and civilian faction, which currently controls the country. That faction was identified by Wang Jisi, one of China's foremost specialists on the United States, who wrote in 2011 that the pervasive anti-Americanism in China is based on a concept espoused by yet another ancient Confucian philosopher, Mencius (372 BC–289 BC), who argued that "a state without an enemy or external peril is absolutely doomed." Thus the United States has been demonized as China's main enemy, along with Japan, to be vanquished through information warfare under a program with the strategic goal of dominating the region. "Its proponents argue that China's current approach to foreign relations is far too soft; Mao's tit-for-tat manner is touted as a better model," Wang wrote in *Foreign Affairs*. "As a corollary, it is said that China should try to find strategic allies among countries that seem defiant toward the West, such as Iran, North Korea, and Russia. Some also recommend that Beijing use its holdings of U.S. Treasury bonds as a policy instrument, standing ready to sell them if U.S. government actions undermine China's interests."

To better understand China's information operations, the Pentagon produced an important study on Chinese information warfare in May 2013 called "China: The Three Warfares." For the first time, a detailed study had revealed Beijing's covert strategy of using legal warfare, psychological warfare, and media warfare. Stefan Halper, a Cambridge University professor and editor of the study, told me the Chinese are far more advanced than the Pentagon in the art of information war. "We're in a period where it's not whose army wins. It's whose story wins, and the Chinese figured that out very quickly," Halper says. "They're way ahead of us in this. We're in an age where nuclear weapons are no longer usable. They understand that. We keep nattering on about nuclear capabilities, and shields and so on, but it's really quite irrelevant."

In the future, an American president must come to the realization that the decades-long policy of appeasing and accommodating the communist regime in Beijing is not just contrary to American national interests, but is in fact advancing a new strategic threat to free and democratic systems everywhere. As I wrote in my 2000 book, *The China Threat*, the solution to the problem of an economic and politically powerful nuclear-armed communist dictatorship in China is to help China transition its system from a communist regime into a free and open democracy, albeit one with Chinese characteristics. To this end, the use of information warfare tools will be essential to backing the forces for democratic change in China, as represented in part by the faction associated with tycoon and popular blogger Ren Zhiqiang.

Michael Pillsbury, a Pentagon consultant on Chinese affairs for several decades, revealed how a Chinese defector disclosed that Beijing, under supposed reformist Deng Xiaoping, successor to Chairman Mao, deceived the United States into believing China's communist rulers were moderates on a slow but steady path to democratic political reform. "I was among those perpetuating the delusion that the arrest of China's party leader was a temporary setback; that China was still on the road to democracy; that this purge was an overreaction; and that we had to protect the 'moderate' faction, led by Deng, who would right the ship and keep our relationship sailing smoothly.

"No one I worked with at the CIA or the Pentagon in the 1980s raised the idea that China could deceive the United States or be the cause of a major intelligence failure," Pillsbury said.

The Obama administration negotiated an agreement with

China to halt cyber espionage against American corporations. In September 2015 an accord was reached during the visit to the United States by Chinese supreme leader Xi Jinping that stated both nations would abstain from government-backed cyber economic espionage. It was part of an administration policy that argued such agreements would produce new "norms" of behavior in cyberspace and stave off cyberattacks like the OPM and Anthem breaches, or future cyberattacks against critical infrastructures. The effort proved to be an utter failure. According to a U.S. defense official, the U.S. Cyber Command produced an intelligence report in early September 2016 revealing that a U.S. software company was hit by Chinese Ministry of State Security hackers to the tune of 1.65 terabytes of the company's valuable proprietary data, a massive amount of information. The data theft had taken place after the September 2015 cyber agreement reached with the Chinese, and the software company cyber espionage left many American security officials extremely doubtful that Beijing had any intention of abiding by the ban on cyber economic espionage.

China today employs strategic information warfare to defeat its main rival: the United States. China's demands to control social media and the Internet are part of its information warfare against America and must be resisted if free and open societies and the information technology they widely use are to prevail. China remains the most dangerous strategic threat to America—both informationally and militarily.

5

RUSSIA

In Russia, President Assassinates You

*The very "rules of war" have changed. The role of
nonmilitary means of achieving political and strategic
goals has grown and in many cases they have exceeded
the power of force of weapons in their effectiveness.*
—GENERAL VALERY GERASIMOV,
CHIEF OF THE GENERAL STAFF, RUSSIAN
FEDERATION, FEBRUARY 27, 2013

Russia under Vladimir Putin has emerged from the decades following the fall of the Soviet Union as a revanchist threatening power that is engaged in strategic information warfare against the United States and its allies. The attacks strike at the heart of the American democratic system and involve a covert action program aimed at influencing the outcome of the nation's most important political contest: the election of the president of the United States.

Putin is a former KGB lieutenant colonel who directed

its successor agency, the Federal Security Service. As Russia's president, Putin has been a leading advocate for the use of secret intelligence operations for information warfare, and the most deadly form has been assassination of political opponents.

On November 1, 2006, Alexander Litvinenko, a former officer of the Federal Security Service, arranged a meeting with two Russians who had offered him a lucrative business deal. They agreed to gather in the bar of London's Millennium Hotel. As an outspoken critic of Russian dictator Putin and a defector very aware of the deadly capabilities of his former employer, Litvinenko was living an uneasy life in exile. Hours before the planned meeting in the Pine Bar of the hotel, the former FSB officer, who at one time specialized in clandestine assassinations, met with a friend, Mario Scaramella. The Italian lawyer brought distressing news: Litvinenko's life was in danger. Russian intelligence had placed his name on a hit list along with several other high-profile critics of the Putin regime to be eliminated. Scaramella said radioactive poisons might be used. The information had come from Evgeni Limarev, a former member of the Russian SVR foreign intelligence service. Litvinenko doubted the threat. "If it's from Evgeni, it means it's not credible . . . it's shit if it's from Evgeni," he said.

The failure to heed the warning was a fatal mistake. Hours later in the bar of the hotel, the two men, Andrei Lugovoy and Dmitri Kovtun, were waiting at a table with a white ceramic teapot. Both were former KGB agents. British police concluded both men poisoned Litvinenko after one of the men had poured a small vial of an extremely poisonous radioactive substance, polonium 210, through the spout of the teapot.

During the twenty-three days he lay dying in a hospital bed, Litvinenko managed to give British investigators his account of what had happened. Several minutes into the meeting one of the Russian agents, Lugovoy, said: "Okay, well, we're going to leave now anyway, so there is still some tea left here; if you want you can have some."

"I poured some tea out of the teapot, although there was only little left on the bottom and it made just half a cup," Litvinenko recalled. "I swallowed several times but it was green tea with no sugar and it was already cold by the way. I didn't like it for some reason . . . well, almost cold tea with no sugar and I didn't drink it anymore."

Later that night, Litvinenko grew violently ill. When he was admitted to the hospital, doctors were unable to determine what made him sick until hours before his death. A doctor had suspected radiation poisoning and the diagnosis was confirmed by Britain's Atomic Weapons Establishment. The poison was polonium 210.

Litvinenko's death was the direct result of what a special British investigative commission concluded had been an assassination operation—likely carried out by the FSB with the direct blessing of Putin. "I have no doubt whatsoever that this was done by the Russian secret services," Litvinenko told British police shortly before his death. "Having knowledge of the system I know that the order about such a killing of a citizen of another country on its territory, especially if it [is] something to do with Great Britain, could have been given by only one person."

And who was the person? "That person is the president of the Russian Federation, Vladimir Putin," the dying man said. Litvinenko signed a statement on November 21, two days before his death, defiantly announcing to the Russian leader, "you may succeed in silencing one man but the howl of protest from around the world will reverberate, Mr. Putin, in your ears for the rest of your life. May God forgive you for what you have done, not only to me but to beloved Russia and its people."

Moscow made no secret that it favored the defector's demise. Sergei Abeltsev, a member of the Russian Duma, noted in a parliamentary speech on November 24, 2006, that "last night Alexander Litvinenko died in a London hospital. The deserved punishment reached the traitor. I am confident that this terrible death will be a serious warning to traitors of all colors wherever they are located. In Russia, they do not pardon treachery." Putin the same day appeared to provide an indirect claim of responsibility, telling state media that "the people that have done this are not God, and Mr. Litvinenko is, unfortunately, not Lazarus," the Bible character who rose from the dead. A former FSB superior, Alexander Gusak, added that Litvinenko deserved to be executed.

Litvinenko had become an enemy of the Russian state and was targeted and killed by Russian intelligence. His crime was revealing that he had been ordered by the FSB to murder Boris Berezovsky, a Russian dissident, wealthy oligarch, and critic of Putin who claimed political asylum in Britain in 2000. Litvinenko in the late 1990s worked in the FSB's secret Department for the Investigation and Prevention of Organized Crime, known as URPO, which was in charge of killing political and business targets in what are known as "wet operations." In late 1997, he was tasked with the Berezovsky hit. Rather than carry it out, Litvinenko went public at a press conference on November 17, 1998, and denounced the FSB. The result was that the FSB chief, Nikolay Kovalyov, was dismissed by then-president Boris Yeltsin. His replacement as FSB director was none other than Vladimir Putin. Litvinenko recalled meeting Putin in July 1998 and described him as someone who "looked not like an FSB director, but a person who played the director." Litvinenko would be arrested and spend eight months in Moscow's Lefortovo prison before fleeing the country in October 2000. He first met with U.S. officials in Istanbul, Turkey, but they turned him away. On November 1, 2000, Litvinenko was granted asylum in Britain.

Video evidence obtained by the British commission that investigated the defector's death included footage of Russian special forces using targets that featured Litvinenko's face for shooting practice. Litvinenko had been a member of the Russian special forces before joining the FSB.

However, the key element of Litvinenko's opposition to Putin was a July 2006 article the defector had published online in a news outlet called *Chechenpress*. In it he accused the Russian leader of being a pedophile. As quoted in the commission report:

A few days ago, Russian President Vladimir Putin walked from the Big Kremlin Palace to his Residence. At one of the Kremlin squares, the president stopped to chat with the tourists. Among them was a boy aged 4 or 5.

"What is your name?" Putin asked. "Nikita," the boy replied. Putin knee[le]d, lifted the boy's T-shirt and kissed his stomach. The world public is shocked. Nobody can understand why the Russian president did such a strange thing as kissing the stomach of an unfamiliar small boy.

Litvinenko went on to explain that Putin had graduated from the KGB's prestigious Andropov Institute, but unusually was not accepted into the foreign intelligence. Instead, Putin was assigned a junior post in the KGB's Leningrad Directorate. Shortly before graduation, Putin was discovered as a pedophile as a student at the institute, according to Litvinenko. After becoming FSB director and preparing to become president, Putin destroyed all the compromising material. "Among other things, Putin found videotapes in the FSB Internal Security Directorate, which showed him making sex with some underage boys."

"The FSB operation to kill Mr. Litvinenko was probably approved by [FSB director Nikolai] Patrushev and also by President Putin," commission chairman Sir Robert Owen stated. Other chilling evidence of the Russian government murder of Litvinenko included a T-shirt obtained by the commission bearing the words "POLONIUM-210 CSKA LONDON, HAMBURG to Be Continued" and on the back, "CSKA Moscow Nuclear Death Is Knocking Your

Door." CSKA is the Russian acronym for Central Sports Club of the Army.

Litvinenko was not the only victim of the Russian intelligence killing operations. Several political killings were also linked to them, including those of journalist Anna Politkovskaya and opposition politicians Sergei Yushenkov and Vladimir Golovlev. All were shot.

Russian intelligence did not stop its operation against Litvinenko with the defector's murder. Another target was the legendary Soviet-era dissident and human rights advocate Vladimir Bukovsky, who had befriended Litvinenko after his defection and testified to the British commission in 2015. Bukovsky was among the few people who had been able to gain access to the KGB archives between the fall of the Soviet Union and the ascension of Putin. Bukovsky revealed some of the documents that influenced Litvinenko about the KGB.

Bukovsky, a survivor of twelve years in Soviet prisons, labor camps, and prison psychiatric hospitals, would be targeted in a Russian disinformation operation shortly before he was to testify before the Owen commission in March 2015. A Russian hacker broke into his laptop computer and planted child pornography photographs on the device. A Russian intelligence agent then tipped off the European Union law enforcement agency, Europol, to the photos. British authorities charged Bukovsky with five counts of producing indecent images of children, five counts of possessing indecent images of children, and one count of possessing a prohibited image. Russian state-run media quickly reported the charges. It was a classic Russian disinformation and influence operation.

Bukovsky adamantly denied the charges and blamed the FSB for the operation. In protest, he launched a defamation lawsuit against the Crown Prosecution Service and in April 2016 went on a hunger strike to protest the charges. "The KGB didn't change at all," he told the *Guardian* newspaper. "It's the same KGB, only been renamed. And I happened to be their enemy for 57 years. . . . I'm on hunger strike not because of trying to prove anything to the FSB. We've known each other for half a century. There's nothing new they can tell me or I can tell them. I'm doing it for the British public." Bukovsky ended the hunger strike after the court proceedings were delayed and told a British court he was targeted in a Russian FSB intelligence operation.

The Litvinenko case highlights the growing danger of Russian intelligence and information warfare operations, which pose a direct threat to the United States. The case of Russian information warfare against the U.S. presidential election shows the threat is not limited to overseas assassination.

On the eve of the Democratic National Convention in Philadelphia in July 2016, Russia carried out one of the most daring information warfare attacks in history. It was a thinly veiled attempt to disrupt the U.S. presidential election process. Using the left-wing antisecrecy website WikiLeaks as a cutout, Moscow's government hackers released some twenty thousand internal documents hacked from the computer network of the Democratic National Committee. The emails revealed that the DNC had used covert smear tactics during the presidential primary campaign to support the eventual nom-

inee Hillary Clinton against democratic socialist candidate
Senator Bernie Sanders. The emails revealed DNC plans to
produce negative publicity for Sanders by revealing the senator was an atheist. The campaign was part of an effort by the
supposedly neutral DNC, which in reality had been working
to back the less-than-electric candidacy of former secretary
of state Clinton, who would accept the nomination at the
national convention overshadowed by the email disclosures.

The FBI launched an investigation into the information
warfare attack and Secretary of State John Kerry raised the
issue of the Russian hacking and influence operations against
the Democrats during a meeting with Russian foreign minister Sergei Lavrov in Vienna. Lavrov indignantly denied
Russia was behind it. Clinton campaign spokesman Robby
Mook blamed Putin for interfering in the election by seeking
to promote the candidacy of New York real estate mogul
Donald Trump, who during the campaign had voiced admiration for the strength of the Russian leader, who in turn had
responded with positive words for Trump.

Putin shrugged off the accusations and responded under
the traditional intelligence principle that lying to protect the
secrecy of operations is a rigid requirement. "Listen, does it
even matter who hacked this data?" Putin asked. "The important thing is the content that was given to the public." By
focusing on the content, the Russian leader was amplifying
the main goal of the operation—to influence the outcome of
the U.S. election in ways that might support someone who
Moscow perceived would adopt more favorable U.S. policies.

"There's no need to distract the public's attention from

the essence of the problem by raising some minor issues connected with the search for who did it," Putin told Bloomberg
news service, referring to the DNC breach. "But I want to
tell you again, I don't know anything about it, and on a state
level Russia has never done this."

Representative Mike Pompeo, Kansas Republican and a
member of the House Permanent Select Committee on Intelligence, told me, "Evidence and experts have pointed to Russia as the culprit behind the hack of the DNC, which is not
surprising. What is new, and what we must act on, is possible
foreign interference in our democratic process."

American government officials disclosed later that the
U.S. intelligence agencies were conducting an investigation
into a widespread Russian covert operation to disrupt the
2016 presidential election by exposing damaging information
on Clinton and thus boost the election fortunes of her Republican rival, Trump.

The Russian operation's first casualty was Debbie Wasser-
man Schultz, the chairwoman of the DNC, who was forced
to resign the day before the convention began. The Russians
had exposed how Schultz was not neutral during the primary
campaign and sought to help Clinton win the nomination
over Sanders.

Forensic analysis by computer security experts revealed
that the Russians hacked the DNC and then orchestrated the
document release to a hacker named "Guccifer 2.0," and to
the antisecrecy website WikiLeaks. WikiLeaks founder Julian
Assange, when questioned if the Russians were behind the
DNC email leak, at first refused to identify the source and

later denied the material was provided by Moscow. Guccifer 2.0 also denied he was linked to Moscow.

The National Security Agency, however, which has formidable cyber-intelligence capabilities, believes the Russians are behind the political information warfare operation, according to American officials close to the agency.

President Barack Obama, as he did throughout his entire presidency, turned a blind eye to the Russian hacking and influence operations, just as he did in the case of China's information attacks. The president made clear after meeting Putin at a summit of the Group of 20 nations in Hangzhou, China, that he did not raise the Russian influence operation targeting the American election with the Russian leader. "We did talk about cybersecurity, generally," Obama said of the meeting with Putin. "I'm not going to comment on specific investigations that are still live and active. But I will tell you that we've had problems with cyber intrusions from Russia in the past, from other countries in the past.

"We're moving into a new era here where a number of countries have significant capacities, and, frankly, we've got more capacity than anybody both offensively and defensively," Obama said, suggesting that U.S. military and cyber-intelligence capabilities, which the president refused to use against adversaries on numerous occasions, might eventually be employed.

However, Obama has taken an extremely conciliatory approach to cyberattacks against America and instead voiced concerns repeatedly that he worries that a tough stance against foreign cyberattacks would lead to a cyber arms race similar to conventional arms races in the past. It was vintage Obama; he had no problem projecting weakness in dealing with America's enemies.

"What we cannot do is have a situation in which suddenly this becomes the Wild, Wild West, where countries that have significant cyber capacity start engaging in competition— unhealthy competition or conflict through these means when, I think, wisely we've put in place some norms when it comes to using other weapons," he said.

The comments revealed that the Obama administration had no intention of attempting to deter strategic information warfare attacks, whether on U.S. computer networks or through covert intelligence and influence operations.

"I don't think there's any doubt that it was the Russian government that was behind the hacks," said James Lewis, a specialist in cybersecurity at the Center for Strategic and International Studies, referring to the DNC cyberattack.

Just over a month before tens of millions of Americans cast their votes in the presidential election of 2016, the U.S. intelligence community issued an extraordinary statement blaming Russia for conducting information warfare attacks aimed at influencing the outcome of the election. "The U.S. intelligence community is confident that the Russian government directed the recent compromises of emails from U.S. persons and institutions, including from U.S. political organizations," the Department of Homeland Security and Office of the Director of National Intelligence announced in a joint statement. "The recent disclosures of alleged hacked emails on sites like DCLeaks.com and WikiLeaks and by the

Guccifer 2.0 online persona are consistent with the methods and motivations of Russian-directed efforts. These thefts and disclosures are intended to interfere with the U.S. election process." The influence operation was not new for the Russians, who are conducting similar tactics and techniques across Europe and Eurasia in seeking to influence public opinion, the statement noted.

It was only the second time the U.S. government publicly linked a foreign government to a strategic cyberattack. The first was the North Korean hack against Sony.

Putin was not named in the statement, but intelligence agencies concluded that "senior-most" Russian officials authorized the attacks. The statement stopped short of blaming Russia for cyberattacks involving two incidents involving the scanning of election-related networks in Arizona and Illinois, and said the ability of hackers to remotely change ballots or election results would be extremely difficult, even for sophisticated nation-state attackers.

As in the Sony hack by North Korea, once again the White House promised a response to Russian government cyber interference in American politics. A senior White House official said the American public and the democratic system remained resilient against foreign attempts to manipulate public opinion. "The U.S. government is committed to ensuring a secure election process and has robust capabilities to detect efforts to interfere with our elections," the official said. "The president has made it clear that we will take action to protect our interests, including in cyberspace, and we will do so at a time and place of our choosing." Operational secrecy, the official added, would mean the public would not know "what actions have been taken, or what actions we will take."

Among the hacked information made public by the Russians in an apparent bid to boost the election fortunes of Donald Trump was an audiotape of Hillary Clinton speaking to a group of supporters in February 2016. In the tape, Clinton stated she would be in favor of canceling a new long-range cruise missile needed as part of the U.S. nuclear modernization program to replace aging nuclear missiles and bombers. "The last thing we need are sophisticated cruise missiles that are nuclear armed," she was heard saying. The audio was posted on the website DCLeaks.com that U.S. officials believe is a conduit for Russian intelligence agencies involved in the election campaign influence operation.

The audio was a scoop for my online newspaper, the *Washington Free Beacon,* and investigative reporter Lachlan Markay, who would be falsely accused by *New York Times* reporters David Sanger and William Broad of "mysteriously" obtaining the audio. Markay had found the audio through dogged reporting—he had searched the large and disorganized files posted by DCLeaks.com. The audio had been attached to an email sent by Clinton presidential campaign volunteer Ian Mellul to Nick Merrill, the campaign's traveling press secretary. The *Times'* suggestion that somehow the *Free Beacon* was a tool of Russian intelligence for publishing the story on the audio was dismissed by *Free Beacon* executive editor Matt Continetti in a tweet: "My reporter found recording on dcleaks.com. Feel free to update weird implication in story." The *Times* did not update or correct its story, an indication of how politicized America's once-great newspaper of record had become.

Not to be outdone by DCLeaks.com, the antisecrecy website WikiLeaks published a batch of emails that the organization said were hacked from among thousands of emails from the account of John Podesta, Clinton's campaign manager between 2008 and 2016. They included details of speeches Clinton had given to banks and financial institutions while secretary of state and for which she was paid some $3 million, including $675,000 for speeches to Goldman Sachs. During the presidential primary campaign, Clinton was asked if she would release transcripts of the speeches and deflected the question by saying only that she would look into the matter. The emails were embarrassing for the former secretary of state, who had moved to the left politically in a bid to compete against democratic socialist Senator Bernie Sanders, who during the campaign attracted widespread support for advocating the reining in of America's banks. Clinton's leaked speeches also revealed controversial support for open borders. WikiLeaks did not disclose how it received the emails, but U.S. intelligence agencies were confident that their disclosure was the work of Russian government hackers.

The Russian operation to influence the election was no match for hardball Democratic presidential campaign politics. The day the official U.S. government joint statement was issued identifying the influence program, Democratic political operatives published details of a 2005 video showing Republican presidential nominee Donald Trump making vulgar comments about women. The news media feeding frenzy that ensued effectively drowned out the latest eye-opening and politically damaging hacking disclosures by the Russians through DCLeaks.com and WikiLeaks.

Russian information warfare capabilities are among the most advanced of any nation and are built on a foundation of similar operations honed to perfection during the Soviet Union, a period that stretched from 1917 to 1991. American intelligence officials believe the current government unit in charge of Moscow's information warfare programs is the Federal Security Service, which in the 2010s emerged as the most powerful spy agency in Moscow, eclipsing the civilian SVR foreign spy service and the once-powerful military spy agency known as GRU. In September 2016, word came from Moscow that Putin was planning KGB 2.0 in the form of a super security and intelligence agency to be called the Ministry of State Security, or MGB. The new ministry would elevate the FSB and combine it with the SVR and Federal Protective Service, which guards Russian leaders. The ministry would be invested with sweeping new powers.

The Russian official behind the presidential campaign operation was identified as Colonel General Sergei Beseda, head of the FSB's Fifth Service, known as the Directorate of Operational Information and International Communications. Beseda was slapped with U.S. Treasury Department sanctions in July 2014 following Russia's military annexation of Ukraine's Crimea—an operation that was among the most strategically significant Russian information warfare operations and one that set in motion all the conditions for the new Cold War with Moscow.

On the night of February 27, 2014, an extraordinary event began unfolding on the Crimean Peninsula, located in the northern part of the Black Sea in Ukraine, a former Soviet republic southwest of Russia and the size of Poland and Germany. Masked troops wearing khaki green uniforms with no military markings or insignia landed at Simferopol International Airport aboard six unmarked helicopter transports and three IL-76 troop transports. Within a few hours, the troops had taken over key military bases in Crimea, including airfields and ports at Sevastopol, and the Supreme Council of Crimea, the local parliament in Simferopol. They hoisted the Russian flag from the top of the building. The covert troops were dubbed "Little Green Men" and turned out to be much more than ordinary Russian armed troops. The Little Green Men were in reality elite Russian special operations commandos, known as Spetsnaz, and were armed with the most modern arms, like AK-74 assault rifles and PKP machine guns. To avoid detection from NATO intelligence-gathering assets, the Little Green Men followed complete radio silence during the operation, which would continue over the next several days.

The covert military operation had come just two weeks after the ouster in Kiev of Ukraine's pro-Russian leader Viktor Yanukovych, who was driven from power by crowds of protesters after he refused to conclude an agreement between Ukraine and the European Union. The deal was sought by a large majority of Ukrainians who wanted Ukraine's closer integration with Europe as protection against the increasingly expansionist and hostile Russia.

In an attempt to counter the negative connotation associated with the term "Little Green Men," Russian government propagandists orchestrating the Crimea coup from Moscow tried to rename the intruding forces the "Nice People," over concerns that "Little Green Men" was viewed as too threatening. By March 18, Russian intelligence agents operating inside Crimea had engineered a unilateral declaration of independence from Ukraine. The takeover of the strategic peninsula that included large and valuable industries was complete.

Russia's Little Green Men were the inaugural players in a new form of Information Age conflict called hybrid warfare. It includes the use of deception, propaganda, covert intelligence and political influence operations, and other information warfare techniques, combined with conventional military forces, and in this case produced the bloodless takeover of a major portion of a foreign country. The annexation of Crimea represented a shift in the geopolitical threat environment. For the first time since Stalin sent Soviet military forces to take over eastern Poland in 1939, Russia assumed an expansionist military posture. The takeover of Crimea is a valuable lesson in understanding Moscow's use of information warfare to achieve strategic objectives in the twenty-first century.

Polish strategic analyst Jolanta Darczewska views the Crimean takeover as a classic case of Russian information warfare aimed at furthering the neofascist vision of Russian president Vladimir Putin, who lamented in a 2005 speech that the fall of the Soviet Union in 1991 was the "greatest geopolitical catastrophe of the century." The remark signaled new Russian aggressiveness in seeking to restore at least some of the closest former Soviet states under Russian control.

"The Crimean operation perfectly shows the essence of information warfare: the victim of the aggression—as was the case with Crimea—does not resist it," Darczewska wrote in a 2014 report, "The Anatomy of Russia Information Warfare." "This happened because Russian-speaking citizens of Ukraine who had undergone necessary psychological and informational treatment (intoxication) took part in the separatist coup and the annexation of Crimea by Russia." Russian information warfare will intensify, she warned, as Moscow has achieved a sense of impunity on the information battlefield and is constantly assessing, modifying, and perfecting its use of information warfare methods and techniques. The information operations will continue because the techniques are central to Putin's new geopolitical doctrine, which is Russian-centered, antiliberal, oriented toward rivalry with the West, and aimed at reasserting Russia's dominance over the Eurasian landmass.

Crimea was just the beginning of Russian covert action against Ukraine, which has continued with the semi-secret military support for pro-Russian rebels in the eastern part of the country, large-scale nuclear forces exercises near the border in Ukraine, and unprecedented threats by Russian leaders, including Putin, to use nuclear weapons against the United States and the West.

For the United States, the Crimea operation was the most visible and alarming manifestation of hybrid information warfare. It was the first large-scale military aggression since Russian forces carried out operations against the former Soviet satellite republic of Georgia in 2008. Russian operations in the information sphere are taking nonkinetic warfare—conflict that limits or eliminates the use of overt military force—to a new level in aggressively working to fan anti-U.S. and anti-Western sentiment both within Russia and globally. Director of National Intelligence James Clapper told Congress in 2015, "Russian state-controlled media publish false and misleading information in an effort to discredit the West, undercut consensus in Russia, and build sympathy for Russian positions."

Along with the operations under Putin, Russia has adopted a new ideology based on the false notion that the country and its culture are under siege from hostile forces in the West, led by the United States.

Understanding the threat of Russian information warfare requires first knowing Putin, his strategic vision, and how he is ordering the comprehensive use of Soviet-style intelligence, covert action, and strategic influence activities in a coordinated campaign of information warfare. The ultimate goal of the Russian leader is to expand Russia's control over an area stretching from the Pacific Ocean across Europe to the Atlantic Ocean over the next two decades.

The ideological roots of Russian strategic information warfare against the West can be traced to a combination of neofascism, Russian nationalism, and opposition to Western liberalism. Its two main theorists have been identified as Igor Panarin, professor at the Russian Foreign Ministry Diplomatic Academy, and Aleksandr Dugin, professor of sociology and philosophy at Moscow Lomonosov University and director of the Center for Conservative Studies at Moscow State University. Panarin was a former colonel in the KGB and was also with the Federal Agency of Government Communications and Information, the signals intelligence service. Both academics are closely tied to the Russian intelligence and security services, including the dominant FSB.

Dugin worked as an officer in the GRU, a military spy agency that is one of Moscow's key information warfare arms. From 1988 to 1989, Dugin was a leader of the notorious anti-Semitic Russian nationalist organization Pamyat. He went on to found the pan-Russian social movement Eurasia, which was funded by Russian intelligence services.

Panarin has labeled what he says were two periods of "information aggression" against Russia. The first occurred under the glasnost—openness—of reform communist leader Mikhail Gorbachev in the mid-1980s and ended with the fall of the Soviet Union in 1991. The second wave took place around 2000 and is predicted to continue until 2020, when Putin's nationalist Eurasian ideal is to be realized. This view regards the so-called Color Revolutions of the early 2000s that rocked the former Soviet republics as information aggression against Moscow, along with the upheavals of the Arab Spring, which took place across North Africa and the Middle East.

Panarin defines information warfare in the Russian

context as the use of influence operations, including social control to influence polities; social maneuvering through the intentional control of publics to achieve certain goals; information manipulation through the use of accurate information in ways that produce false implications; disinformation, or the spreading of manipulated or fabricated information; information fabrication, or the production of false information; and lobbying, blackmail, and extortion of sought-out information.

The secret and open tools of information warfare include propaganda, intelligence operations, analysis of media and monitoring the effects, and organizational elements. The organizational methods include coordination and steering of operations, secret agents of influence to shape the opinions of political leaders, and media acting in line with state goals. Special channels for information warfare include special operations military forces that can conduct activities disguised as a foreign state. Panarin calls the single center used to carry out information warfare as "the information KGB," and he has claimed that the anti-Russian protests in Ukraine leading up to the ouster of Yanukovych were Western information aggression.

Dugin's information warfare theories reflect a more military orientation. He regards the Color Revolutions as part of American "net-centric warfare" and has proposed a "Eurasian" network warfare system to engage in counter-information warfare. To defeat Western information operations, Dugin called for creating a special group of senior officials from the Russian intelligence services, along with academics, scientists, journalists, and cultural activists, to wage information warfare on a U.S.-led "Atlantic network."

Russian information warfare is aimed at defeating what the nationalists regard as the dominant Western ideology of liberalism, based on individualism, technocracy, and globalism, and which took down the ideology of communism.

Panarin too is a Russian supremacist who advocates defeating Western liberalism. Panarin bases his views on Putin's 1999 manifesto, "Russian at the Turn of the Millennium," which urged returning Russia to superpower status. An ideological trinity of spiritualism, state power, and cyber sovereignty are key elements. The Russian theorists also use the term *netcode* to describe the basis of information warfare; the U.S. netcode is said to be global hegemony and anti-Russian statehood. The Russian netcode seeks to defeat the West and establish a Russia-centered civilization, with the new Moscow-dominated Pacific-to-Atlantic sphere of influence. In their thinking, pro-Western Ukraine is a main impediment to achieving the goal.

Phillip Karber, a former U.S. arms control official and national security expert, says Russian hybrid warfare spans the spectrum of conflict domains and levels of conflict. On the low end, Moscow is using political subversion, such as seizing government buildings, sabotage, assassination and terrorism, propaganda and media campaigns, and supporting agents of influence. For certain campaigns, such as the ongoing destabilization in eastern Ukraine, Russian hybrid warriors are deploying paramilitary forces posing as volunteers and militias to conduct attacks and destroy government infrastructure. The Russians also use threats of military force and preparations for military incursions, along with cyberattacks. For soft power, negotiations and legal warfare are being used in an attempt to legitimize Russian activities and to inhibit Western counterattacks and countermeasures. Russia's nuclear forces, currently undergoing major modernization, also provide a coercive information warfare weapon. Russian leaders frequently hype Moscow's nuclear strength, and nuclear bombers have sharply increased provocative flights near U.S. coasts.

The United States is ill-prepared to deal with the threat, according to Karber, president of the Potomac Foundation. "Modern decision makers in Western democracies are neither prepared for Russian disguised operations, denial, duplicity, and deception on the low end of conflict, nor steeled against brazen nuclear posturing and direct threats at the high end," Karber told me. "This hybrid combination often leads to 'decidophobia' and fear of 'escalating' even when that only means reciprocal matching of behavior the Russians are already practicing."

On the cyber front, Moscow's cyberwarfare operators are regarded by U.S. intelligence agencies as the world's most sophisticated. The basis of Russia's advanced cyber operations stems from the skilled technological base left over from the Soviet Union. Many Soviet-era KGB and GRU intelligence service personnel have launched cybersecurity companies that provide ideal cover for Russian government cyberattacks, according to defense officials. "Anyone who would risk using a Russian cybersecurity company should have his head examined because the risks are great," a senior U.S. military officer familiar with intelligence reports about Russian cyberwarfare capabilities told me.

The military annexation of Crimea also demonstrated that the Russians are leading the way with cyberattacks, including the first known cyberattack against a foreign nation's electrical power grid, which temporarily turned out the lights for tens of thousands of Ukrainians. On December 23, 2015, covert Russian cyber actors struck Ukraine's power grid in what a U.S. State Department security report called the "first blackout to be caused by malicious software."

"While cyber attacks on critical infrastructure systems have long been viewed as digital aggression with physical consequences, very few have been documented to date, making the late December events in Ukraine a hallmark incident," the report by the Overseas Security Advisory Council, which supports American businesses overseas, stated. "Subsequent reports indicate that airport, rail, and mining system networks were also targeted, leading some to believe the hackers were focused on disrupting Ukraine's critical infrastructure."

The Ukrainian power supplier Prykarpattyaoblenergo, which provides electrical services to customers across the western Ukrainian region of Ivano-Frankivsk, announced that the utility suffered a "large-scale breakdown" on December 23 that left 700,000 homes across the region without power for several hours. Ukraine's Energy Ministry announced the outage was caused by interference with the supplier's automated control system.

The linkage to Russian hackers emerged from a forensic

analysis of the malicious software found on the networks. A computer virus called a backdoor Trojan—because the software can infiltrate a system by appearing to be a non-threatening program—and known as BlackEnergy 3 was first observed in 2007 and has been linked directly to Russian government hackers. It specifically affects remotely controlled networks used to operate critical infrastructure systems, which include electrical grids, financial networks, telecommunications, transportation, water and waste management, and other strategic functions. The software contains a unique feature, called KillDisk, that permits remote cyberattackers to rewrite files on the infected systems with random data, and then to block any user from rebooting the system, thus making the computer inoperable. BlackEnergy 3 also allows remote cyberattackers to search infected computers for software used in electric control systems—the signature that the virus is aimed at taking down electric grids.

Security researchers at the SANS Institute, a nonprofit company that specializes in information security, determined that hackers remotely accessed the Ukraine power companies and disguised the malicious activity, directed changes in electrical power distribution, and then conducted activities that made it more difficult for Ukrainian network administrators to restore power. The cyberattack coincided with another Russian information warfare operation to flood telephone help desks at Ukrainian electric companies so that support staff were distracted from responding to the ongoing technical attack.

From an information warfare perspective, the Russians

were further engaging in political messaging over Crimea. Specifically, Moscow was warning Ukraine not to attempt to isolate Russian-occupied Crimea or attempt to cut off electrical power to the peninsula. The cyberattacks coincided with other activities aimed at Ukrainian government and private sector networks, while providing the Russian government with deniability as it continued to carry out information-based strikes and activities.

To highlight the Russian cyber threat, the DIA issued an internal warning in early 2016 stating that industrial security software being developed by a Russian-origin company, Kaspersky Lab, could result in American critical infrastructures becoming vulnerable to Russian cyberattacks. The DIA stated that the software, if adopted by American utilities, would create vulnerabilities inside U.S. industrial control systems, specifically a category of controllers called supervisory control and data acquisition software, known as SCADA, systems. The DIA report disclosed that U.S. electrical and water utilities, as well as other critical industrial sectors, were considering the purchase of the software, which the intelligence agency said could allow Russian government hackers, considered among the most advanced nation-state cyber spies, to get inside industrial control networks, specifically remote-controlled SCADA programs that are used to operate the electrical grid, oil and gas networks, water pipelines and dams, and wastewater systems. Kaspersky denied its software could create vulnerabilities. "The alleged claims are meritless as Kaspersky Lab's products and solutions are designed to protect against cybercriminals and malicious threat actors, not enable attacks against any organization or entity," the company said in a statement. "We are not developing any offensive techniques and have never helped, or will help, any government in the world in their offensive efforts in cyberspace." Efforts by Kaspersky to enter the American industrial network security market continued that same year when the company looked to partner with American defense contractors as a way of winning lucrative U.S. government information security contracts.

Another alarming aspect of Moscow's preparation for future information warfare operations was disclosed by senior U.S. intelligence officials who revealed that the Russians are conducting "cyber reconnaissance" against critical U.S. infrastructures, including the electric grid. James Clapper, the director of national intelligence, disclosed that Russian cyberwarfare specialists had broken into the computer supply chain of U.S. infrastructure companies and were able to gain access to industrial control networks as a result. "Unknown Russian actors successfully compromised the product supply chains of at least three [industrial control system] vendors so that customers downloaded malicious software designed to facilitate exploitation directly from the vendors' websites along with legitimate software updates," Clapper testified to the House Permanent Select Committee on Intelligence. "Politically motivated cyberattacks are now a growing reality, and foreign actors are reconnoitering and developing access to U.S. critical infrastructure systems, which might be quickly exploited for disruption if an adversary's intent became hostile," he added.

The BlackEnergy malware linked to Russian hackers also has been detected in U.S. industrial control system software since at least 2011. According to a Department of Homeland Security notice from October 2014, industrial control systems used to operate critical U.S. infrastructure, including water and energy systems, have been under attack from cyber actors using malicious software since 2011. DHS and its Industrial Control System–Cyber Emergency Response Team (ICS-CERT), a unit devoted to protecting industrial infrastructures, revealed in the notice what it called "a sophisticated malware campaign that has compromised numerous industrial control systems (ICSs) environments using a variant of the BlackEnergy malware."

The most serious concern is that the Russians are hacking the systems and using the penetrations to prepare for damaging cyberattacks in a future conflict. The activities include reconnaissance operations and implanting clandestine malware inside the industrial control networks. The network intrusions would be used to attack systems in a future conflict, or for coercive information warfare, such as threatening to take out the power grid or other critical infrastructure unless the United States gives in to Russian demands on a particular issue.

Russian hackers also have broken into the White House military office, which is used to coordinate presidential travel, and the Joint Chiefs of Staff email network, shutting down the military command center's ability to send unclassified emails for at least two weeks.

At the same time Russian government hackers have been

conducting cyberattacks against industrial control systems, governments, and private sector networks, Moscow has sought to use the United Nations to limit America's ability to both defend and counterattack against the Russians, a key feature of a broad-based information warfare campaign, often referred to as legal warfare, or lawfare. In February 2016, Major General Yuri Kuznetsov, director of the eighth directorate of the Russian Armed Forces General Staff, told a security conference in Moscow that the Russians are seeking a United Nations cyber nonaggression agreement. "The global informatization of society enables the use of modern technologies to destabilize the social situation inside countries and influence people," he said. "The leaders of major countries have come to realize that there is a need for legislative regulation in this field. The first step on the path to establishing these conditions will be a cyber nonaggression pact that is expected to be signed under the auspices of the UN." The agreement would delineate nations' obligations to follow principles and norms of conduct in cyberspace.

In regard to Russian information warfare campaigns, the idea of a UN agreement on cyberspace was like music to the ears of the arms control–enamored national security policy makers within the administration of President Obama. Christopher Painter, the State Department's cybersecurity policy maker, has promoted the idea of establishing norms of behavior in cyberspace. The idea is to negotiate an agreement with states like Russia and China that would limit cyberattacks. In May 2015, Painter told a Senate hearing the Obama administration is seeking an international call for "voluntary measures of self-restraint," such as state promises not to attack critical infrastructure, not conduct cyberattacks on systems used to respond to cyberattacks, and cooperation on investigating cyber crime. But relying heavily on international agreements with Russia would not work because Moscow systematically has violated or circumvented all its arms agreements, most recently the 1987 Intermediate-Range Nuclear Forces Treaty, which limits the United States and Russia from building missiles with ranges of between 310 miles and 3,400 miles. Moscow was caught cheating on the accord several years ago in building a new ground-launched cruise missile called the SSC-X-8. The missile has a range of more than 310 miles.

The danger posed by Russian cyberattacks against U.S. critical infrastructures comes amid alarming indications the governments and utilities in charge of the American infrastructure are woefully unprepared to deal with cyberattacks.

"It is only a matter of the 'when,' not the 'if' we're going to see a nation-state, group, or actor engage in destructive behavior against critical infrastructure in the United States," Admiral Mike Rogers, commander of the U.S. Cyber Command and director of the National Security Agency, warned in a speech in March 2016. Rogers called the cyberattack against the Ukrainian electricity grid a "very well-crafted attack" that included monitoring the response by Ukrainian recovery technicians. "And their strategy also focused on how they could attempt to slow down the [electrical power] restoration process," he said.

"Seven weeks ago it was the Ukraine. This isn't the last

we're going to see this, and that worries me," Admiral Rogers added.

The problem with critical infrastructure control networks is that they use "operational technology" (OT), which is very different from traditional information technology (IT) found in most computers and networks, according to Idan Udi Edry, chief executive officer of the Israeli cybersecurity firm Nation-E. As a result, critical infrastructures for the electric grid, water system, and other sectors are highly vulnerable to cyberattacks. "When you have an existing IT network and now you are connecting the OT part into the existing network, all of a sudden you've created millions of points that are completely vulnerable for cyberattacks," Edry said. "This is exactly where I see the potential threat in the United States. The potential damage from such attacks is huge and that's exactly where hackers want to put the effort," he said.

The threat of infrastructure cyberattacks prompted two military commanders to sound the alarm in a letter to the secretary of defense in early 2016. "We respectfully request your assistance in providing focus and visibility on an emerging threat that we believe will have serious consequences on our ability to execute assigned missions if not addressed—cyber security of [Defense Department] critical infrastructure Industrial Control Systems," Northern Command's Admiral William Gortney and Pacific Command's Admiral Harry Harris stated in the February 11, 2016, letter to Ashton Carter. "We must establish clear ownership policies at all levels of the department, and invest in detection tools and processes to baseline normal network behavior from abnormal behavior," the four-star admirals stated, adding that once completed "we should be able to track progress for establishing acceptable cyber security for our infrastructure [industrial control systems]."

The commanders' worries were prompted by Department of Homeland Security statistics showing a sevenfold increase in cyberattacks on critical infrastructure between 2010 and 2015. The attacks were carried out against what the Pentagon calls "platform information technology"—critical national security hardware and software, including industrial controls and SCADA. They identified several types of malware— including Shamoon, Shodan, Havex, and BlackEnergy—that they warned could potentially "debilitate our installations' mission critical infrastructure."

"As geographic combatant commanders with homeland defense responsibilities and much at stake in this new cyber connected world, we request your support," they added. As shown in Ukraine, BlackEnergy remains the most sophisticated malware used in infrastructure attacks. Shamoon was linked to the 2012 cyberattack against the state-run Saudi Aramco oil company that damaged thirty thousand computers and was believed to have been carried out by Iran. Havex malware has been linked to cyberattacks on industrial control systems, and Shodan is a search engine that is believed to have helped foreign hackers map remote industrial control networks for possible attacks.

Admiral Rogers, the Cyber Command leader and NSA director, has been discussing the infrastructure cyber threat in meetings with executives and security officials in the electri-

cal power and water industries. Power companies are working to develop micropower grids and "island-able" power
grids, along with distributed storage and power generation,
to mitigate the effects of a large-scale cyberattack.

Western intelligence agencies are just beginning to focus on
Russian information warfare programs. A NATO official in
charge of monitoring Russian information revealed that Moscow adopted a comprehensive approach to achieving what he
termed "information dominance," spending up to $500 mil-
lion a year on warfare that employs lies and disinformation,
hoaxes, and the use of Internet trolls. In Russian information
warfare campaigns, television under state control is a major
outlet. "In Russia television is God," the NATO official, an
information operations specialist, told me. The major television channels are government owned and others are run by
oligarchs, like the oil and gas conglomerate Gazprom, that
broadcast only content that is in line with the government.
"In our countries, this would be free media, but they're not
free media. If you switch on the Russian TV, there are others
like five, six, seven different channels and you hear the same
narratives. All the same topic. So that's pretty clear that they
are getting the same instructions."

This is not simple or crude propaganda. It is a highly
sophisticated endeavor. For example, Russian television
producers often set up phony debates on news programs
that present what appear to be differing points of view, in an
attempt to boost credibility. In reality, the faux debates are

carefully staged as part of information warfare themes. Entertainment programs also are geared to influencing publics, with many shows featuring "heroic" government officials. No more tractor films, as in the Soviet days; modern Russian propaganda programming is targeted, sophisticated, and effective—at least internally, within Russia. It also is broadcast abroad to countries with large ethnic Russian populations, such as Ukraine and the Baltic states of Lithuania, Latvia, and Estonia.

Overseas, RT, formerly known as Russia Today, a well-funded, twenty-four-hour Russian channel, and Sputnik, the digital news service, serve as Moscow's main propaganda outlets for information campaigns. Moscow also is trying to control the Internet, since the free unfiltered information it provides has been categorized by the government as a threat to the state. Like China, the government hires thousands of Internet trolls to promote propaganda and disinformation themes.

An internal British government report on Russian hybrid warfare and influence operations I obtained reveals Moscow is expanding its reach beyond Ukraine. "Now there are increasing worries this tactic is being used elsewhere, as part of a broader strategy to undermine the U.S. and Europe," the March 25, 2016, report says.

In Finland, journalist Jessikka Aro exposed Russia's use of pro-Kremlin trolls—those who seek to discredit people through online attacks. Russian trolls targeted Aro in an online campaign of vilification on social media, the key battleground in the information war. The campaign used Russian operatives sending complaints about her to media leaders, ombudsmen, and government officials, including Finland's president. The campaign also used cyberstalking, along with the use of threatening phone calls and even protests outside her office. The trolls also resorted to sending fraudulent text messages to her that appeared to be from her deceased father. "My private life, family affairs, and nonexistent political background have been under scrutiny," she says. "During the last year I have been accused of destroying the freedom of speech probably hundreds of times, an absurd claim coming from anonymous profiles or public propaganda figures, who bully people and spread Russian lies." Finnish police eventually investigated the smear campaign and identified two people behind the effort who were linked to pro-Russian activists in Finland. A Russian dissident, Lyudmila Savchuk, also has exposed Russian online trolls after infiltrating a front company called the Internet Research Agency, later renamed Glavest, located in St. Petersburg, Russia. Savchuk disclosed that she and others at the company were paid to produce false posts and comments on blogs, social media, and news websites, using proxy servers to mask their IP addresses. The posts all praised the Russian government and Vladimir Putin and attacked opposition political figures and pro-European Ukrainian and Western leaders. They also spread disinformation—including the false claim that Malaysian Airlines flight MH17, a commercial airliner shot down over Ukraine, was attacked by Ukrainian government forces. The July 17, 2014, airliner attack in reality was the work of pro-Russian rebels who used a Moscow-supplied SA-11 surface-to-air missile. All 283 people on board the aircraft were killed. Moscow propaganda organs shifted into high gear in denying Russian involvement in the disaster.

In the United States, pro-Kremlin trolls tweeted false news of several disasters, such as a chemical accident at a Louisiana factory and an outbreak of the Ebola virus in Atlanta. The ruse employed fake screenshots of established news websites and some of the tweets were addressed to media outlets and politicians. The motive behind the campaign appeared to be to trigger a public panic. The *New York Times* traced the fake tweets to the Internet domain add1.ru, which is connected to the Glavest disinformation operation in St. Petersburg.

U.S. Air Force general Philip M. Breedlove, commander of the U.S. European Command and NATO commander from 2013 to 2016, sees Russia's use of hybrid warfare as a combination of diplomacy, information warfare, and military and economic measures, along with traditional warfare, covert action by military and intelligence operatives, and cyberwarfare. A key feature is spreading lies and disinformation through state-run Russian news outlets and attacking the credibility of target states.

"Informationally, this is probably the most impressive new part of this hybrid war, all of the different tools to create a false narrative," Breedlove said. "We begin to talk about the speed and the power of a lie, how to get a false narrative out, and then how to sustain that false narrative through all of the new tools that are out there."

Russia used military forces differently in hybrid warfare,

as the Little Green Men in Crimea showed. They were successful in creating ambiguity as to whether they were official Russian military forces. Breedlove argues that intelligence means should be employed to publicize the truth behind such actions, and then to forcefully disseminate the information to global publics. "What the military needs to do is to use those traditional military intelligence tools to develop the truth," he says. "The way you attack a lie is with the truth. I think that you have to attack an all-of-government approach with an all-of-government approach. We need to, as a Western group of nations or as an alliance, engage in this information warfare to . . . drag the false narrative out into the light and expose it."

Breedlove rejected the Obama administration's approach of doing little to counteract Russian information warfare over concerns the efforts could be destabilizing. "In Ukraine, what we see is diplomatic tools being used, informational tools being used, military tools being used, economic tools being used against Ukraine," he said. "We, I think, in the West, should consider all of our tools in reply. Could it be destabilizing? The answer is yes. Also, inaction could be destabilizing."

Breedlove himself was a target of suspected Russian information warfare when his private Gmail account was hacked and the emails leaked online. The outspoken general was revealed as having taken a much harder line on Russia than President Obama or his aides, according to the emails. "I may be wrong, . . . but I do not see the WH really 'engaged' by working with Europe/Nato," Breedlove wrote on September 30, 2014. "Frankly I think we are a 'worry', . . . ie a threat to get the nation drug into a conflict . . . vice an 'opportunity represented by some pretty stalwart allies.'" The four-star general made the remarks in an email to former general and secretary of state Colin Powell in seeking advice on "how to work this personally with the POTUS [president of the United States]."

In another email, Breedlove told academic Harlan Ullman, "I think POTUS sees us [the U.S. military and NATO] as a threat that must be minimized, . . . ie do not get me into a war????"

Russian intelligence services play a major role in information warfare and one service developed an Internet influence and monitoring system, according to a report by the CIA-based Open Source Center. "Russia's Foreign Intelligence Service (SVR) is developing an automated system to monitor blogs and social media to influence public opinion via social networking websites," the report says. The SVR announced plans for the system through three contracts in January 2012 for an automated system to shape public opinion. The program was to be developed in three stages and completed by 2013, at a cost of around $1 million. The first phase is called "Disput," or public debate, and "analyzes intelligence gathering methods in 'Internet-centers' and regional segments of social networking website." Disput also will produce analysis to "identify factors that affect the popularity and spread of messages." Phase 2 is called "Monitor-3" and relies on "a virtual community of experts" devoted to developing methods of effectively creating and disseminating messages. Last is

Shtorm-12 (Gale Wind-12), which fires off automatic messages produced using Disput and Monitor-3.

According to the Open Source Center report, the system is directed at influencing both foreign audiences and internal Russian audiences. A main target is Eastern European countries made up of former Soviet republics or Warsaw Pact states that Russia refers to as the "Near Abroad" and the main target of Putin's pan-Eurasian vision. The report said the SVR system appears based on Russian officials' belief that social media–enabled foreign covert influence campaigns triggered the Arab Spring and other antigovernment movements. "Russian officials, including Putin, have publicly opposed the use of the Internet to influence foreign audiences, but the establishment of this program in the SVR, Russia's external intelligence arm, contradicts officials' public stance," the report said.

One of the more menacing aspects of Russian information warfare has been Moscow's ongoing campaign to threaten nuclear attacks against the United States. The campaign included stepped-up flights by nuclear-capable Russian bombers and dangerous aerial intercepts of U.S. reconnaissance aircraft around the world, including northern Europe, the east and west coasts of the United States, and Asia. Beginning in early 2013, Russian Tu-95 nuclear-capable Bear bombers began flying very close to U.S. coasts and borders, in several cases conducting simulated attacks on the United States. One of the practice strikes targeted the U.S. missile defense interceptor base at Fort Greely, Alaska. Another took place off the Atlantic coast and practiced simulated long-range cruise missile strikes on Washington, D.C.

After I disclosed the existence of Russia's development of a new underwater nuclear drone submarine, code-named Kanyon by the Pentagon and capable of delivering a massive nuclear warhead against U.S. harbors, Russian information warfare specialists took the unusual step of confirming the existence of the experimental drone submarine by leaking details during a televised press conference with Putin in November 2015. The disclosure on Russian state television of what the Russian military is calling the Status-6 unmanned underwater vehicle was the latest attempt at nuclear intimidation against the United States. Konstantin Sivkov, a member of the Russian Academy of Missile and Artillery Sciences, wrote in a state-run news outlet that the drone leak was aimed at forcing negotiations. "Russia is creating a system of strategic deterrence against which even in the remote future there will be no acceptable defense," Sivkov wrote. "This will compel our 'partners' to sit down at the table for constructive negotiations."

A Russian government spokesman claimed the leak of the Kanyon by a senior Russian military officer on television was a mistake. But Sivkov asserted that explanation is false. "In no way is it possible to believe that a military leader of the highest rank disclosed such important information by mistake—this would certainly cost him his career at the very least," he said. Instead, the leak was actually an "information bomb" aimed at intimidating the United States.

"The aim is to scare the adversary by means of a 'bubble,' to make him agree to certain concessions or undertake work on resource-intensive defense programs in totally unproductive areas," Sivkov stated in an article published in *VPK Voyenno-Promyshlennyy Kuryer Online,* a weekly newspaper on military and defense industry issues associated with the arms manufacturer Almaz-Antey. Sivkov compared the Kanyon to the Reagan administration's Strategic Defense Initiative, which was largely credited with forcing the Soviet Union into spending large sums preparing to counter U.S. strategic missile defenses. Sivkov also believes the Kanyon leak was intended to send the strategic message that the weapon will be built in the distant future. "The aim is the same: to grab the adversary's attention, to push him in the direction of concessions."

A third message is that the Russians are moving ahead with the weapon, which will deploy with a nuclear charge estimated to be in the "tens" of megatons—or the equivalent explosive force of tens of millions of tons of TNT. "In this instance we are letting the partners know that it is time for them to stop and begin a constructive dialogue with Russia," he stated.

A report produced by a defense consulting firm for the Pentagon's Office of Net Assessment revealed an even more alarming nuclear weapons program by Moscow: the development of low-yield, precision-guided tactical nuclear weapons that unlike their strategic arms counterparts can be more easily used in future regional conflicts. Instead of city-busting warheads with the nuclear blast equivalent of tens, hundreds, or millions of tons of TNT, Russia is developing nuclear weapons with yields in the range of between 10 tons and 150 tons of TNT for use in regional conflicts Moscow anticipates could break out along Russia's periphery in the future. "In effect, Russia's nuclear developments are making the unthinkable thinkable," the 2010 report said of the prospects for future nuclear conflict.

The drone submarine is estimated to be around 82 feet in length, with a diameter of around 30 feet, and it will be capable of ranging some 6,200 miles after being dropped from a larger submarine.

Russia and China together pose the most potent danger to American security through the use of information warfare. The immediate danger, however, comes from the Islamic State terrorist group, which is working to develop similar cyber and information warfare skills.

The Russian information warfare threat is real and growing and must be countered with a vigorous and well-funded American program designed to expose its operations, murders, and lies.

6

ISLAMIC TERROR

When Jihad Johnny Comes Marching Home

The struggle with revolutionary Islam will only be
won when the West begins to methodically analyze the
ideological religion that empowers it and forms its basis.
—STEPHEN P. LAMBERT, "THE SOURCES OF
ISLAMIC REVOLUTIONARY CONDUCT," 2005

Pakistan-born Tashfeen Malik opened the top of her laptop computer inside the Redlands, California, home where she and her husband lived. It was December 2, 2015, another typically warm and sunny day in Southern California. Around 8:46 a.m. she began searching social media for documents and videos posted by the Islamic State terrorist group. Less than two hours later, around 11:15, Malik posted this message on her Facebook page: "We pledge allegiance Khalifa bu bkr al bhaghdadi al quraishi." It was a public declaration of jihad— or holy war—in support of the Syrian-based Islamic State terror group leader, Abu Bakr al-Baghdadi.

Minutes earlier Malik and her husband, Syed Rizwan Farook, a specialist with the San Bernardino County Department of Public Health, had opened fire on a group of some eighty people who had gathered for a training event and Christmas Party for employees of the San Bernardino County Environmental Health Department at a state-run nonprofit center. Farook earlier had stopped by the meeting and left a backpack containing several pipe bombs that he had planned to set off during his attack.

Around 11 a.m., Malik and Farook, dressed in all black to hide their identities, burst through the door of the center firing AR-15 semiautomatic rifles. After more than one hundred rounds were fired, fourteen people were dead and twenty-two others wounded.

Several people ran for a door in the large room and another person screamed "Get down!" while others, frozen in terror, just stood there. Survivors initially thought the attack was a training exercise but then realized what was happening and fled the scene.

According to a Justice Department report issued months after the attack, "As the chaos unfolded, a round hit a fire sprinkler pipe causing water to pour out of the ceiling. The water and smoke that filled the room made it difficult for people to see. The shooters walked between tables. If someone moved or made a sound, the shooters fired one or multiple shots into their body."

Many of the high-velocity .223-caliber bullets passed through the conference room walls, striking one woman, and another woman was shot as she tried to escape through a glass door. The bodies of two people were lying outside the room—the first people killed as the terrorists arrived at the building.

"It was the worst thing imaginable," one police officer who arrived at the scene recalled. "Some people were quiet, hiding, others were screaming or dying, grabbing at your legs because they wanted us to get them out, but our job at the moment was to keep going. That was the hardest part, stepping over them."

The first official response was a tweet by the San Bernardino County sheriff at 11:51 a.m.: "ACTIVE SHOOTER: Area of Orange Show Rd/Waterman Ave near Park Center, & surrounding area remains VERY ACTIVE. AVOID!"

The attack lasted four minutes. Most of those killed were shot in the back. Malik and Farook fled in an SUV and a short time later would die in a shoot-out with police.

Neighbors interviewed by local media in the aftermath of the shooting revealed that fears of a possible terrorist plot were not reported to authorities. A group of Middle Easterners seen at the couple's house was not reported over fears the informants would be accused of racial bias by "profiling" the potential terrorists, and fears of being labeled "Islamophobic."

The Justice Department report made no mention that neighbors' fears of being labeled anti-Muslim as a result of liberal political correctness had hampered law enforcement from discovering the plot to carry out the attack. The omission reveals just how deadly the doctrine of political correctness can be when it comes to dealing with Islamic terrorism.

Both racial profiling and Islamophobia are targets of liberals and Muslim activists who insist there is no link between terrorism and Islam. Had the suspicions been reported to police or FBI counterterrorism agents, the attack might have been headed off. A search of the couple's residence prior to the attack would have revealed pipe-bomb-making materials and thousands of rounds of rifle and pistol ammunition that were used in the attack. The pipe bombs either failed to detonate or were not triggered.

Days later the official Islamic State radio network Al-Bayan hailed Malik and Farook as "soldiers of the caliphate," the name used for the group's territory.

San Bernardino marked the deadliest terror attack on American soil since the September 11, 2001, attacks on the World Trade Center and Pentagon—that is, until six months after San Bernardino, when another American jihadist, Omar Mateen, a twenty-nine-year-old Islamist security guard, killed forty-nine people and wounded fifty-three others in an Orlando nightclub. That massacre also exposed the fact that poor FBI training involving Muslim terrorist suspects could have prevented that attack, since Mateen was investigated not once but twice by the FBI before the deadly shooting.

Americans are dying at the hands of Islamic terrorists in attacks that are increasing both at home and abroad. And American government leaders have refused to take action against the deadly ideas behind the murders as a result of false and politically correct fears that attacking Islamist ideology will fuel religious bigotry against Islam.

The failure to wage information warfare against the hateful and murderous Islamic ideology of jihad—holy war—has doomed the United States to endless conventional warfare that is both costly and deadly and is being waged with no formula for achieving victory and the peace that comes with it.

American security is endangered by leftist policies that prohibit recognizing the terror threat, the vital first step in taking action to defeat it.

Two of the deadliest attacks on Americans could have been stopped before they occurred but for the damaging notion of "Islamophobia"—leftist code for religious bias against Muslims—which prevented authorities from disrupting the terrorist attacks in San Bernardino and Orlando.

The root cause of these failures can be traced to June 4, 2009. On that date, President Barack Obama made an extraordinary speech that at the time appeared to be of little consequence. But the remarks would shake the foundations of Middle East stability and ultimately lead to the emergence of perhaps the deadliest Islamic terrorist group in the modern era: the Islamic State. On that date in Cairo, the American president spoke before an audience at Al-Azhar University and blamed the United States for the poor relations between the West and Muslim-dominated North Africa and the Middle East. The president had come into office only six months earlier with little foreign policy experience and harboring a worldview shaped by associations with the radical politics of the 1960s and '70s, when the New Left radicals promised a Chinese communist–style Long March through the institutions of America in a revolutionary Marxist coup d'état. In Cairo, Obama claimed falsely that the terrorist attacks in 2001 on New York and Washington "led some in my country to view Islam as inevitably hostile not only to America and Western countries but also to human rights." Never before in history had an American president traveled abroad and attacked his own country and people in such a fashion. In effect, the president was tarring Americans as racists and religious bigots opposed to radical Islam out of ignorance and prejudice. For the president, the 9/11 attacks that killed three thousand innocent people at the World Trade Center, the Pentagon, and on United Airlines Flight 93 triggered an American backlash against Islam that "led us to act contrary to our traditions and our ideals."

The comments were fundamentally false, as there was no anti-Muslim backlash after the 9/11 terror and Muslims continue to be protected, along with followers of other faiths, under American principles of religious freedom.

What has come to be called Obama's apology speech was the first item on the president's liberal left agenda; Obama called for a new beginning between America and Muslims around the world, based on mutual interest and respect. He insisted that "America and Islam are not exclusive and need not be in competition." Throughout history, he said, Islam has featured both religious tolerance and racial equality. Vowing to fight against negative stereotypes of Islam, the speech set in motion a series of disastrous U.S. government policies. "We are taking concrete actions to change course," Obama proclaimed in what was surely a presidential understatement.

Within a few short years of the Cairo speech, the president's misguided liberal left policies and a commitment to making the United States liked by the Muslim world had produced the most destructive period of instability since the administration of President Jimmy Carter, whose own misguided policies facilitated the Soviet invasion of Afghanistan and in that same year, 1979, the fall of the shah of Iran, an American ally, and the takeover of that key Middle East state by hostile Islamic theocrats.

Within a decade of Obama's one-sided nuclear deal, Tehran will be free to develop nuclear weapons that can be used by the Islamist regime to carry out its threat against Israel, America's key ally in the Middle East. Iran has vowed to wipe Israel off the earth. The disasters of the Carter administration show that liberal political idealism and utopianism are no substitute for global American leadership, and that the consequences of failed policies can be destructive, long-lasting, and deadly.

From an information warfare standpoint, Obama failed from the outset of his presidency at one of the most fundamental duties of a commander in chief: knowing your enemy. The president has misunderstood the nature of the Islamist forces arrayed against both the United States and the West in general. By sympathizing with Islam and misunderstanding its key tenets, Obama forced his administration into ideological disarmament that limited all descriptions of Islamist foes by mandating the use of a vaguely defined term for Islamic terrorism, "violent extremism." His worldview was derived from resentment-based concepts espoused in Marxist dogma that assert that America is not a great or even good nation but a racialist and imperialist power that must be brought to heel through liberal left policies. The president utterly failed to understand the ideology of Islamism—the political form of religious Islam that combines elements of fascism, Marxist historical resentment, and a supremacist view of inevitable Islamic world domination under fundamentalist principles dating back centuries. As a result, the president has doomed Americans to endless war.

The current battle against Islamist terror forces can be compared in some ways to the immoral foreign policies that for decades dominated American foreign policy during the Cold War. By treating the struggle between the Soviet Union and its global satellites on the one hand and the U.S.-led free world on the other with a kind of moral equivalence between the two competing systems, the United States facilitated Soviet oppression and continued rule.

It took President Ronald Reagan to produce the kind of moral clarity that was needed to bring about the eventual collapse of the Soviet Union in 1991. So too with the worldwide Islamist danger: unless its evil supremacist ideology is effectively countered, there will be no similar victory.

In essence, Obama's policies provide a case study in how not to fight and defeat Islamic terrorism through information warfare. The result is a Middle East in tatters, with hundreds of thousands of people dead, and an expanding force of ideologically motivated Islamists gaining both followers and territory at an alarming rate.

For his first term and most of the second, the president kept the country in the dark about the fundamental change in course he had initiated in American foreign and security policies. The lone exception was his plan to close the prison in Guantanamo Bay, Cuba, where al Qaeda terrorists captured in Afghanistan and elsewhere had been taken, some of them harshly interrogated. Obama and his advisers falsely believed the prison was the main recruiting tool for al Qaeda and other terrorists. But that view was mistaken, part of a calculated program of jihadist propaganda designed to fool international publics into opposing the United States. For jihadists—holy warriors following the tenets of Islam—imprisoning enemies and beheading and torturing them is an accepted practice. Only the misguided liberal infidels of the West, they argued, failed to exploit their enemies.

In 2016, the president finally tipped his hand regarding his prejudiced views. In a revealing interview with the *Atlantic Monthly*'s Jeffrey Goldberg, Obama for the first time helped place into context why he and his administration were so feckless in dealing with the problem of Islamic State terrorism, which in 2016 was rapidly spreading from central power bases in Syria and Iraq to the United States and Europe in the

West, to Afghanistan, Egypt, North Africa, and as far away as Southeast Asia. The tens of thousands of refugees flooding into Europe from the Middle East carnage spawned new networks for terrorist attacks like those in Paris and Brussels.

The headline on the White House–sanctioned *Atlantic* article was "The Obama Doctrine." It distilled the president's policies down to the bumper-sticker mantra of "Don't do stupid shit." It was not really a doctrine but an antidoctrine, based primarily on opposition to President George W. Bush's ill-fated 2003 invasion of Iraq. Obama had exploited the failure to create a stable Iraq into his own ideology. The article revealed that the president disdained the Washington foreign policy and national security establishment, which he claimed had scripted a "Washington playbook" that he opposed. And Obama dismissed the notion that maintaining the credibility of American power around the world as a force for keeping the peace mattered at all, whether in Syria or elsewhere. For Obama and his advisers, there was in effect a policy of "Don't do anything that risked the use of force," and adamant opposition to any action that might remotely lead to war with Muslim countries. The president expressed resentment toward American military leaders who had given him advice on what to do militarily in places like Syria. He first threatened to strike the Bashar Assad government in Damascus if they used chemical weapons; it was a strategic red line, the crossing of which would require U.S. action. But after announcing plans for military strikes using standoff missiles and bombers, the weak president never followed through with the threat. Since then, the Islamic State cancer centered in Syria has continued to metastasize.

As Obama explained, the resistance to using military force was a crowning achievement of his presidency. As he told the *Atlantic*:

> *Where am I controversial? When it comes to the use of military power. That is the source of the controversy. There's a playbook in Washington that presidents are supposed to follow. It's a playbook that comes out of the foreign-policy establishment. And the playbook prescribes responses to different events, and these responses tend to be militarized responses. Where America is directly threatened, the playbook works. But the playbook can also be a trap that can lead to bad decisions. In the midst of an international challenge like Syria, you get judged harshly if you don't follow the playbook, even if there are good reasons why it does not apply.*

Goldberg described Obama's 2013 decision not to bomb Syria as a landmark in preventing the United States "from entering yet another disastrous Muslim civil war." But that conclusion badly missed the most important point: Obama never understood that the key to defeating the growing threat of Islamic terrorism is the use of information warfare tools to discredit and defeat the ideology of radical Islamic jihad. This was a fact he could never bring himself or his administration to admit because he was so wedded to misguided notions both about America and the nature of the threat posed by radical Islam. For Obama, the questionable and scientifically unproven notion of man-made climate change posed a bigger threat than the spread of the Islamic State from Syria and Iraq into Libya, Egypt, Pakistan, Afghanistan, and ultimately Europe and the United States.

"ISIS is not an existential threat to the United States," Obama said. "Climate change is a potential existential threat to the entire world if we don't do something about it," he added in the next breath. Designating the notion of climate change as a world threat has been dubbed the "church of climatology," since there is a dearth of honest scientific study. Climate change is yet another liberal shibboleth in the Left's panoply of tools seeking more centralized political power. Yet in the same conversation with Goldberg, the president described himself as a foreign policy "realist" who believes he cannot relieve all the world's misery and noted that choices were required where they "can make a real impact."

The president also made clear he is opposed to American leadership, whether in regard to jihadist terror, Russian expansionism, or Chinese communist hegemonism. Obama instead favors what one of his aides termed "leading from behind," a policy first enunciated with disastrous effect during Obama's reluctant foray into foreign military intervention when he ordered U.S. military forces to aid rebels fighting Libyan strongman Moammar Gadhafi.

The Libyan intervention would prove to be nearly as dangerous as Bush's intervention in Iraq, and that danger continues to increase. Gadhafi, who had ordered the bombing of Pan Am Flight 103, which exploded over Lockerbie, Scotland, in 1988, killing all 243 people on board and 16 crew members, and who was never held accountable, would be killed and his body dragged through the streets of the coastal Libyan city of Sirte during the Libyan revolution.

The intervention left bands of marauding militias to rule the country and turned an oil-rich state into a failed Islamist redoubt. "Libya has become a terrorist safe haven," an American counterterrorism official told me. So much for leading from behind.

The one area where Obama was not averse to the use of force was in ordering attacks by armed drones. This single weapon has proved so powerful and effective that it has forced terrorists around the world to completely alter the way they operate, requiring them and their security minders to listen intently for the telltale hum of hovering unmanned aerial vehicles—the deadly signature of Predator and Reaper drones, which deliver deadly accurate guided missiles against cars or houses.

Yet this tool too had been restricted under Obama as a result of pressure from international human rights groups and others who lobbied against use of the weapon as *unfair to the terrorists* and because the strikes caused too much collateral damage—mainly because terrorist leaders began surrounding themselves with women, children, and captured prisoners to dissuade the drone targeters and operators and their commanders from striking.

Obama ordered a sharp curtailment in drone strikes, like those planned against Islamic State leader Abu Bakr al-Baghdadi several times in 2015 and 2016 but never carried out, over concerns about killing civilians close to the terrorist leader. Baghdadi had been spotted in the open at least three times at or near his headquarters in Raqqa, Syria. Under Obama's orders, the CIA and U.S. military, which operate the armed drones, must first meet strict rules of engagement that limit causing civilian and collateral damage, and require confirmation that the target is located in a specific strike zone. The curtailment highlighted the failure of the president and his administration to understand that warfare must be waged with a specific strategic objective—defeating the enemy, ending in victory, and producing peace.

Drone strikes have been the central element of the president's counterterrorism policy since he took office in 2009. And they are a fundamental reason his counterterrorism policies have failed. Obama claims to harbor no illusions about radical Islam but his worldview was poisoned by his bias *against America* and the outdated and false notion that America is a colonialist, imperialist power rooted in the evil of slavery.

The key failure was his unwillingness to use information warfare tools and techniques to attack the ideological underpinnings of Islam's tenet of jihadism, which permits killing to advance the cause of Islamic supremacy. As shown, the president was more concerned about stoking anti-Muslim xenophobia among what he regarded as racist Americans by the use of any type of counter-jihad ideological warfare campaign.

During his 2012 reelection bid, Obama's central campaign theme was that "a new tower rises above the New York skyline, al Qaeda is on the path to defeat, and Osama bin Laden is dead." But as the September 11, 2012, terrorist attack on two U.S. government facilities in Benghazi, Libya—a CIA base and U.S. diplomatic compound—would show, the narrative of a declining al Qaeda was totally false. A terrorist group linked to al Qaeda, Ansar al Sharia, launched a deadly, military-style assault on the compound and a nearby CIA facility that resulted in the deaths of four Americans, including the U.S. ambassador to Libya, J. Christopher Stevens. The others were Foreign Service officer Sean Smith and CIA contractors Tyrone S. Woods and Glen Doherty. To protect his political fortunes, aides to the leftist former community organizer from Chicago floated false and deceptive stories that the attack was really the result of an anti-Islamic video—a meme that again bolstered Obama's false propaganda narrative against America.

Fears of anti-American bias and worries of fueling anti-Muslim sentiment prevented the president and the rest of the American government from adopting an effective strategy. And this key failure is a central reason Obama will be remembered most for his failed foreign policies. Throughout his presidency, Obama adamantly refused to apply an effective counter-ideological warfare approach to, first, al Qaeda, and then its ultraviolent successor, the Islamic State. In Obama's worldview, globalization made notions of American national interest outdated. The liberal cosmopolitan leader has turned the twentieth-century precept that nations do not have friends, only interests, on its head. For Obama, the world should be friends and transcend all concept of nationalism. The exception was the policy for dealing with

transnational terrorists. And here the president and his advisers refused to address the religious ideology behind Islamic
extremism, because of a postmodern liberal left philosophical
bias that argues the concept of religious truth should be rejected as outdated. In its place leftists now advocate a radical-
ized moral relativism and individualism that are applied to all
spheres of human existence. Instead of tackling the difficult
task of waging ideological war against the Islamist ideology,
Obama favored the policy of killing terrorist leaders as the
primary means of addressing the problem, a strategy that
harked back to the Vietnam War, when news reporters attended daily briefings dubbed the "five o'clock follies" on the
roof of a Saigon hotel, where military spokesmen would give
out the latest body count of Viet Cong insurgents killed in
battle by U.S. forces.

The war on Islamic terror that began after the 9/11 attacks
has been based completely on the mistaken idea that killing
terrorist leaders is akin to cutting off the head of a snake and
causing the rest of the body to die. Both the George W. Bush
administration and the Obama administration frequently
touted statistics on the deaths of al Qaeda and later Islamic
State leaders as signs of progress against the enemy. Bush
liked to say that 75 percent of al Qaeda leaders had been
killed or captured. By 2011, Obama was using the same questionable statistics, albeit slightly modified by the fact that the
United States was no longer capturing enemy combatants,
as a result of his opposition to Guantanamo detentions and
interrogations.

By 2015, Obama boasted that drone strikes and special

operations commando raids had killed twenty-two of the top thirty al Qaeda leaders, or 73 percent, including Osama bin Laden. "How many times do 75 percent of al Qaeda's top leaders need to be killed before the terror group is dead?" remarked Bill Roggio, editor of the online *Long War Journal*.

The flaw of the snake-head approach completely misunderstands the persistence and nature of an ideologically armed jihadist enemy that is driven to killing not by its radical Islamist leaders, who are quickly replaced once removed from the battlefield, but by the greater appeal of a death-cult-like Muslim ideology that feeds on the resentments of Muslims going back over one thousand years.

The jihadists have adopted sophisticated information warfare techniques to promote their ideological cause and recruit suicide bombers and others willing to die in promoting their cause. The terrorists' apocalyptic jihadist ideology argues that of the three monotheist religions of Judaism, Christianity, and Islam, Islam is the historically ordained successor to both Christianity and Judaism, simply based on the belief that Muhammad, who lived from AD 537 to 632, was the most recent central figure in the three faiths' religious history.

The train pulling the Obama counterterrorism strategy went off the rails in 2011, when the president outlined a key element of his strategy against al Qaeda in a secret directive called Presidential Study Directive–11, or PSD-11. An American official familiar with the still-secret directive told me the order was used as the basis for the administration's support of the international Islamic extremist group known as the Muslim Brotherhood, which advocates what has been labeled a "pre-violent" iteration of same jihadist revolutionary creed in use by the Islamic State and al Qaeda. The ultimate goal is the imposition of fundamentalist Islamic religious and political systems worldwide under sharia law, the totalitarian legal creed followed by terrorists and fundamentalist Muslims.

Backing the Muslim Brotherhood was an utter failure of American information warfare efforts against terrorism. The idea behind PSD-11 was for the Obama administration to support the Muslim Brotherhood as a nonviolent alternative to al Qaeda. The policy met with a disastrous end in Egypt, where Obama repeated the mistake of Jimmy Carter in Iran by misunderstanding the nature of the opposition movement opposing the authoritarian regime of Egyptian president Hosni Mubarak, a longtime Middle East ally. As the Arab Spring demonstrations resulted in mass protests in Cairo's Tahrir Square, Obama failed to support prodemocracy protests and instead gave American support to the better-organized and ideologically committed Muslim Brotherhood as the successor regime. Muslim Brotherhood leader Mohammed Morsi was elected in the aftermath and had quietly begun consolidating power and preparing for the imposition of sharia law and other extreme Islamist policies when the Egyptian military ousted him in July 2013. The move came after protesters took to the streets again to oppose the effort to end traditional rule of law. Then–secretary of state Hillary Clinton revealed how naïve and uninformed she was about the antidemocratic nature of the Muslim Brotherhood regime in Egypt under Morsi during a meeting with the Egyptian leader in July 2012 in Cairo. Secret State Department talking points for the meeting, released under the Freedom of Information Act, note that Clinton planned to tell Morsi that "We stand behind Egypt's transition to democracy," and that "we are ready to work with you." She also offered Morsi covert police assistance to help keep him in power.

Since the events of Egypt, the Muslim Brotherhood has been labeled a terrorist organization by the governments of Saudi Arabia, Egypt, and the United Arab Emirates—but not the United States, an indication that the dangerous PSD-11 remained in force at the end of the Obama administration. The UAE government went further and labeled two American groups they viewed as affiliates of the Muslim Brotherhood, the Council on American-Islamic Relations (CAIR) and the Muslim American Society, as terrorist groups. Both groups denied they are either Brotherhood outlets or otherwise terrorist organizations. Islamism gained ground in Turkey, a NATO ally, under President Recep Tayyip Erdogan, who moved the country from a secular, Western-oriented democracy toward the budding Islamist state it has become. The failed military coup against Erdogan in July 2016 triggered an acceleration of the Islamicization process by Erdogan. Civil liberties were curtailed and non-Islamic opposition figures were repressed in its aftermath.

"This dangerous foreign policy was launched by PSD-11 and the administration's open embrace of the Muslim Brotherhood, and now we can see its catastrophic effect," counterterrorism analyst Patrick Poole told me. The Center for Security Policy has documented Muslim Brotherhood subversion efforts, both in the United States and abroad, including several Brotherhood supporters whom the center has identified as key advisers to Obama. The Obama administration's support of the Muslim Brotherhood exemplifies a failure to understand the ideologically driven enemy facing the United States in the early decades of the twenty-first century and helped foster the emergence in 2014 of the Islamic State.

The strategy of killing al Qaeda leaders created a major problem. Its new leader after bin Laden, the Egyptian Ayman al-Zawahiri, joined the Muslim Brotherhood at age fourteen and ended up playing a role in the 1981 assassination of Egyptian leader Anwar Sadat. He would go on to found Egyptian Islamic Jihad, which merged with al Qaeda in 1998. By 2009, he would become al Qaeda's chief operational and strategic commander and in 2011 the overall leader of the terrorist group. Unlike bin Laden, Zawahiri lacked the appeal of his deceased predecessor, which led to divisions within the various chapters, most notably the Iraqi affiliate group known as the Islamic State of Iraq and Syria, also known as the Islamic State of Iraq and the Levant. It would differentiate itself by becoming a full-fledged insurgent group—not just a shadowy terrorist organization like al Qaeda.

The starting point of the Islamic State takeover of Iraq, a pivotal event in the rise of the organization, can be traced to the night of July 22, 2013. On that date, dozens of gunmen armed with assault rifles, mortars, and rocket-propelled grenades made a surprise attack on two prisons near Baghdad, at Abu Ghraib—notorious in the mid-2000s as the place where U.S. Army soldiers had photographed other soldiers abusing terrorist captives—and a second prison north of the capital, called Taji. The Iraqi government was slow to respond to the attacks, which prompted uprisings at both prisons and led to the release of some five hundred prisoners, half of them known to be hardened al Qaeda terrorists and key leaders. The prison break was carried out by al Qaeda, operating under the Islamic principle espoused by Muhammad ibn Abd al-Wahhab, the eighteenth-century Muslim behind the current Islamic supremacist movement promoted by Saudi Arabia called Wahhabism. Wahhab taught that Muslims had a responsibility to recover their prisoners from captivity. And at Abu Ghraib and Taji that is what they did, to great effect. The approximately two hundred jihadists freed from the prisons represented the first and second generation of the Islamic State in Iraq, headed by Abu Bakr al-Baghdadi, who began rebuilding IS in 2010 and merged his group with a Syrian branch to become the Islamic State of Iraq and the Levant in April 2013. The group, also known as the Islamic State of Iraq and Syria, orchestrated the July 2013 prison break.

Less than a year later, on June 6, 2014, Baghdadi's forces, numbering some 1,500 fighters, equipped with pickup trucks and machine guns and rocket-propelled grenades and utilizing suicide car bombs, attacked Mosul, a city in northern Iraq that is the country's second largest. Despite outnumbering the ISIL fighters 15 to 1, two entire Iraqi military divisions, about 30,000 troops, simply fled the city rather than fight against the ISIL forces. It was a stunning victory for the terrorists. The fleeing Iraqis shed all their equipment, including artillery, tanks, armored vehicles, and tons of other weapons, which was quickly integrated into the lightly armed terrorist group's forces. Two more prisons in Mosul that held hundreds of ISIL terrorists were attacked by the advancing ISIL insurgents, which freed at least 1,200 additional fighters.

The takeover was followed by a bloodbath of gruesome mass killings and executions, filmed and distributed on the Internet and involving thousands of Iraqis. The murderous rampage was unlike any witnessed in modern history and was key propaganda for the group in instilling fear and terror in its enemies. By the end of June 2014, after controlling large sections of Iraqi territory, Baghdadi declared the creation of a caliphate—a region under Islamic control—that aspired to restore the last Muslim caliphate under the Ottoman Empire, which lasted until 1924 and once stretched from Spain through North Africa and as far east as current-day Pakistan and parts of Russia. The group was renamed the Islamic State.

Unlike bin Laden, who issued directives as an insurgent photographed carrying a signature AK-47 assault rifle, Baghdadi issued his declaration of the caliphate from the Grand Mosque of occupied Mosul, wearing a black turban and black clerical robe. The presentation highlighted key differences between the new Islamic State and al Qaeda. "Where Al Qaeda was primarily a terrorist enterprise and brand, ISIS presents itself first and foremost as a theocratic enterprise, with the goal to reestablish the Caliphate and return all Muslims to a pure form of Islam as it was lived during the time of

Mohammed," counterterrorism experts Sebastian Gorka and Katharine Gorka stated in a report on the group.

Obama, who had undermined American influence in Iraq by withdrawing all U.S. troops by 2011, was slow to react, initially limiting the U.S. government's response to vapid official pronouncements voicing "concern" for events in Iraq. After realizing the takeover of Mosul and the rise of the Islamic State was a major setback, and under pressure from his military commanders to prevent the complete takeover of Iraq, Obama took to national television and announced he was launching a new counterterrorism strategy. The speech on September 10, 2014, like earlier mutterings, once again included an oft-repeated falsehood asserting the Islamic State was not Islamic. "No religion condones the killing of innocents, and the vast majority of ISIL's victims have been Muslim," he said. As one U.S. intelligence analyst told me: "The president may be couching terms. Clearly IS fighters are Islamic in prayers, devotion, and ritual. Hundreds to thousands of followers were Islamic before joining IS and there is no evidence of renunciation or apostasy from their earlier Islamic beliefs or practices." As for the massacres, Obama said that "no religion condones the killing of innocents," again carefully couching the truth to avoid offending Muslims and attempt to prevent Americans from seeing Islam in a negative light.

As the intelligence analyst explained:

The operative word is "innocents" and to a great extent, this is accurate. However, it should be noted that Muhammad himself, the founder of Islam, was a prolific killer. IS's march

throughout Iraq and Syria is arguably similar to Muham-
mad's initial twenty-seven campaigns, and Islam's breakout
across Arabia under the subsequent Caliphs, where post-
hostilities slaughters occurred, icons destroyed, booty taken,
and women raped and parceled out, with their children, to
the fighters. We may be seeing the president using a rhetori-
cal device to objectify IS so that they can be legitimately, in
the eyes of a larger audience, targeted.

Obama emphasized that the vast majority of IS's victims
were Muslims. But what he conveniently did not disclose was
that the vast majority of the killings involved Shia Muslims,
and that taking sides against IS in Iraq had effectively aligned
the United States with Shia Muslims who are engaged in a
bitter struggle with their Sunni coreligionists for dominance
of the faith. Many blame the unthinking policy of siding with
Iraqi Shias on Obama's closest White House adviser, Valerie
Jarrett, who was believed to harbor greater sympathy for
Shiite Muslims based on her affinity for Iran, where she was
born and spent her early childhood.

Unlike its covert predecessor, the Islamic State terrorists
proved to be aggressive insurgent fighters. "ISIL has proven
to be an effective fighting force," Matthew G. Olsen, director
of the National Counterterrorism Center, said in a speech in
2014, using one of two acronyms for the group, the Islamic
State of Iraq and the Levant and the Islamic State of Iraq and
Syria. "Its battlefield strategy is complex and adaptive, employing a mix of terrorist operations, hit-and-run tactics, and
paramilitary assaults to enable the group's rapid gains."

But more important than its fighting capabilities, IS had become the undisputed heavyweight champion of the global jihadist movement. "It operates the most sophisticated propaganda machine of any extremist group," Olsen said, noting:

> ISIL disseminates timely, high-quality media content on multiple platforms, including on social media, designed to secure a widespread following for the group. We have seen ISIL use a range of media to tout its military capabilities, executions of captured soldiers, and consecutive battlefield victories. More recently, the group's supporters have sustained this momentum on social media by encouraging attacks in the U.S. and against U.S. interests in retaliation for our airstrikes. ISIL has used this propaganda campaign to draw foreign fighters to the group, including many from Western countries. As a result, ISIL threatens to outpace al Qaeda as the dominant voice of influence in the global extremist movement. Today, ISIL has more than 10,000 fighters and controls much of the Tigris-Euphrates basin—the crossroads of the Middle East—an area similar in size to the UK. And its strategic goal is to establish an Islamic caliphate through armed conflict with governments it considers apostate— including Iraq, Syria, and the United States.

In his "My fellow Americans" speech to the nation that September, Obama promised for the first time to "counter [IS's] warped ideology." But his administration did nothing in the counter-ideology sphere. Once again, the president's fear of creating a backlash against Muslims hindered the only real tool capable of defeating Islamic jihadism over the long term. One of the architects of the failure was Quintan Wiktorowicz, a behind-the-scenes counterterrorism strategist for the Obama administration. "While the government has tried to counter terrorist propaganda, it cannot directly address the warped religious interpretations of groups like ISIL because of the constitutional separation of church and state," Wiktorowicz told me.

The statement was false and showed Wiktorowicz's lack of understanding of the American system. The constitutional provision for the separation of church and state was added *to prevent the creation of a state religion—not to prevent warfare or policies against the threat of terrorism.*

Islamic advisers brought into the White House and other institutions of power in Washington also succeeded in preventing any U.S. government discussion of the Islamic roots of radical jihadism.

It was revealed in a *New York Times Magazine* article on White House senior adviser Ben Rhodes just how important these Islamic sympathies were for Obama, who grew up in predominantly Muslim Indonesia, as well as his key adviser Jarrett. As Jarrett told David Samuels, the author of the *Times Magazine* piece, their early upbringing overseas influenced both hers and the president's policies toward all things Muslim. Jarrett, who has been dubbed Obama's "work wife," was asked about the "point of connection" between her and the president. She said that having lived abroad was a bond between them. During their first conversation over dinner, Obama and Jarrett shared "what it was like for both of us to live in countries that were predominantly Muslim countries at formative parts of our childhood," Jarrett said, noting "I remember [Obama] asking me questions that I felt like no one else has ever asked me before, and he asked me from a perspective of someone who knew the same experience that I had. So it felt really good. I was like, 'Oh, finally someone who gets it.'"

What their foreign experience did not give them, unfortunately, was an honest understanding of radical jihadism; such understanding is the ultimate key to defeating the threat posed by Islamic terrorism. By the fall of 2015, the Islamic State had become the most well-armed and well-funded terrorist organization in the world. Intelligence estimates put its holdings of cash at about $1 billion, and its raids in Iraq had netted the group an estimated $50 billion in captured weapons and equipment. "ISIL's sophisticated military skill and brutality has been key to its success in Iraq and Syria," stated an October 19, 2015, report by the State Department–led Overseas Security Advisory Council, a group that supports American businesses overseas. "However, its ability to generate cutting-edge propaganda to promote its ideology and gain sympathizers and members across the globe, added to its largely self-reliant, robust financial system, has contributed heavily to its success as well."

Foreign nationals sympathetic to the Islamist organization and encouraged by its early battlefield victories flooded into Syria and Iraq by the thousands beginning in 2015, many recruited by the estimated 46,000 Twitter accounts of members and sympathizers. "Halting the flow of foreign fighters is incredibly difficult," the State Department report says, noting that travel bans imposed by Western countries were not effective at curbing foreign fighters from joining the group since they could easily enter Syria, mainly through Turkey.

Congress criticized the failure to attack the Islamic State ideology but appeared powerless to spur the Obama administration to take more effective action. Senate Armed Services Committee chairman Senator John McCain, an Arizona Republican, accused the president of "self-delusion" in asserting that the U.S. strategy of limited bombing against Islamic State targets was producing results. "Since U.S. and coalition airstrikes began [in 2014], ISIL has continued to enjoy battlefield successes, including taking Ramadi and other key terrain in Iraq, holding over half the territory in Syria and controlling every border post between Iraq and Syria," McCain said. "Our means and our current level of effort are not aligned with our ends. That suggests we are not winning, and when you're not winning in war, you are losing."

A covert U.S. intelligence program to train Syrian rebels at first failed miserably because of restrictions placed on the program by the president: the United States would train only Syrian rebels who would agree not to seek the overthrow of Syrian leader Bashar Assad, a condition most adamantly rejected. As a result, fewer than one hundred fighters were trained, despite planning to produce an opposition force of seven thousand Syrian rebels to fight only against the Islamic State. The failure also highlighted how the CIA's covert action capability had been decimated. "The lack of coherent strategy has resulted in the spread of ISIL around the world to Libya, Egypt, Nigeria, and even to Afghanistan," McCain said. "We have seen this movie before, and if we make the same mistakes, we should expect similarly tragic results."

Duane "Dewey" Clarridge, the former CIA operations officer and first director of its Counterterrorism Center, told me the administration's Syrian training program was a waste of time. Instead, the Pentagon should have funded and organized a regional military force of Egyptians, Saudis, Jordanians, and troops from Persian Gulf militaries based on the Sunni Arab National Front for the Salvation of Iraq, also known as the Awakening Movement, which was developed in Iraq from 2008 to bring stability to the country. According to Clarridge a major shortcoming was the failure of the Obama administration to counter IS propaganda and recruitment efforts.

"Everyone says you can't win this war militarily. But where is the psychological warfare effort? I have people monitoring this day in, day out, and there is none, zero," he said. "There are people standing by with large capabilities, Muslims, ready to put their capabilities to work, if someone would organize it," Clarridge said, noting that no radio broadcasting was being carried out in Iraq and Syria.

The bombing campaign against the Islamic State also proved to be feckless. One reason it was ineffective surfaced in an analysis of the scores of air strikes carried out in Iraq and Syria by the United States and allies. Details released on the strikes revealed that an extremely small percentage of the estimated sixty Islamic State training camps that were producing thousands of fighters each month had been targeted in the bombing campaign as of August 2015. According to the website of the U.S. Central Command, the military command in charge of counterterrorism operations, a total of 6,419 air strikes were carried out in the twelve months between August 2014 and 2015, including 3,991 in Iraq and 2,428 in Syria. But astoundingly, only 19 attacks, or .3 percent of the total air strikes, were carried out against terrorist training areas. The camps were spread throughout Islamic State–controlled areas of Iraq and Syria but were placed off-limits by Obama's political appointees, who were concerned about causing collateral damage and killing civilians who were being used by the terrorists as shields. And U.S. intelligence agencies reported in classified channels that training within camps was so successful that it allowed the group to expand from Syria into Libya and Yemen. "If we know the location of these camps, and the president wants to destroy ISIS, why are the camps still functioning?" one intelligence official critical of the policy told me.

Defense Department officials lamented how information warfare efforts against the Islamic State had been stifled by the Obama policy of avoiding any mention of Islam, and by resistance within the government bureaucracy to countering the jihadist threat. Bureaucratic red tape within the military, especially at the Central Command, and at the Pentagon had prevented rapid responses to Islamic State propaganda and activities. The cumbersome approval process for taking information warfare action against IS all but ensured that efforts to counter the group would fail. Several layers of approvals and a lengthy chain of command are required for an information operation to be carried out. That resulted in delays of weeks for operations designed to counteract Islamic State propaganda and recruitment activities. As a result, terrorist recruitment and propaganda flourished and new fighters joined the group or were inspired to carry out deadly attacks. Fears of exposing a U.S. government hand in the counter–information warfare also hampered effective action; also, risk-averse bureaucrats—both military and civilian—opposed any counterattack on IS propaganda, because of fears they would trigger stepped-up IS information warfare and terrorist attacks. The command was able to address obvious lies propagated by IS, but the propagandists for the jihadist movement used information techniques that mixed truth with falsehoods as a way to avoid giving the Americans an easy way to disprove their open lies. Urgently needed aggressive online programs to dissuade would-be jihadists and expose IS propaganda programs and activities were blocked both at Central Command and the Pentagon.

Officials involved in the programs revealed that the military's information warfare campaign was derailed not just over issues of restrictions on mentioning Islam but by a more banal cause: simple government bureaucratic opposition to conducting what are perceived to be distasteful propaganda activities that bureaucrats mistakenly associated with being contrary to American traditions of freedom, honesty, and openness. "What we're finding is it's very difficult to address these guys because of our own process," one American counter-IS official told me. "Every time CENTCOM tries to address this directly, we get slapped down."

One example of IS's online information warfare agility is how the group uses Twitter. IS operatives and supporters use multiple Twitter accounts to disseminate well-crafted videos and propaganda materials. Usually, IS online jihadists open up to six Twitter accounts at a time and shift to successive accounts after one or more are shut down by the social media giant. The terror group also produced what have been described as very professional videos in multiple languages and aimed at various international audiences; the videos seek to recruit new fighters, including those willing to carry out the most deadly form of attack, suicide vehicle or body vest bombing. The group also has begun shifting from the use of social media sites like Facebook and Twitter to specialty apps like Telegram, which are well suited to disseminating material and communicating through mobile handheld devices, such as smartphones, and have security features including encryption for messages. Telegram, as mentioned earlier, is a Russian-origin messaging service that uses commercial-grade data encryption to prevent electronic interception. It is easily available to anyone with a smartphone. Another application used by terrorists is called Surespot, also downloadable to handheld devices. While the encryption is breakable, decoding intercepted messages from terrorists now requires the use of great computer power and lengthy periods of time that limit the ability to find actionable intelligence on pending attacks or operations.

IS jihadists are also using the Dark Web, the part of the Internet used by criminals, to share information and recruit members. Judging by its many video and online products, government analysts say IS appears to have learned information dissemination methods used by neo-Nazi political groups to communicate and spread their messages throughout the English-speaking world on the Dark Web.

Counterterrorism expert Sebastian Gorka believes it is urgent that the United States develop and employ a massive counter–information warfare program against terrorism. The information warfare campaign must be covert—not revealed as linked to the U.S. government—and provide support and backing for brave Muslim reformers around the world, as well as launch major programs of support for private sector initiatives that would be infinitely more efficient than government-run programs. "This is what we did against the USSR and this is what we have to do against the new totalitarian ideology of jihadism," Gorka says.

Until early 2016, one of the most powerful information warfare tools of the U.S. government—the ability to conduct cyberattacks against Islamic State information systems—had been denied. That changed with the unusual announcement by the Pentagon in the spring that the U.S. Cyber Command, the military subcommand based at Fort Meade, Maryland, had begun using cyberattacks to disrupt Islamic State command-and-control and recruiting efforts. It was the first time the Pentagon had ever conducted cyberwarfare. Secretary of Defense Ashton Carter announced the cyber operations, which he said were targeted at "disrupt[ing] ISIL's command and control, to cause them to lose confidence in their networks, to overload their network so that they can't

function, and do all of these things that will interrupt their
ability to command and control forces there, control the
population and the economy." Further details were not disclosed, but the use of cyber, while welcome, appeared to have
had a limited impact on the Islamist enemy.

The chairman of the Joint Chiefs of Staff, General Joseph
Dunford, explained that the operations aim to isolate the Islamic State both physically and virtually; to limit the group's
ability to command and control its forces and its captured
territory; to disrupt communications; and generally to stifle
the terrorist organization's ability to conduct operations. In
declining to provide further details, Dunford said, "We don't
want them to have information that will allow them to adapt
over time. We want them to be surprised when we conduct
cyber operations, and frankly, they're going to experience
some friction that's associated with us, and some friction
that's just associated with the normal course of events in dealing in the information age."

It was the first use of what Cyber Command calls Cyber
Mission Force teams, which are being deployed with military commands and other units around the world devoted to
cyberattacks.

By mid-2016, the U.S. government had been loudly asserting that the conflict against the Islamic State was advancing. But the facts on the ground provided a different story. As
the noose tightened around the group's strongholds in Iraq
and Syria, terrorists simply moved to safer ground. In Libya,
the number of fighters grew from around one thousand in

2015 to four thousand by the spring of 2016. The group Boko Haram, based in northern Nigeria, renamed itself in early 2016 as the Islamic State West Africa Province.

U.S. Army general Joseph Votel, head of the Central Command, revealed that the strategy of targeting terrorist leaders was simply driving the problem out of Syria and Iraq and into other lands and ultimately toward Europe and the United States. "Certainly in both Iraq and Syria, in a lot of locations, we are continuing to target their leadership," Votel said at a Pentagon briefing in 2016. The four-star general said that after gains against the group are made in those two locations, the Islamic State "will continue to adapt and we will continue to deal with the next evolution of ISIL, whether they become more of a terrorist organization and return to more of their terrorist-like roots."

The commander's comments reveal that the current U.S. counterterrorism strategy, based on targeting terror leaders and fighters on the ground without waging information warfare against Islamist ideology, is doomed to failure. Worse, this failed strategy continues to force America into waging an endless war—war that will result in victory only when the ideas behind the murderous terror group are attacked and defeated. This requires adapting the counter-ideology programs used to defeat Soviet communism to a comprehensive offensive against Islamic terror.

7

IRAN

I Went to the Store and They Still Don't Have Whiskey. What Kind of Nuclear Deal Is This?

Iran employs the concept of "soft war," using the Internet and other technical platforms to combat perceived enemies.
—INTERNAL STATE DEPARTMENT
SECURITY REPORT, MAY 8, 2015

The Islamic Republic of Iran remains the world's deadliest state sponsor of international terrorism, a regime responsible for the killing of thousands of Americans. And within a few years, as a result of the nuclear agreement orchestrated by President Barack Obama, the extremist regime in Tehran will be capable of firing missiles armed with nuclear warheads against American cities, threatening the lives of millions of Americans. In developing these weapons of mass destruction, the hard-line Islamic rulers of Iran remain steadfast in their goal of making "Death to America" a reality. In the process, the Iranians have conducted a highly effective information warfare program to deceive the United States into lifting crippling economic sanctions and paying billions of dollars in ransom, in exchange for the false promise of improved relations between the United States and Iran. In pursuing this objective, Obama utterly failed to understand the true nature of the danger posed by Iran. And in an unprecedented move by an American president, Obama carried out his own information warfare operation against the American people to conclude the nuclear agreement, which guarantees the ruling mullahs in Tehran will be permitted under an international treaty to produce nuclear weapons in ten years or less. The mishandling of the nuclear danger posed by Iran was blatant appeasement of a kind not seen since British prime minister Neville Chamberlain declared "peace for our time" after caving in to Nazi Germany in 1938—less than a year before German forces invaded Poland, marking the start of World War II.

On July 14, 2015, in Vienna, Austria, representatives of the Islamic Republic of Iran, the United States, China, France, Germany, the European Union, Russia, and the United Kingdom gathered to sign an agreement that had been twenty months in the making. And according to its preamble, the agreement would "ensure that Iran's nuclear program will be exclusively peaceful, and mark a fundamental shift in their approach to this issue." In reality, the agreement will go down in history as among the worst diplomatic failures in American history. It legitimized an illegal nuclear program for Iran and permits the hard-line Islamist state to take all the technological steps needed to produce nuclear weapons within a decade.

It was the deal of the century. Iran was a rogue Islamist state that at the time of the signing remained one of the most active state sponsors of international terrorism, backing such groups as Lebanon's Hezbollah and the Palestinian terror group Hamas. Iran also had harbored several key al Qaeda leaders throughout the 2000s. Iran is a state that since its Islamic revolution in 1979 has been linked to the killing of thousands of Americans, including at least 1,100 U.S. soldiers killed in Iraq as a direct result of Tehran's supplying deadly armor-piercing bombs to Iraqi militias and terrorists.

The nuclear deal triggered deadpan humor on Iran's vibrant social media, one of the few areas of society where Iranians opposed to the violent theocratic regime express themselves. "I went to the store now and they still don't have whiskey! What kind of a deal is this?" went one wry text message circulating on WhatsApp and Viber.

The appeasement of Iran was a deliberate policy of President Barack Obama and his administration to seek normal relations with Iran, at the same time pretending the nuclear agreement would mitigate perhaps the most serious danger of Iran developing nuclear weapons and thus emerging as a nuclear weapons state. By participating in what became known as the Joint Comprehensive Plan of Action, Tehran received through negotiations what it had been seeking for years—relief from crippling international sanctions imposed for its illegal nuclear program, sanctions that had prevented the purchase of foreign military weapons and equipment. The kicker, however, came when the U.S. government agreed as part of the deal to allow Iran to recover at least $100 billion in cash that had been frozen in various banks around the world under U.S. sanctions.

The Iran deal was a clear case of a successful information warfare campaign waged against the United States and the world; it involved infiltrating key pro-Iranian influence agents within the Obama administration. For President Obama, the Iran nuclear deal was cast as the crowning achievement of his second term in office, a foreign policy gambit he and his aides regarded as the equivalent of his controversial national health care program of the first term.

Obama ignored a strategic opportunity to support democratic reform in Iran during the mass demonstrations that broke out in Iran following rigged elections in 2009. As Iranians took to the streets by the thousands to protest the fraud, Obama remained silent. The protesters were supporting official Iranian government reformers who, while not advocating democratic changes or opposing the theocratic regime, could nonetheless have been utilized in an information warfare program to advance the emergence of a democratic regime in Iran if given covert American intelligence support or financing. The president instead regarded any covert intervention to back the protesters as harking back to what he viewed as unwelcome American imperialism. The CIA successfully had worked behind the scenes in Iran in 1953 to overthrow Prime Minister Mohammad Mosaddegh and install the shah Mohammad Reza Pahlavi.

Hillary Clinton, as Obama's secretary of state, wrote in her book *Hard Choices* that Obama rejected arguments from his advisers to help the protesters, who would end up being brutally suppressed and attacked by Iranian security forces. Clinton wrote that "the president grudgingly decided that we would better serve the aspirations of the Iranian people by not putting the United States in the middle of the crisis. It was a difficult, clear-eyed tactical call." An inveterate dissembler, Clinton also falsely stated that the failure to back the Iranian protests was not based on Obama's desire to engage the Islamist regime. She then stated that "in retrospect, I'm not sure our restraint was the right choice."

In reality, Iran's Green Revolution, as it was called, was a golden opportunity for the United States to change the power structure in the Middle East by forcing democratic reform on the terrorist-backing regime in Tehran. Had the United States government and intelligence community had a highly developed information warfare capability at the time, the peaceful regime change could have been carried out without firing a shot. But the president and his team squandered the chance to not only improve the lives of millions of Iranians, but to serve U.S. interests as well. Instead of doing the right thing, Obama pressed ahead with a secret program of engaging Iran, sending at least four secret letters to Iran's dictator, Ayatollah Ali Khamenei. The letters naïvely offered American cooperation with the hard-line regime. In 2014, Obama asked Khamenei to work with the United States in countering terrorism, apparently oblivious to Iran's role as a leading state sponsor of Islamist terror itself.

As noted earlier, Ben Rhodes operated as the president's chief liberal left communications strategist, waging a kind of information warfare against the American public in mustering support for the Iranian nuclear deal. As a thirty-year-old White House official working for Obama, Rhodes was dubbed the Boy Wonder. Under the grandiose title Deputy National Security Advisor for Strategic Communications, it was Rhodes who served as the puppet master, pulling the strings of the entire Obama foreign and international security apparatus. The neophyte aide peeled back the veil of secrecy surrounding his operations in a revealing *New York Times Magazine* profile published in early 2016. The article exposed how Rhodes had boasted of manipulating Congress and the news media into supporting the Iran nuclear deal, whose skeptics included both Republicans and Democrats alike.

Rhodes's Iran nuclear deal operation was central to Obama's gigantic disinformation program, especially against Congress, which gave up its constitutional prerogative to approve treaties in exchange for a promise from the White House to submit the final accord to a much easier up-or-down Senate vote. By contrast, formal treaty ratification would have required the nearly impossible to obtain two-thirds majority of the divided one hundred senators. Along with CIA detailee to the White House Ned Price, who served as Rhodes's sidekick and spokesman at the National Security Council, Rhodes ran a propaganda and deception campaign that rivaled the propaganda efforts of Nazi Joseph Goebbels. As writer David Samuels explained in his *Times Magazine* piece:

Price turns to his computer and begins tapping away at the
administration's well-cultivated network of officials, talking
heads, columnists and newspaper reporters, web jockeys and
outside advocates who can tweet at critics and tweak their
stories backed up by quotations from "senior White House
officials" and "spokespeople." I watch the message bounce
from Rhodes's brain to Price's keyboard to the three big
briefing podiums—the White House, the State Department
and the Pentagon—and across the Twitterverse, where it
springs to life in dozens of insta-stories, which over the next
five hours don formal dress for mainstream outlets. It's a tu-
torial in the making of a digital news microclimate—a storm
that is easy to mistake these days for a fact of nature, but
whose author is sitting next to me right now.

To manipulate the press into reporting stories Obama
wanted, Rhodes and his team worked to spin reporters
through tightly controlled and coordinated official press briefings held daily or several times a week at the State Department, Pentagon, and White House. Rhodes then amplified the
propaganda themes through "force multipliers"—propaganda
agents within the Washington media milieu who could be
counted on to spout administration talking points, especially
against critics of the administration. "We have our compadres,
I will reach out to a couple people, and you know, I wouldn't
want to name them," Price told Samuels.

The White House–backed reporters could be counted on
to tweet and otherwise propagate digital propaganda directly
in line with administration themes. With the decline of news-

papers and traditional news outlets over the past decade—the wire services, the major newspapers, and the major broadcast outlets—Rhodes and his information warfare team successfully fooled millions of Americans about the Iran deal. Samuels wrote that it likely will be the model for future presidents' efforts.

In the case of the Iran deal, Rhodes presented the lie that the deal directly resulted from the emergence in 2013 of alleged Iranian "moderates" within the regime, led by Hassan Rouhani, and who Rhodes asserted had provided a strategic opening for U.S. engagement with the longtime enemy. According to Samuels, this meme was largely manufactured for the purpose of selling the deal. Rhodes described Obama's Iranian efforts as beginning in 2012 and as the apogee of an arc of his entire second term. As Rhodes put it:

> We don't have to kind of be in cycles of conflict if we can find other ways to resolve these issues. We can do things that challenge the conventional thinking that, you know, "AIPAC [American Israel Public Affairs Committee] doesn't like this," or "the Israeli government doesn't like this," or "the gulf countries don't like it." It's the possibility of improved relations with adversaries. It's nonproliferation. So all these threads that the president's been spinning—and I mean that not in the press sense—for almost a decade, they kind of all converged around Iran.

The president's claim that 2013 marked the key starting point for the Iran deal was false, since the negotiations had begun in mid-2012 and informal talks stretched as far back as 2011—*months before Rouhani came to power*. The notion that Rouhani was a moderate was also disinformation, since all Iranian candidates for elective office are picked by the supreme leader—dictator Khamenei. The idea of a leadership split was a deception ploy used by Obama and Rhodes to make it appear to Americans that a nuclear deal was a real chance to influence the Islamist state.

To help sell the deal, Rhodes used a false straw-man argument that there were only two choices related to the nuclear deal—reject the agreement and bring about war, or support it and bring about peace. Key media influencers were Jeffrey Goldberg, the staff writer at the *Atlantic* who wrote the flattering article on the Obama foreign policy doctrine, and Laura Rozen, a liberal pro-Iran advocate who wrote for the online *Al-Monitor* and who according to the *Times Magazine* article was counted on by the White House to reliably promote their propaganda.

Rhodes boasted of creating the echo chamber for the press and pro-Iran activist supporters. It included groups like the liberal Ploughshares Fund, an arms control advocacy group that promoted the utopian antinuclear program Global Zero, which found favor with Obama but was resoundingly rejected by senior defense and military leaders worried about the nuclear modernization under way in China, Russia, and, soon, Iran. Also co-opted to propagandize the Iran deal was a group called the Iran Project, which billed itself as "independent" and "nonpartisan" yet worked covertly with the Rhodes information warfare machine to push the Iran nuclear agreement on an unsuspecting public and Congress. Rhodes seemed unconcerned that Iran could cheat on the agreement without any real penalty, or by the fact that it ultimately will be permitted to develop all the infrastructure for arming itself with nuclear weapons. For Rhodes, as for Obama, the urgent mission was to strive for the utopian notion of a reoriented, pro-Iran foreign policy in the Middle East.

Leon Panetta, who held significant posts within the Obama administration as CIA director and secretary of defense, would turn against Obama by disclosing his disagreement with the fiction that the fortunes of moderate Iranians would be boosted by concluding the Iran nuclear deal. Hard-liners remained firmly in power and Panetta viewed Obama's shift in sucking up to Iran as reflecting the president's liberal left antiwar policies of seeking to end the wars in Iraq and Afghanistan regardless of the security situation on the ground. Obama also falsely believed that continuing to impose U.S. and international sanctions on Iran would lead to war. In Panetta's telling, the pacifist, liberal Obama could not be convinced otherwise. The president thought that "if you ratchet up sanctions, it could cause a war. If you start opposing their interest in Syria, well, that could start a war, too," Panetta said.

In other words, Obama's policy was based on rank appeasement.

A day after the *New York Times Magazine* article appeared, Rhodes moderated an interagency government videoconference with a large group of Obama administration officials. The thirty-eight-year-old propaganda wizard opened the meeting by joking about the article. "You're my echo chamber," he quipped, according to a person in the meeting. "It was disgusting," the official told me. "He was making fun of how he deceived the American people."

The Iran deal came on the heels of an unsuccessful U.S. information warfare operation against Iran's nuclear program. It began in 2010, when Obama authorized a clandestine cyberattack on Iran's program of enriching uranium through thousands of centrifuges—precision machines linked together in groups called cascades that spin a uranium gas into highly enriched uranium that can be used in nuclear weapons. The clandestine program, code-named Olympic Games, secretly planted sophisticated malicious software, later called Stuxnet, into the centrifuge control system. The computer virus caused around one thousand of the five thousand centrifuges located at the nuclear complex in Natanz to spin out of control and self-destruct. As fallout from the secret operation, the Stuxnet computer worm had managed to escape the Natanz industrial control system network and began appearing on the Internet by the summer of 2010. It was quickly identified by security researchers as a nation-state-developed malware with capabilities beyond those of the average or even advanced nonstate hacker. The disclosure of Stuxnet caused the president to consider shutting down the secret operation, part of a program developed by the CIA and National Security Agency during the administration of President George W. Bush around 2006. "Should we shut this thing down?" Obama asked, according to the first account of the secret program disclosed by *New York Times* reporter David Sanger. Obama would stay the course and keep the operation going for a few more years with some new variants of the cyber weapon. But the program was not producing the urgently needed result: complete destruction of Iran's nuclear infrastructure.

The Stuxnet program employed a device called a beacon, which was planted inside Iran's Siemens industrial controller and sent back technical details of the system to cyber spies at NSA headquarters in Fort Meade, Maryland. Through Stuxnet, a detailed map of the entire Natanz centrifuge network was obtained. Israel's military cyberwarfare group, called Unit 8200, also played a key role in the operation. But the cyber covert action program was never understood by its operators as a total solution to the Iran nuclear problem. A very high-ranking U.S. intelligence official disclosed to me that Olympic Games was assessed by both intelligence officials and policy makers as unable to eliminate the threat posed by the growing Iran nuclear program.

However, for a while the clandestine program helped convince the Israelis that the United States was supporting its Middle East ally in working to block Iran from developing nuclear weapons. That goal was critically important because Israel correctly views Iran and its nuclear ambitions as posing an existential threat to the Jewish state that must be countered, preferably through nonmilitary means, but ultimately through the use of force if needed.

In the end, Obama abandoned the cyber covert action

program in favor of his naïve approach of seeking engagement diplomacy with Iran. The reality is that the president
was guilty of appeasing one of the world's most dangerous
regimes, which will become more dangerous through the use
of a nuclear agreement that by any objective measure provided the regime with both cash and arms in the near term,
and the technology, equipment, and international backing for
producing nuclear weapons in the longer one.

Behind the scenes, Obama had authorized his administration to secretly begin supplying large payments of cash to
the Iranian regime—cash that almost certainly will be used to
fuel Iran's arms buildup and covert support for international
terrorism.

The most dangerous payment involved the transfer of
$1.7 billion in foreign cash paid to settle claims made by Iran
involving weapons sales to the predecessor regime. In January 2016, an unmarked chartered aircraft flew into Tehran
carrying the first installment, $400 million in cash stacked on
wooden pallets in euros, Swiss francs, and other currencies.

The same day the cash arrived, January 16, Iran released
four Americans who had been unjustly held prisoner by the
regime. It was clearly a ransom payment for their freedom.

Months later Obama would lie to the American people
about the cash ransom, claiming it was no such thing. The
cash was to pay back Iran for pre-1979 arms purchases that
were not fulfilled. "We do not pay ransom for hostages,"
Obama said. Days later he would be contradicted by his State
Department spokesman, John Kirby, who, under questioning
from reporters, admitted the cash transfer was delayed until

the prisoners were released, in other words, that the money was paid as part of a prisoner ransom. Iran's state-run media had already described the cash as ransom, further boosting the Iranian information warfare narrative that the mullahs had outmaneuvered the Obama administration on the nuclear deal.

The failure to stop Iran's nuclear program through cyber operations and other information warfare is an American foreign policy disaster. It was the result of a combination of two factors. First, the Iran deal grew out of Obama's misguided foreign policy realism, which he asserted was based on views of former White House national security adviser Brent Scowcroft, under President George H. W. Bush. As noted earlier, Scowcroft's brand of realpolitik produced the embarrassing secret visit to Beijing in support of China's rulers—days after the blood of unarmed protesters, crushed under the tracks of People's Liberation Army tanks in Tiananmen Square, had been washed clean. The second factor was Obama's open sympathy for Muslim states, a kinship based on his experience growing up in Jakarta, Indonesia, from 1967 to 1971. Obama asserted in 2007 that he believed America's biggest failure since the end of World War II was a lack of sensitivity to other nations, and that the United States needed to project respect rather than arrogance—coincidentally, a favored word of Iran's rulers to describe their hatred for America.

Just what American arrogance Obama referred to was never mentioned in the 2007 interview. But it highlighted Obama's bias against the United States, a bias steeped in the false liberal left nostrum that America remains a racist and imperialist power to be brought to heel in world affairs. It was in that same *New York Times* interview in 2007 that Obama made his often-quoted statement that the Muslim daily call to prayer is "one of the prettiest sounds on Earth at sunset."

Appeasement of Iran also had its roots in Obama's 2009 Cairo university speech, when he made the false statement to the world that radical Islamic terror was not to blame for tensions between Islam and the West, but rather colonialism was. Obama dismissed the threat of Islamic terrorism as the work of a "small but potent minority of Muslims." Obama suggested, as he did repeatedly during his presidency, that it is Americans who are racist and bigoted. Obama promised that as president he would "fight against negative stereotypes of Islam wherever they appear."

During his presidency, few news reporters with regular access to Obama asked what he meant in the Cairo remarks, or how he would go about addressing the alleged anti-Islam bias Obama claimed was ingrained within Americans. The first time the public would learn more about these inner views was the interview the president gave to Jeffrey Goldberg of the *Atlantic*. Obama for the first time explained that in his worldview, the United States needs to be hardheaded and bighearted. He asserted that the U.S. military had been overused in seeking to solve world problems and that America was overextended around the world and needed to cut back. In terms of the Cairo speech, Obama asserted that Muslims needed to stop blaming Israel for all the Middle East's troubles and address problems of regional governance—code for corrupt rulers—along with Islam, which he asserted must adapt to modernity. "My thought was, I would communicate that the U.S. is not standing in the way of this progress, that we would help, in whatever way possible, to advance the goals of a practical, successful Arab agenda that provided a better life for ordinary people," Obama said.

One of the most alarming disclosures occurred late in his presidency when Obama revealed he did not believe America's enemies were really enemies, nor America's friends its friends, such as Israel. During his tenure in the White House, he downgraded close U.S.–Saudi Arabia ties in favor of closer ties to Iran, an Islamist state with extremist views that sees the United States as its main enemy.

Formally, we won't know until 2022 whether the Iran deal's hoped-for goal of a less dangerous Iran comes true. That is when most restrictions on Iran's nuclear development will end. On August 5, 2015, Obama gave a speech at American University in Washington, D.C., that contained numerous falsehoods about the Iran nuclear deal. First, he stated the detailed arrangement would permanently prohibit Iran from obtaining a nuclear weapon. In the text of the 159-page deal it states that the Tehran government "reaffirms that under no circumstances will Iran ever seek, develop or acquire any nuclear weapons." Thus with only *a promise* not to develop nuclear weapons "ever," Iran was able to win a string of concessions, including more than $100 billion in cash, access to arms and other markets, and regional prestige that is boosting one of the worst regimes in modern history.

The Israel-based Institute for National Security Studies challenged the White House meme that the deal was an unprecedented victory for those seeking to permanently prevent Tehran from getting nuclear weapons. "Our sense is that a string of P5+1 [the acronym for the six nations that signed the agreement] concessions over the past year on the critical issues of the sunset clause, verification, the possible military dimensions issue, and Iran's continued work on its nuclear infrastructure, coupled with Iran's proven non-compliance with its [Nuclear Non-Proliferation Treaty] obligations, make it uncertain that the deal will keep a nuclear weapon out of Iran's hands," INSS analysts Ephraim Asculai, Emily B. Landau, and Shimon Stein stated. "When one adds to the mix the $100 billion (or more) Iran will receive at the outset, Iran's enhanced regional position, and Iranian attitudes that reject the notion of a changed relationship with the U.S., the basis for concern only grows."

A close examination of the fine print of the Joint Comprehensive Plan of Action reveals Iran will be free to develop nuclear weapons within a decade—even without the anticipated violation of the accord. The nuclear agreement contains numerous loopholes and vague provisions, such as references to Iran's "voluntary" compliance with terms of the accord, rather than mandatory adherence. The overly bureaucratic process for addressing violations and noncompliance outlined in the agreement also means Iran would not be penalized for cheating. Under the agreement, three Iranian entities were freed from international sanctions. They include three elements of the Islamic shock troops that play a dominant role in keeping the theocratic regime in power and for exporting terrorism and Islamist ideology: the Islamic Revolutionary Guard Corps (IRGC) air force, the IRGC's Al Ghadir Missile Command, and the Quds Force, the covert action force that has been linked to terror attacks and terrorist support throughout the world. The Quds Force is regarded as Iran's main foreign policy tool for special operations and terrorist support to Islamic militants, including Hezbollah and the Taliban.

Iran's 20,000 centrifuges were to be reduced to 5,000 centrifuges, and nuclear research and development were permitted to continue at Natanz under the agreement. Most of Iran's stockpile of low-enriched uranium was to be shipped out of the country, but the means of producing enriched uranium would be only temporarily curtailed. After ten years, under the provisions of the Joint Comprehensive Plan of Action, limits on uranium enrichment *will be lifted, allowing Iran to design and develop more advanced centrifuges.* The International Atomic Energy Agency, which was unable to enforce Iranian compliance with international controls on nuclear technology before the nuclear agreement, was given the main role of monitoring previously known and other declared facilities with a team of up to 150 inspectors. Uranium mines will be watched and dismantled centrifuges will be stockpiled.

After eight years of the agreement, the United States and the European Union agreed to lift conventional arms sanctions on Iran. This will permit Tehran to both export and import advanced conventional arms and ballistic missiles, opening the way for destabilizing arms transfers from Iran's three main weapons backers—Russia, China, and North Korea. In Annex 1 of the accord, Iran will be allowed in fifteen years to again reprocess spent nuclear fuel, and to build plutonium and uranium from spent fuel, key sources of fuel for nuclear weapons. After fifteen years, a ban on producing or acquiring plutonium or uranium metals ends completely, and research on plutonium and uranium metallurgy, casting, and forming will be allowed. *These critical functions are key elements for developing nuclear weapons.* By 2024, Iran's limit on possessing 5,060 centrifuges in thirty cascade units at Natanz also ends, and the ban on uranium enrichment of no more than 3.67 percent ends after fifteen years. Enrichment of 20 percent is needed for nuclear bombs. Iran's stockpile of low-enriched uranium will be limited to 300 kilograms. The remaining stockpile likely will be used in covert efforts by Iran to produce highly enriched uranium for bombs and missile warheads, if IAEA monitoring is circumvented, something Iran showed itself easily able to do in the past. Considering that Iran violated its original obligations under the Nuclear Non-Proliferation Treaty, which violation gave it the means to gain the technology for a nuclear program in the first place, Iranian cheating on the nuclear agreement is almost a certainty.

Since the Iran nuclear deal was signed, approved by Congress, and bolstered by a United Nations Security Council resolution, Iran has continued to violate both the spirit and the letter of the agreement. Germany's domestic security service, the Bundesamt für Verfassungsschutz (BfV), revealed in its 2015 annual report that Iranian agents aggressively sought to acquire nuclear-weapons-related technology and goods in the federal republic. Despite the Iran agreement, "the illegal proliferation-sensitive procurement activities in Germany registered by the Federal Office for the Protection of the Constitution persisted in 2015 at what is, even by international standards, a quantitatively high level," the report said, noting pursuit of "items which can be used in the field of nuclear technology."

The Iranians also sought missile technology—a capability that was never addressed in the Iran nuclear agreement because it remained a steadfast Iranian demand throughout the negotiations. The missile program provides the clearest indication that Iran is pushing ahead with nuclear weapons development because its long-range missiles are a strategic weapons capability principally used as a nuclear delivery system. In April 2016, Iran conducted the first launch of a space-launch vehicle that U.S. intelligence agencies concluded was in reality cover for future development of a long-range nuclear missile. The Simorgh launch was closely monitored by intelligence agencies, and was carried out in violation of the UN Security Council resolution that required Iran to forgo nuclear missile tests for eight years.

Similarly, Iranian activities in support of terrorism showed no signs of lessening after the Iran nuclear agreement. Iran continued to support Hezbollah, the Iranian proxy terrorist group centered in Lebanon, and to back the Palestinian terror group Hamas. The Washington Institute for Near East Policy assessed that after the signing of the nuclear accord, Iranian-backed terrorism *actually increased*. "It is clear that

Iran's support for terrorism has only increased since the deal was reached, and officials cannot feign surprise on the matter," wrote Washington Institute analyst Matthew Levitt on the one-year anniversary of the nuclear accord in 2016. "Given Iran's ongoing support for terrorism and regional instability and the administration's repeated insistence that it would hold Tehran's feet to the fire on these very issues, the [Joint Comprehensive Plan of Action's] first anniversary presents Washington with a perfect opportunity to reassess the regime's menacing behavior and take steps to hold it accountable."

Not surprisingly, the Obama administration and participants in Ben Rhodes's information warfare echo chamber were silent on all these issues.

At the same time the White House was vigorously pursuing the Iran nuclear deal in 2012, the Pentagon sounded the alarm on the growing threat posed by Iran's increasingly capable cyberattacks against financial institutions, government information networks, and critical infrastructure computers used to control the electrical grid and other vital systems. The Iranian cyber threat is real and growing. In the fall of 2012, the NSA detected a major cyberattack against a U.S. financial institution that represented much more than a relatively minor attempt to temporarily disrupt the institution's operations. "Iran's cyber aggression should be viewed as a component, alongside efforts like support for terrorism, [to] the larger covert war Tehran is waging against the west," the classified Joint Staff report, dated September 14, concluded. The J-2, the intelligence directorate of the Joint Staff, stated that the specific bank cyberattack had been unsuccessful. But the operation signaled the beginning of a major covert information warfare campaign by the Iranian government against the United States. The report was an indication that the U.S. military was more honest in dealing with the threat posed by Iran and was less impacted by the propaganda and disinformation campaign of Obama and Rhodes, which had as an overriding goal the obscuring of all Iranian threats and avoidance of any public discussion of them, in order to facilitate completion of the nuclear deal with Tehran. Officials disclosed the bank cyberattack to me to demonstrate that the military would not be silenced despite Obama's attempt to obscure the mounting Iranian information warfare threat.

As with Russia and China, Iran too learned beginning in the early 2000s that cyber and information warfare were asymmetric weapons for attacking their main enemy, the United States. By the mid-2010s, Iran had emerged as an increasing strategic threat to the United States because of the grave risks it posed to vital U.S. information networks and industrial control systems that operate critical infrastructures, such as the electric grid, financial networks, communications systems, transportation, and other vital functions. James Clapper, the director of national intelligence, testified in Congress in February 2016 that Iran was using covert information warfare. "Iran used cyber espionage, propaganda, and attacks in 2015 to support its security priorities, influence events, and counter threats—including against U.S. allies in the region," Clapper said. An earlier threat assessment in 2012 concluded that "Iran's intelligence operations against the United States, including cyber capabilities, have dramatically increased in recent years in depth and complexity." American intelligence agencies categorized Iran as falling within the second-tier category of dangerous cyber threats. Intelligence agencies identified two broad categories of cyber threat states: advanced nations like China and Russia, and the less technically capable states like Iran and North Korea, described as still "more aggressive and more unpredictable." Cybersecurity experts agree that Iranian cyberwarfare actors are technically proficient and well funded and have placed a high priority on developing and implementing both cyber offense and defense activities.

Since at least 2009, American intelligence has closely tracked Iran's cyber capabilities. A classified State Department cable made public by the antisecrecy group WikiLeaks revealed Iran's aggressive efforts to steal U.S. technology and learn about U.S. activities through cyberattacks. "Several Iranian institutions and organizations conduct OSINT [open-source intelligence] against USG [U.S. government] programs," states a March 31, 2009, cable labeled "secret." "Most of the Iranian universities involved in this activity maintain longstanding ties to the IRGC," the Islamic Revolutionary Guard Corps, the regime's pivotal security and intelligence force. The programs run by the Iranians likely were used in further cyberattacks. The cable noted that "persistent attempts to collect U.S. information could jeopardize the security of U.S. operations and personnel"—no doubt a bureaucratic understatement of the danger. The cable identified Internet Protocol addresses associated with the Farhang Azma Communication Company, one of the Iranian entities used for directly spying on a number of U.S. Navy unit websites. The company "systematically downloaded over 100 U.S. Navy unit webpages using software 'Web Downloader/8.1.'" Additionally, students and researchers at a number of prominent Iranian universities and companies conducted open-source intelligence collection operations against U.S. information for several years. The targets included academic research, databases, forums, official and draft documents, online publications, reference material, Web logs, and websites.

The March 2009 cable also disclosed a strong and continued interest in and knowledge of U.S. capabilities and operations from both Iranian institutions and government hackers. The spying included the practice known as social engineering—making phone calls and sending emails seeking information from defense contractors that would provide insights into sensitive U.S. military and defense programs. The targeted information included Pentagon equipment, weapons systems, unmanned vehicle technologies, communications, and intelligence systems. "This information could then be used to develop similar programs for the [government of Iran], shared with third-party entities (e.g., Islamic extremist groups), or exploited through additional Iranian computer network operations activities," the cable said, adding that the operations by the Iranians had been ongoing since at least January 2007.

The Iranians also searched online for information on U.S. facilities in Iraq and Afghanistan—which could be passed to the Taliban for use in attacks—along with information on vehicles, vessels, and individual leaders. The hackers used the Web Downloader open-source software program to gather vast amounts of data from multiple sources. Other Iranian institutions linked to the cyber spying were identified as the Amirkabir University of Technology (AUT) and Malek-Ashtar University of Technology (MUT) in Tehran, which focused on stealing data on unmanned aerial vehicles (UAVs) and autonomous underwater vehicles.

"Information and countermeasures derived from the collection and analysis of this type of information have been incorporated into AUT and MUT research programs and capabilities," the cable said, noting the AUT has had close ties to the IRGC since 1998. Researchers at MUT were linked to the Iranian Defense Ministry and projects related to UAVs and small aircraft.

Iranian data miners at Isfahan University of Technology (IUT) were also spotted gathering sensitive technology and information from U.S. computer networks. "Although the majority of the information sought through Iranian OSINT collection efforts pertains to military capabilities and technological development, other USG departments and agencies could also become (or continue to be) targets of foreign actors' extensive online research," the cable said. "Users must remain alert to and minimize the potential threats associated with the misuse of personal and professional information posted to online resources," the cable said.

From relatively passive cyber spying, Iran would escalate its cyberattacks to large-scale operations on Internet access points to disrupt the functioning of websites, a tactic known as distributed denial-of-service attacks, or DDoS. The attacks work by using hijacked servers that are linked together electronically and operated as remote robot cyberattackers programmed to launch multiple attempts to gain access to public Internet portals of banks or financial institutions. The massive flood of automated log-in requests is designed to overwhelm the computer operating systems and force the servers to shut down, thus denying their use for online banking and other remote financial activities.

The NSA took a leading role in warning about the danger posed by Iran's growing use of cyberattacks and cyber espionage. A top-secret memorandum dated April, 12, 2013, that was disclosed by renegade NSA contractor Edward Snowden revealed a set of talking points used by NSA director general Keith Alexander on Iranian cyber capabilities. "NSA has seen Iran further extending its influence across the Middle East over the last year," the memo says. "Iran continues to conduct distributed denial-of-service (DDOS) attacks against numerous U.S. financial institutions, and is currently in the third phase of a series of such attacks that began in August 2012."

NSA signals intelligence uncovered evidence showing that the attacks were carried out in retaliation for Western cyber activities against Iran's nuclear facilities, and that senior officials of the Iranian government were aware of the attacks—an indication NSA had succeeded in getting inside Iranian communications and was able to read or listen to the communications of senior officials. "NSA expects Iran will continue this series of attacks, which it views as successful, while striving for increased effectiveness by adapting its tactics and techniques to circumvent victim [computer network] mitigation attempts," the memo said.

The memo also provided the first official confirmation that the August 2012 cyberattack against the Saudi Arabian national oil company, Saudi Aramco, was linked to Iran's information warfare program. "Iran's destructive cyber attack against Saudi Aramco in August 2012, during which data was destroyed on tens of thousands of computers, was the first such attack NSA has observed from this adversary, Iran, having been a victim of a similar cyber attack against its own oil industry in April 2012. [Iran] has demonstrated a clear ability to learn from the capabilities and actions of others," the agency stated.

Iran's Shia Muslim rulers are rivals of Saudi Arabia's Sunni rulers. NSA also concluded from its intelligence analyst that Iran did not appear to be planning similar cyberattacks against U.S. oil companies' networks. But the agency warned that "we cannot rule out the possibility of such an attack, especially in the face of increased international pressure on the regime."

At the time of the memo, the United States intelligence community had completed a major assessment, called a National Intelligence Estimate, on global cyber threats. The estimate was based on highly classified intelligence outlining foreign cyberattack and cyber espionage threats. Officials familiar with the top-secret NIE, a consensus of all spy agencies, described it as highlighting the growing danger of cyberattacks and espionage from the main adversary states, including China, Russia, North Korea, and Iran.

Iranian bank cyberattacks and the destructive cyber strike against the Saudis were followed by a major cyberattack in the United States, perhaps Iran's boldest and most politically motivated. The attack was carried out against the Sands Corporation in Las Vegas in February 2014. However, in a bid to avoid upsetting its secret diplomatic effort to conclude the nuclear deal with Tehran, the Obama administration kept the attack secret. The Iranian connection to the cyberattack was not made public until nineteen months later, on September 10, 2015, during testimony before Congress by Clapper, the DNI. Clapper had never mentioned the Iranian Sands attack in his public testimony before the House Permanent Select Committee on Intelligence and none of the House members present asked a single question about it. But tucked away in his formal statement submitted in advance of the testimony was a short paragraph that was the first official mention that in addition to the 2012–13 financial institution cyberattacks, Iran had been linked to "the February 2014 cyber attack on the Las Vegas Sands casino company." No details were provided.

"Iran very likely views its cyber program as one of many tools for carrying out asymmetric but proportional retaliation against political foes, as well as a sophisticated means of collecting intelligence," Clapper stated.

Details of the Sands incident had been first revealed in a

detailed investigative report by the news agency Bloomberg Business more than a year earlier but never officially confirmed by the U.S. government. The Iranian hack was politically suppressed by the Obama administration, unlike the other high-profile cyber strike on an American company, Sony Pictures Entertainment (see Chapter 2), which attack was quickly attributed to North Korea as a state sponsor. The playing down of the Sands Corporation attack was no doubt the work of Rhodes's White House information warfare program, which covertly manipulated American news reports on the Iran threat.

The Sands attack was not trivial. It cost the company some $40 million in destroyed computers and stole data, including sensitive employee data and Social Security numbers.

The attack began in the early morning hours of February 10, 2014, when hundreds of Sands computers began crashing, leaving blank screens and rendering systems inoperable. Email could not be sent or received and most of the landline telephones stopped working. The $14 billion casino company was thrown into chaos. "PCs and servers were shutting down in a cascading IT catastrophe, with many of their hard drives wiped clean. The company's technical staff had never seen anything like it," Bloomberg revealed. The highly networked and technology-reliant casino suffered information systems failures throughout its complex, including computers that handled loyalty rewards, programs used to check the performance and payouts of slot machines and table gambling games, and the company's multimillion-dollar information storage systems. In a bid to prevent a ripple effect, employees were sent racing throughout the huge casino corporation's offices unplugging as many network connections as possible in a bid to minimize damage.

For the Iranian hackers, the goal of the information warfare operation was not an attempt to hack funds or otherwise seek financial gain, as was suspected by security officials initially. This was a physically damaging and politically motivated cyberattack. The main target: Sands owner and billionaire Sheldon Adelson. The conservative Adelson was one of the staunchest American defenders of Israel, the key democratically governed American ally in the Middle East. Born in 1933, he was listed by *Forbes* as being worth some $28 billion. His title is chairman and chief executive officer of the Las Vegas Sands Corporation, which owns the Marina Bay Sands in Singapore and is the parent company of Venetian Macao Limited, which operates the Venetian Resort Hotel Casino and the Sands Expo and Convention Center. Adelson also owns the Israeli daily newspaper *Israel Hayom* and the *Las Vegas Review-Journal*. He was also a close associate of Israel's prime minister at the time of the cyberattack, Benjamin Netanyahu.

It immediately became apparent to security technicians that the cyberattack was retaliation for a controversial speech Adelson gave in October 2013 at Yeshiva University in Manhattan. He told the gathering that his solution to the nuclear negotiations with Iran—then ongoing and incomplete—would be for the U.S. military to fire a nuclear missile into a desert near Iran, and then tell the Iranians that would be their fate if they ever threatened Israel. "And then you say, 'See?

The next one is in the middle of Tehran,'" Adelson said, adding that the message to Iran needs to be "we mean business. You want to be wiped out, go ahead and take a tough position and continue with your nuclear development."

In response, two weeks after the speech Iranian supreme leader Ali Khamenei gave a speech that called on the United States to stop all such comments from being made, as if the U.S. government had the power to impose such speech constraints. A month after the Khamenei remarks, Iranian hackers launched the operation to attack the Sands. They began by conducting reconnaissance on ways to penetrate Sands information systems in an operation the company would later code-name "Yellowstone 1."

The first breach occurred around January 8, 2014, not in Las Vegas but at the Sands Bethlehem casino in Pennsylvania, with a cyberattack against the Pennsylvania casino's virtual private network. The hackers broke in using password-cracking software and repeated log-in attempts carried out with automated trial-and-error combinations of user identification credentials and passwords. By the end of that month, the Iranians had succeeded in what cyber sleuths call a brute-force log-in-cracking attack. The intrusion attempts paid off. On February 1, 2014, the hackers broke through to a Web development server. Once inside the electronic system, the Iranians used another password-hacking program, called Mimikatz, to obtain additional passwords and log-in credentials that were in turn used by the Iranians to eventually gain administrator-level control on February 9. One day later, the Iranians launched their large-scale cyber-

attack in Las Vegas. Thousands of servers, desktop computers, and laptops were damaged or rendered useless. Worse,
sensitive company data was exfiltrated, including private
documents and credit checks on high-profile gamblers. In
the clearest link to Iran, the hackers left images on the pirated
network showing Sands casinos in flames, as messages were
posted on some company websites that read, "Encouraging
the use of Weapons of Mass Destruction, UNDER ANY
CONDITION, is a Crime." The message was signed the
"Anti WMD Team."

From cyber-intelligence gathering, to denial-of-service
attacks, to targeting the Sands, Iran's information warfare
forces have been systematically escalating operations against
the United States.

Despite clear evidence of an increasing threat, the Obama
administration took no action and said nothing—all to
protect the feckless policy of Obama to avoid upsetting his
effort to be friends with the mullahs. During a hearing on
cyber threats in September 2015, Representative Joe Wilson,
a South Carolina Republican, pressed Deputy Secretary of
Defense Robert Work on whether the Obama administration had imposed sanctions on Iran for the Sands attack.
"I'm going to have to take that for the record," Work said
in sidestepping the question. Admiral Michael Rogers, the
commander of the U.S. Cyber Command and director of
the NSA, who testified at the same hearing with Work, was
only marginally more candid. Rogers indicated "no specific
sanctions" were tied to Iranian cyberattacks. But the Cyber
Command chief suggested he favored U.S. action against Iran

for the attack. "Clearly a broader discussion about what's acceptable, what's not acceptable" is needed, he said, noting that Iranian cyberattacks against financial websites had subsided somewhat after the U.S. government began identifying publicly the activities of nefarious cyber actors. Rogers also praised greater cooperation between government and financial institutions "to see what we could do to work the resiliency piece here to preclude the Iranians' ability to actually penetrate, which, knock on wood, we were successful with."

As the U.S. government refused to denounce Iranian information warfare, an internal State Department security report I obtained revealed that Iranian cyberattacks were posing a growing danger to American security. The report includes the chart below showing a detailed timeline of several Iranian cyberattacks. The activities included the targeting of government personnel involved in arms nonproliferation from 2011, the financial cyberattacks of 2012, further attacks on large banks in 2012, the hack of the Marine Corps intranet, and what the report described as the "wiper malware" attack on the Sands Corporation.

The report was produced by an analytic group in the State Department for the Overseas Security Advisory Council and went on to identify key trends in Iranian cyber operations, the main element being retaliation, first for the Stuxnet virus, which damaged centrifuges at Natanz, and then in the Sands attack, carried out to punish Adelson for his critical remarks. "In similar fashion, the multi-stage 2012 attacks against U.S. banks and financial institutions were assessed to be a response to economic sanctions," the report said. "Iran em-

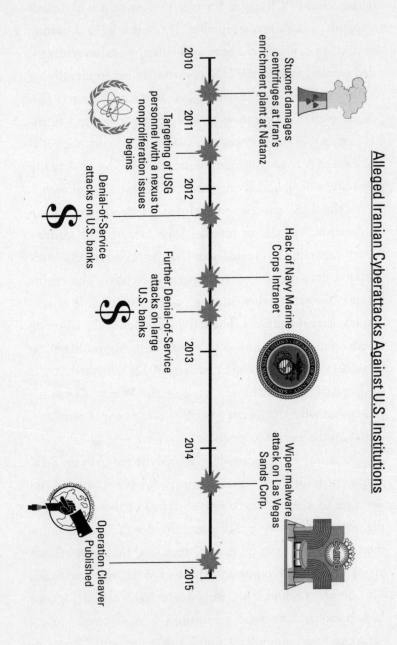

Alleged Iranian Cyberattacks Against U.S. Institutions

2010 — Stuxnet damages centrifuges at Iran's enrichment plant at Natanz

2011 — Targeting of USG personnel with a nexus to nonproliferation issues begins

2012 — Denial-of-Service attacks on U.S. banks

Hack of Navy Marine Corps Intranet

Further Denial-of-Service attacks on large U.S. banks

2013

2014 — Wiper malware attack on Las Vegas Sands Corp.

2015 — Operation Cleaver Published

ploys the concept of 'soft war,' using the Internet and other technical platforms to combat perceived enemies. Other case studies also draw parallels between tracked cyber operations and the Iranian government's political objectives." The report warned that "Iran is rapidly improving its cyber warfare capabilities" as a "direct result of Tehran's investment in its cyber offensive [capabilities] noting that a growing number of Tehran-based hackers are being blamed for high-profile incidents.

"It has been assessed that these hackers have progressed from making low-level website defacements with the use of publicly available malware, to using customized and targeted implants intended for specific victims," the report said. "As these techniques continue to increase in sophistication and focus, researchers also deduce that Iran may be preparing for future operations by growing their available technical infrastructure."

In an ominous warning, the report revealed plans by Iranian information warriors to target critical U.S. infrastructures in the future. Several case studies noted Iran's desire to attack critical American infrastructures—those used for everything from electricity to financial transactions, communications, and transportation—in some capacity. "Assessments continue to place critical infrastructure, supervisory control and data acquisition (SCADA) and transportation systems at the top of the list for potential targets of Iranian cyber operations," the report said, noting that the Tehran government and the IRGC are "backing numerous groups and front entities to attack the world's critical infrastructure."

It was a stark warning of what was to come.

In the months after the Sands cyberattack, the Iranian information warfare threat mounted. Iran was linked to cyber threats against the American electrical grid, and then a group of Iranian hackers were indicted by a U.S. federal grand jury that linked them to a cyberattack against the water control system for a dam in upstate New York.

In California, Iranian-origin hackers struck a contractor for Calpine, a company that bills itself as the largest electrical power provider in the state and uses natural gas and geothermal resources. The hacking took place over several years beginning around August 2013 and the data theft included the downloading of design drawings on dozens of power plants, including at least one that was described as "mission critical."

The activities were a classic example of what the U.S. military calls cyber reconnaissance—covertly breaking into computer networks to map their connections and links so that in a future conflict or crisis the information could be used to sabotage the American power grid, which provides vital electrical power to millions of homes and businesses.

The Calpine attack was followed by an even more serious Iranian cyberattack that attempted to gain control of the Bowman Dam, near Rye, New York, a small suburban town located about thirty-five miles north of New York City. The dam hacking was outlined in the federal indictment of seven Iranian hackers charged on March 24, 2016, with both the Bowman intrusions and the earlier denial-of-service attacks on American financial institutions. It was the first time Iranian hackers had been targeted in a legal proceeding and followed years of silence and inaction by the Obama administration, which, as we have seen, feared that any action it took against Iran would scuttle the nuclear talks and resulting deal.

The indictment was largely symbolic, given that the likelihood of ever prosecuting the seven hackers is remote. While it provided the first official and public identification of Iranians involved in hacking U.S. networks, it was a White House attempt to give the appearance that it was not completely ignoring the threat posed by Iranian cyberattacks. American intelligence and defense officials had been demanding the White House do something to counter the escalating cyber threat. Two Iranian hacker groups were identified. One is called the ITSec Team and the second is the Mersad Company. The two entities are ostensibly private computer security companies based in Iran that "performed work on behalf of the Iranian government," including the IRGC, which the indictment recognized as one of several Iranian intelligence units.

The botnet strikes on U.S. financial institutions that took place between December 2011 and around May 2013 were orchestrated by the ITSec Team. They involved weekly attacks, usually on Tuesdays and Thursdays, that flooded banks with 140 gigabytes of information per second—up to three times the entire operating system capacity of the banks' computers. Some forty-six major financial institutions were hit, causing hundreds of thousands of customers to be blocked from banking online, and inflicting tens of millions of dollars in damage on the companies. The ITSec Team and

Mersad's cyber targets included major financial institutions, among them Bank of America, Capital One, the New York Stock Exchange and NASDAQ stock exchange, ING Bank, BB&T, U.S. Bank, and PNC Bank.

The Mersad hackers were linked to financial institution attacks conducted between September 2012 and May 2013, targeting different institutions, including Ally Bank, American Express, Ameriprise, Bank of America, Bank of Montreal, BB&T, Banco Nilbao Vizyana Argentaria, Capital One, JPMorgan Chase, Citibank, Citizens Bank, Fifth Third Bank, FirstBank, HSBC, Key Bank, NYSE, PNC, Regions Bank, State Street Bank, SunTrust Bank, Union Bank, U.S. Bank, Wells Fargo, and Zions First National Bank. The Mersad hackers were formed from two other Iranian hacking groups, the Sun Army and the Ashiyane Digital Security Team—both of which claimed credit for cyberattacks on U.S. government servers, with Ashiyane claiming its work on behalf of the Iranian government. The Sun Army claimed credit for hacking NASA in 2012.

The attack on the Bowman Dam took place between August and September 2013 with repeated intrusions into the remote computer controls of the dam, the supervisory control and data acquisition system, or SCADA. The intrusions were traced to Iranian national Hamid Firoozi, one of the ITSec hackers. Once inside, Firoozi gathered data on the water levels and temperature, and the status of the sluice gate that controls the water flow from the dam. What Firoozi did not know, according to the indictment, was that the dam control system had been manually disconnected for maintenance before he gained access to the controller. Firoozi for a year "would and did attempt to cause a threat to public health or safety" by gaining access to the controller of the Bowman Dam, the indictment stated.

If they had succeeded, the Iranians might have been able to cause a major flood that would have caused mass casualties among the people living nearby.

In Iran, the information warfare system struck back in response to the indictments. The Iranian Foreign Ministry, through spokesman Hossein Jaberi Ansari, stated on March 27, 2016, that "Washington is not in any position to accuse other countries' citizens without providing documentary evidence." Ansari added that the United States has a "history of cyber attacks against Iran's peaceful nuclear facilities." The response also played up Iran's demand that non-U.S. governments be allowed to control the Internet in their own countries.

The Bowman Dam cyberattack, however, was a stark reminder for American security officials that ever-increasing Iranian cyber and information warfare threats will require more than feckless and unprosecutable indictments.

Former CIA director James Woolsey believes Iran's information warfare capabilities will be combined with nuclear weapons in the future to produce a major attack: a nuclear burst in near-earth space to create a devastating electromagnetic pulse, or EMP, shock wave capable of knocking out all electronics for a thousand miles in all directions.

"Our cyber and information warfare doctrines are dangerously blind to the likelihood that a potential adversary making an all-out information warfare campaign designed to cripple U.S. critical infrastructures would include an EMP attack," Woolsey said. The Iranians who are working on long-range missile capabilities under cover of space launch vehicles also are likely to employ nuclear EMP attack from freighters sailing near U.S. shores that would launch 620-mile-range mobile Shahab missiles over the United States to knock out power. A congressional commission several years ago revealed that Iran's military doctrine includes explicit writings on the use of nuclear EMP attacks that could eliminate the United States as a major actor on the world stage through information warfare. "Nuclear weapons . . . can be used to determine the outcome of a war . . . without inflicting serious human damage [by neutralizing] strategic and information networks," states one Iranian military report. "Terrorist information warfare [includes] . . . using the technology of directed energy weapons (DEW) or electromagnetic pulse (EMP)."

"Today when you disable a country's military high command through disruption of communications you will, in effect, disrupt all the affairs of that country," the Iranians threatened. "If the world's industrial countries fail to devise effective ways to defend themselves against dangerous electronic assaults, then they will disintegrate within a few years."

From the damaging, pro-Iranian information warfare operation launched against the American people by Barack Obama and his administration in pursuit of a dangerous nuclear deal with Iran, to successively more damaging

Iranian-origin cyberattacks, the strategic nature of the Iranian information warfare threat is a direct outgrowth of the hard-line Islamist regime in Tehran. Mitigating the threat of information warfare will require a U.S. offensive and defensive information warfare program.

The Obama administration's information offensive against America was part of a larger ideological assault on the nation, as will be shown in a look at the ongoing leftist information war on the homeland.

8

THE LEFT

Workplace Violence, Safe Spaces, and Other Politically Correct Nonsense

The strategy of the long march through the institutions: working against the established institutions while working in them.
— New Left Marxist philosopher Herbert Marcuse, *Counterrevolution and Revolt,* 1972

Information warfare is not limited to foreign powers. An ideological enemy within the United States also is employing systematic ideological information warfare against American culture and traditions. It is based on revolutionary Marxist ideology carried out through the seemingly innocuous practice of political correctness. Today, political correctness is fundamentally transforming the United States from a country built by American founders who believed in the ideas of freedom, prosperity, and limited government, to one based on aggravating past resentments and self-centered identities.

Instead of supporting patriotism, anyone who declares the United States of America to be a great nation is denounced for failing to understand the dominant, false leftist narrative that America must be pummeled, ceaselessly, as a racist, imperialist power whose culture and traditions are to be destroyed and replaced with socialistic and hedonistic values.

Typical of this view is Hillary Clinton. Clinton, driven to the political left during the early 2016 campaign by democratic socialist senator Bernie Sanders, denounced her Republican challenger, Donald Trump, and his supporters. "To just be grossly generalistic, you can put half of Trump supporters into what I call the basket of deplorables," Clinton announced in the fall of 2016. "Racist, sexist, homophobic, xenophobic, Islamophobic, you name it." In other words, Clinton, a liberal politician operating under the canons of ideological information warfare, simply dismissed the millions of Americans who supported Trump as evil retrogrades.

The dominant liberal left narrative gained unprecedented prominence during the administration of President Barack Obama, who enforced the most radical agenda in the history of any American presidency. Obama was greatly assisted by an elite media, like the *New York Times*, *Washington Post*, and others, that became his unquestioning facilitators.

"Run! Get out! There's a guy with a gun!" So screamed Pascal Mignon, a patron at the gay nightclub Pulse, to crowds of people on a busy night in Orlando, Florida. It was around 2 a.m. on June 12, 2016, and Pascal was trying to alert people that a militant Muslim extremist had begun opening fire with a rifle and pistol. The terror attack would later expose the deadly nature of the liberal Left's political correctness agenda as never before. The gunman, twenty-nine-year-old Omar Mateen, was a radical Muslim who systematically crossed the main dance floor at the Pulse nightclub firing methodically at revelers along the way. Around 2:09 a.m., the club posted a terse message on Facebook: "Everyone get out of pulse and keep running." Three local police officers working security at the club reacted by firing at Mateen, who by 2:15 had retreated to a bathroom at the back of the building. Around fifteen minutes later he dialed 911 on his smartphone and informed the dispatcher that the attack was a protest against what he said was "the bombing of my country," a reference to U.S.-led military air strikes in Syria. Additionally, Mateen announced the shooting rampage was being carried out on behalf of Abu Bakr al-Baghdadi, leader of the Muslim terrorist organization known as the Islamic State. The ultraviolent group had burst on the scene two years earlier in Syria and Iraq and quickly began spreading radical Muslim–inspired death and hatred throughout the Middle East, while declaring the restoration of an Islamic caliphate, a geographical region led by a Muslim caliph—none other than Baghdadi. Mateen had pledged loyalty to the terrorist group during the call. Earlier murderous attacks by Islamic State terrorists had struck the heart of Europe in Paris and Belgium. Now a supporter of the group had carried out the worst mass killing by a terrorist organization in the United States since the September 11, 2001, suicide airline bombings.

Not content with having made the 911 call, fifteen minutes later Mateen phoned a local television station. "I'm the shooter. It's me," he announced. Mateen again explained the attack was being conducted in support of the Islamic State terrorist group—to hammer home the message. As the standoff ensued over the next three hours, Mateen would conduct Internet searches on his smartphone, scanning reports about his terrible killing spree. On Facebook, he posted: "America and Russia stop bombing the Islamic state. The real Muslims will never accept the filthy ways of the west. . . . You kill innocent women and children by doing us airstrikes . . . now taste the Islamic state vengeance." His final post issued an ominous warning: "In the next few days you will see attacks from the Islamic state in the usa." In a conversation with a police negotiator, Mateen threatened to put four of the hostages he held in bomb-laced vests, and also said he was wearing an explosive suicide bomb vest. The threat prompted police to end negotiations and storm the club. After breaking through a wall near the restroom, police opened fire, killing Mateen. At 5:53 a.m., Orlando police tweeted: "Pulse Shooting: The shooter inside the club is dead."

When the deadly terrorist attack was over, a total of forty-nine people lay murdered; fifty-three others were wounded, many critically, and certainly scarred, both emotionally and physically, for life. The club floor was covered in blood and bodies. Reports from survivors revealed Mateen fired at least one hundred rounds, taking time to fire extra rounds into some of the wounded to ensure he had killed them.

In the days that followed, the mass murder would be revealed as one of the worst failures—if not the worst—in the illustrious history of the Federal Bureau of Investigation. Formed in July 1908, the FBI was reoriented after the 2001 terror attacks from a predominantly law enforcement and investigatory agency into one whose primary mission, as stated on the FBI website, is to "protect the United States from terrorist attack." In the Orlando shooting case, the FBI did not stop the attack and FBI director James Comey later disclosed that Mateen *was investigated twice for links to Islamic State terrorism and in both cases let go.* Comey irrationally defended the bureau in a statement at FBI headquarters, insisting his agents had done the best job they could in the two investigations of Mateen.

Warning signs of the attack had been missed. Mateen was the U.S.-born son of an Afghan refugee who had voiced support for the Taliban terrorist organization in Afghanistan. Mateen first came onto the FBI's radar in May 2013 when a coworker at the local Florida courthouse where he worked as a security guard reported to authorities that he had voiced sympathies with Islamic terrorism, indeed saying that he was a member of al Qaeda and the Iran-backed group Hezbollah, at the time, two of the world's most deadly terrorist organizations. According to the informant, Mateen had said he hoped law enforcement agents would raid his apartment and assault his wife and child so he could martyr himself— commit suicide in the cause of jihad—in response.

FBI agents questioned Mateen and he admitted making the statements. But he claimed the comments were made in anger because Mateen felt discriminated against by co-workers for being Muslim. The FBI investigation was not perfunctory. It employed both confidential informants and electronic surveillance. The probe was dropped after Mateen's admission. However, the bureau mistakenly accepted his claims of Muslim discrimination by coworkers as leading to the outburst. Two months later, in July 2014, the FBI investigated Mateen a second time for links to an American suicide bomber in Syria, Abu Hurayra Al-Amriki, also known as Moner Mohammad Abu-Salha, a member of the al Qaeda–affiliated terrorist group Al-Nusra Front. Mateen and Abu-Salha attended the same mosque in Florida, the Islamic Center of Fort Pierce. Again the FBI dropped its investigation based on what Comey said were "no ties of any consequence" between the two Islamists.

During the 2014 investigation, an informant told the FBI that Mateen mentioned watching videos produced by Islamic terror recruiter and American Anwar al-Awlaki, an al Qaeda member in Yemen (killed in a U.S. drone strike in 2011). Awlaki figured prominently in three deadly terrorist attacks in the United States and yet the FBI ignored the clues.

Mateen was watching videos of the same al Qaeda terrorist in Yemen, Awlaki, who had communicated with army major Nidal Hassan, the Muslim extremist who killed thirteen people at Fort Hood, Texas, in 2009.

Awlaki's terrorist recruiting activities had also surfaced during the investigation into the attack six months earlier in San Bernardino, California. Court papers revealed that one of the terrorists who killed fourteen people in the December

2015 shooting, Syed Rizwan Farook, introduced a Muslim convert, Enrique Marquez Jr., to the Islamic teachings of Awlaki in 2007.

According to Comey, the FBI also dropped that investigation because investigators had no indication of an imminent attack.

It was the second botched domestic terrorism case. Similarly, the two terrorists who carried out the bombing of the Boston Marathon in April 2013, Chechen immigrants Dzhokhar and Tamerlan Tsarnaev, were missed by the FBI despite warnings from Russian security services that the two could be terrorists.

Why was the FBI unable to prevent deadly terrorist attacks? Two words explain it: political correctness. By 2016, liberal left ideologues within the U.S. government had systematically blocked the FBI from training its agents on how to investigate and respond to Islamist terror suspects. Former FBI agent John Guandolo believes the FBI mistakenly closed the Mateen investigations as a result of a lack of training for agents on how to properly investigate jihadist threats. Under pressure from liberal advocacy groups, the FBI stopped teaching its agents about the internal aspects of Islamist threat and warfare doctrine, such as jihad and sharia law, that guide terrorist activities and operations. "This investigation was closed because FBI leadership has systematically refused to look at and teach sharia to its agents because it is getting its advice on Islam from Muslims who are hostile to us and our system of government," Guandolo told me.

A source within the FBI angered by the Orlando failure

also revealed that beginning three or four years before the nightclub attack, the FBI halted all counterterrorism radicalization classes for both special agents and bureau counterterrorism analysts. The training was stopped because of fears of discrimination lawsuits filed against the bureau by Muslim employees and outside liberal activist groups. "The threat of internal complaints has killed the training," the source told me.

The main force at work behind the deadly policy, which prevents urgently needed training for agents and analysts in the tenets of Islamist terrorism, was the political correctness agenda imposed aggressively on the entire U.S. government by the White House under President Barack Obama, the source said. The FBI had become very afraid of religious discrimination lawsuits based on the liberal notion that teaching Islamic warfare tenets and principles might create a "hostile work environment"—vague code that has been used in liberal left lawfare to limit training and impose leftist policies. As a result, the FBI canceled all classes and removed all instructors who taught the subject.

"The FBI has a documented track record of mishandling reports of credible derogatory information and failing to rigorously follow referrals from other law enforcement and intelligence services concerning terrorism suspects," Judicial Watch investigator Chris Farrell, a former counterintelligence officer, said. "The impression the public is left with is of an agency that is overwhelmed, underresourced, inattentive, or all of the above."

For the Left, the Orlando shooting had to be spun for

political reasons as not the result of Islamic terrorism. Instead, the false narrative was spread to portray it as the result of lax American gun laws and to promote the liberal left policy of tighter government gun control. Mateen, whose terrorism ties had been documented, at one time was placed on a terrorism watch list, and when he was taken off after the FBI ended its investigations, he was able to purchase the AR-15–style carbine rifle used in the killing spree. Still others on the left falsely promoted the theme that the cause of the attack was rooted in antihomosexual prejudice. Despite clear evidence of Mateen's Islamist terrorist motives, the *New York Times* produced an incredible and false editorial blaming the Orlando attack on antigay hate. Other false news stories were circulated that Mateen was a homosexual and had patronized the gay nightclub. The FBI later declared there was no evidence Mateen was gay.

President Obama revealed his administration's true devotion to the deadly leftist canon of political correctness less than a week after the grisly massacre in Florida. Following a meeting of his National Security Council, Obama launched into an angry tirade—but not against the Islamic State terrorist group, which inspired the attack. The president, in a pattern followed during his tenure in office, *instead criticized Republicans.* Such partisanship and deception had been a hallmark of the liberal commander in chief.

A day before the president's rant, the *Washington Free Beacon* had published my report analyzing the Florida killing spree under the headline "Orlando Attack Is a Failure of Obama's 'Politically Correct' Policy, Analysts Say." It identified three major failures by U.S. authorities prior to the attack, including the two botched FBI investigations, the failure of the Department of Homeland Security tip line program known as "See Something, Say Something" (a coworker had alerted authorities but no action was taken), and finally, the failure of the Obama administration to warn the public of a direct threat by the Islamic State to attack the United States and Europe during the Islamic observance of Ramadan, which began in early June. The group issued a video threat on May 21, 2016, calling for Islamic State sympathizers to launch attacks in Europe and the United States. No nationwide warning was issued, most likely because it would be linking the group to the Muslim religious observance. Once again, politically correct policies had turned deadly.

"Political correctness is endangering the lives of Americans," said Sebastian Gorka, a counterterrorism specialist. "I have spoken to many law enforcement officers who are angry and not just frustrated that a political matrix and narrative is being forced upon them, and they are not allowed to speak accurately and truthfully about what the threat is and who the enemy is," Gorka added.

Critics of Islamic terrorism who blame the ideology of jihadism for the threat are falsely labeled by the Left as bigots and "Islamophobes," in much the same way that those who view homosexual orientation as contrary to Judeo-Christian religious beliefs are called "homophobes." The *New York Times* editorial on the shooting claimed that "while the precise motivation for the rampage remains unclear, it is evident that Mr. Mateen was driven by hatred toward gays and lesbians." The piece was headlined "The Corrosive Politics That Threaten L.G.B.T. Americans." The *Times* had completely missed Mateen's public declarations linking the attack to Islamic State terrorism.

The acronym *LGBT* is the latest evolution in liberal left efforts to control public debate through semantics. The same is true for the terms *racism* and *Islamophobia*. Once someone is tarred with these epithets, political campaigns of public denunciation ensue with little regard for whether the allegations are true.

Whether the president saw my article on the politically correct failures on Orlando, I do not know. More likely, Obama attempted to counteract the comments made a day earlier by Republican presidential nominee Donald Trump, who had criticized the current politically correct response to terrorism as crippling the government's ability to talk, think, and act clearly. After announcing once again the ratcheting up of another round of halfhearted military efforts against the Islamic State, Obama launched into the diatribe against Republicans as a "final point" of his public remarks, asserting that "the main contribution" of Republicans in the fight against IS had been to "criticize the administration and me for not using the phrase 'radical Islam.'"

"That's the key, they tell us. We cannot beat ISIL unless we call them radical Islamists," a visibly upset Obama claimed. He went on to ask rhetorically how the use of the term would contribute to the battle against IS, and specifically if it would make the terrorists less committed to killing Americans, or bring in more allies. He also wondered whether "there is a military strategy that is served by" use of the term.

In Obama's worldview there was no good reason to do so because, as he asserted, Islam had been perverted by terrorists to justify terrorism. "There has not been a moment in my seven and a half years as president where we have not been able to pursue a strategy because we didn't use the label 'radical Islam,'" he thundered. "Not once has an adviser of mine said, 'Man, if we use that phrase, we are going to turn this whole thing around,' not once. So someone seriously thinks that we don't know who we are fighting?" The president went on to explain that his nonuse of the term *radical Islam* "has nothing to do with political correctness and everything to do with actually defeating extremism." And according to Obama, calling terrorists Islamists would make it more difficult to solve the terror problem.

The diatribe revealed for the first time why America was losing the war against Islamist terror. Political correctness was to blame for subverting efforts to destroy the ideology behind Islamic extremism. The president made clear that day that he does not understand that countering the ideology of Islamic extremism is the ultimate key to victory. And contrary to the president's assertion, the ideology of political correctness is to blame and must be countered.

Critics were quick to respond to the president's angry denunciation of users of the term *radical Islam*. "To suggest, as the White House does repeatedly, that calling jihadis by their name bestows religious legitimacy, or that recognizing radical Islamists as Muslims somehow bestows religious legitimacy on them is as arrogant as it is wrong," American Enterprise Institute analyst Michel Rubin countered. "No Muslim looks to the United States to define religion or bestow religious legitimacy." Afghan war veteran and retired army lieutenant colonel Joseph Myers, a former DIA analyst and counterterrorism expert, called the president's stance on avoiding the term *radical Islam* the key to preventing effective counter-ideology programs from attacking the Islamist ideology. "We can kill terrorists every day, but if we do not engage and confront the ideas that are generating new terrorists tomorrow, we will not win this war," Myers told me. "If our national security policy and strategy prevents us from engaging the enemy on the ideological battlefield and separates Islamic doctrine as a causal factor in Islamic jihad-based terrorism, then we are disarming ourselves and conceding that key terrain to the enemy," Myers added.

A Department of Homeland Security report reveals that the president's ban on the use of Islamic religious terms was incorporated in a multimillion-dollar program designed to dissuade American youth from becoming terrorists. The June 2016 report by the Homeland Security Advisory Council called for spending up to $100 million in new funding for programs aimed at American millennials in response to the Islamic radicalization threat. But the report urged that to avoid creating an "us versus them" mentality in what was supposed to be a war of ideas, the government must limit its description of the problem to the vague rubric "Countering Violent Extremism," or CVE. A section of the report on the use of terminology recommended that the Department of Homeland Security "reject religiously-charged terminology and problematic positioning by using plain meaning American English" instead of "religious, legal and cultural terms like 'jihad,' 'sharia,' 'takfir' or 'umma.'"

Jihad is the Islamic concept of holy war, the primary call to arms for Islamic terrorist groups around the world, including the Islamic State, al Qaeda, and the Muslim Brotherhood. Sharia law is the antidemocratic, Islamic supremacist legal code that analysts say has kept many American Muslims from assimilating into American society and opened them up to terrorist recruitment. *Takfir* is the Arabic term for apostasy, and *umma* is the word used to describe the entire Muslim community. Thus tens of millions of dollars devoted to anti–Islamic radicalization programs would be wasted by ignoring the root cause of the problem.

Political correctness remains the major impediment to successful information warfare against terrorism. The American failure to turn back the Islamic State was highlighted by one of the president's most politically correct acolytes, CIA director John Brennan. In testimony before the Senate Select Committee on Intelligence two days after the president's defense of the non-Islamic nature of the program to defeat the Islamic State, Brennan said this: "Unfortunately, despite all of our progress against [the Islamic State] on the battlefield and in the financial realm, our efforts have not reduced the group's terrorism capability and global reach." It was a damning indictment of failed politically correct counterterrorism policies.

Obama consistently misjudged the Islamic State threat, no doubt because of the foolish hope that his policies would lead Muslims around the world to favor the United States. Yet he never once admitted the failings or changed course. In a remarkably wrong statement reported by *New Yorker* editor David Remnick in January 2014, as Islamic State forces were taking over the Iraqi city of Fallujah, Obama tried to dismiss the group as nonthreatening: "The analogy we use around here sometimes, and I think is accurate, is, if a JV [junior varsity] team puts on Lakers uniforms that doesn't make them Kobe Bryant." Obama tried to spin the embarrassing comment months later by denying he was referring to the Islamic State. Remnick, however, later contradicted the president by insisting the comment was referring to the Islamic State take-over of Fallujah in January.

Obama's politically correct posture toward radical Islam surfaced during the 2016 presidential campaign when Hillary Clinton announced she too would refuse to speak the term *radical Islam* because doing so would be harmful to Muslims. "No. 2, it helps to create this clash of civilizations that is actually a recruiting tool for ISIS and other radical jihadists who use this as a way of saying, 'We are in a war against the West—you must join us,'" Clinton explained. After the Orlando massacre, Clinton cleverly distanced herself from Obama by announcing she prefers the term *radical jihadism*—something that represents a slight improvement in dealing with the problem and possibly a positive step for the future toward more effective information warfare.

The source of deadly politically correct policies can be traced to the New Left radicals who read Herbert Marcuse during the 1970s and followed his advice of abandoning street protests and demonstrations in favor of long-term infiltration and subversion. Within several decades, Marxist and leftist sympathizers had moved into positions of power in American institutions, first in academia and the universities, then in the news media and entertainment industry, and finally into government. It was a remarkable use of information warfare techniques to impose Marxist ideas on a nation built on Judeo-Christian values and American traditions of independence and freedom. American national culture is now dominated by what has come to be known as "opinion morality," which seeks to obscure traditional concepts of right and wrong. Leftist proponents of opinion morality argue there is no right or wrong; morality is whatever your personal opinion may be. The leftist street radicals of the 1970s, such as those who took part in the Youth International Party and were called Yippies, once sought safe houses to hide from authorities. Today's radicals, by contrast, demand "safe spaces" on campuses for protection from even the slightest offensive speech—especially speech emanating from those espousing conservative, pro-American or patriotic beliefs, or literally anything that could lead to the slightest emotional upset. Leftists today also promote the bogus concept of "white privilege" as an information warfare weapon to be used in campaigns of weaponized shaming that seek to discredit any and all things favorable to American traditions, freedoms, and culture.

By 2015, the destructive politically correct movement had reached its zenith on college campuses. The conservative *National Review* published a list of what it termed the "13 Most Ridiculously PC Moments on College Campuses." It included such inane incidents as the Swarthmore College student who declared that anyone who said they hate pumpkin spice lattes must be labeled "sexist" because doing so was tantamount to saying "girls don't have valid emotions." The University of New Hampshire issued a "bias-free language guide" that declared use of the word *American* as offensive and to be avoided. Western University in London declared the word *skinny* to be "violent," because of liberals' concerns it was somehow insulting to those who are overweight.

And in the ultimate leftist semantic subversion, the University of Wisconsin–Milwaukee launched a "just words" campaign that declared use of the term *politically correct* to be offensive because it "has become a way to deflect saying that people are being too 'sensitive.'"

The success of the destructive leftist agenda in the U.S. education system was highlighted by a poll conducted in 2016 that found millennials have little understanding about socialism or communism. The poll showed that 45 percent of young people between the ages of sixteen and twenty said they would vote socialist, and 20 percent would vote communist. Equally disturbing and indicative of the power of the liberal-left narrative was the survey's finding that a third of millennials mistakenly believed more people were killed under the administration of President George W. Bush than under the Soviet Union's Joseph Stalin. Under Soviet rule, an estimated 20 million people were killed or died as a result of communist policies.*

Marion Smith, executive director of the Victims of Communism Memorial Foundation, which commissioned the poll, said his organization has been concerned that an emerging generation of Americans has little understanding of collectivism and its dark history. "Unfortunately, this report confirms this worrisome impression," Smith said. "This report clearly reveals a need for educating our youth on the dangerous implications of socialist ideals."

Clare Fox, head of the British think tank Institute of Ideas, called the hypersensitive crybabies of today's younger generation "Generation Snowflake," melting at the slightest emotional distress. But Fox incorrectly blamed parents of snowflakes for such stupidities as Oxford University's policy of notifying law students they will be informed beforehand if content during a lecture could upset them, or Cambridge University's canceling an Africa-themed dinner over fears the meeting would offend students. Mexican sombreros worn by students also were banned at some schools as insulting to Mex-

---

* For details on deaths under communism, see *The Black Book of Communism: Crimes, Terror, Repression*, by Stephane Courtois, Nicolas Werth, Jean-Louis Panne, Andrzej Paczkowski, Karel Bartosek, Jean-Louis Margolin. Harvard University Press, 1999.

icans, and more than one politically incorrect Halloween costume has come under fire from the mavens of PC. In October 2015, Walmart was pressured to halt sales of an Israeli soldier costume for children, and a "Sheik Fagin Nose," after critics claimed both were offensive. The liberal American-Arab Anti-Discrimination Committee opposed the Israeli soldier costume, calling it a "symbol of violence" against Palestinians, while the hooked Sheik Fagin Nose allegedly had to be stopped for promoting anti-Arab racism. The same month, Amazon and eBay were criticized for a "Lady Boy" Halloween costume deemed insensitive to cross-dressers.

"Anti-bullying" also has become a rallying cry of the new fascists behind political correctness. In recent years bullying has expanded from being defined as physical abuse or beating to include such questionable acts as teasing and name-calling, spreading rumors, verbal sexual commentary, "homophobic taunting," graffiti, insensitive jokes, bullying gestures, and exclusion from friendship groups. In overreaction, schools are subjecting children to endless anti-bullying assemblies, books, programs, and stories of victims.

"By the time they get to university, our overprotected children are so loaded up with emotional angst that they are ill-equipped to deal with the basic challenges of adult life," Fox laments. Students at the University of Missouri forced the school's chancellor and president to resign amid charges the administrators were insensitive in responding to alleged racial incidents on campus.

And in a scene reminiscent of the 1970s' mass Communist Party purges during China's Cultural Revolution, Mizzou student protesters, echoing the Red Guards of China, issued this outrageous demand:

> We demand that the University of Missouri System President, Tim Wolfe, writes a handwritten apology to the Concerned Student 1950 demonstrators and holds a press conference in the Mizzou Student Center reading the letter. In the letter and at the press conference, Tim Wolfe must acknowledge his white male privilege, recognize that systems of oppression exist, and provide a verbal commitment to fulfilling Concerned Student 1950 demands.

The university president did not meet all the demands but few noted its outrageousness on campus or off. Wilfred M. McClay, a University of Oklahoma history professor, sees the case as an example of the Left's weaponized shaming. "One of the many advantages of shaming as a technique for gaining political advantage is that it does not need to trouble itself with the niceties of argument or debate," McClay wrote in the *Claremont Review of Books.* "P.C. discourse, with its wooden abstractions and its servile obedience to ideological desiderata, is its natural home."

Some traditional liberals began to oppose the politically correct mania. Several comedians, including Jerry Seinfeld and Chris Rock, announced they would no longer perform shows on some college campuses over concerns about their facing a politically correct backlash against their politically incorrect humor. The novelist Lionel Shriver came under an information assault after giving a speech in which she opposed the leftist idea that writers should avoid engaging in "cultural appropriation"—the bogus notion that majority cultures are illicitly exploiting minorities by stealing their intellectual property. In particular, Shriver was criticized by Yassmin Abdel-Magied, a twenty-five-year-old Sudanese-born Australian writer who protested by walking out of Shriver's speech and later angrily denouncing the novelist in the *Guardian* newspaper. Shriver's rejoinder in the *New York Times* questioned whether the Left would survive the wrath of politically correct millennials. As she stated: "Viewing the world and the self through the prism of advantaged and disadvantaged groups, the identity-politics movement—in which behavior like huffing out of speeches and stirring up online mobs is par for the course—is an assertion of generational power. Among millennials and those coming of age behind them, the race is on to see who can be more righteous and aggrieved—who can replace the boring old civil rights generation with a spikier brand."

Several police shootings of African Americans spawned a racist antipolice movement that has further undermined law and order nationwide, as police in major cities began turning away from enforcing the law over concerns their liberal political leaders would accuse them of racially motivated policing. The policy was deadly. By May 2016, homicide rates in twenty major U.S. cities increased sharply and the FBI director, James Comey, attributed the rise in murders to intimidated police.

The liberal *New York Times* would profess ignorance in its story on the crime increase with this opening about the murder rate, asserting, "experts cannot agree on what to call a recent rise in homicides, much less its cause." Police killings accelerated in the summer of 2016 after two black men were killed in confrontations with police. Five Dallas police officers were killed, followed by three in Baton Rouge. The attacks were carried out by black racists.

The liberal left political juggernaut reached absurd levels over the use of bathrooms by those professing to be transgenders, physically born males and females who "self-identified" as the opposite sex and often had surgery and hormone treatment to try to change their sex. Using the classic information warfare tactic of legal warfare, or lawfare, transgender rights advocates demanded that public schools allow boys claiming to be girls to use bathrooms and locker rooms designated for schoolgirls. When North Carolina refused to go along with the politically correct demand and passed a law requiring men born as men to use the men's room and women born as women to use the ladies' room, a liberal political backlash ensued. Threats of sports boycotts were made unless the law was reversed. Rock stars canceled concerts in the state.

In Silicon Valley, the technological breadbasket of the United States, the tech community millionaires and billionaires also became hostages to leftist information warfare, under what writer Michael Anton called "San Francisco Values." Liberal San Francisco information warfare goals were identified as support for gay marriage, medical marijuana, universal health care, immigrant sanctuary, "living" minimum wage, bicycle-friendly streets, and stricter environmental and consumer regulations. The list summarizes the incoherent impulses underlying the liberal Left: hedonism, utopianism, suicidal altruism, triviality, and overblown responses to sensible concerns.

"As should be obvious to everyone by now, in America (and in the developed world more generally), the very rich are different from you and me. They're far more left-wing," Anton said in describing how Silicon Valley's titans of industry were cowed into adopting the leftist political dogma now dominating much of the establishment in the United States—not just California. The rich in America and especially in California have been bought off by the political Left mainly to keep them at bay and focused on attacking conservatives instead of them. As Anton stated in the *Claremont Review of Books:*

> Politicians decline to stoke populist outrage against this partnership because the rich pay them not to and because, in a democracy, they must court the Left for reasons not dissimilar to Willie Sutton's rationale for robbing banks. Sutton, though, couldn't count bankers as backers or allies. Today's Democratic Party, by contrast, enjoys near universal support not just from Wall Street but from the 1 percent in every industry, save Big Oil and Big Pharma. Yet as good postmoderns, our S.F. elites are uneasy with the concept of eternal, objective truth, which they assume inevitably leads to Babbitry, absolutism, slavery, fascism, the Inquisition, and

other dreadful things people flee red states to get away from.
Their solution to this paradox is not to think about it.

Technology millionaires and billionaires are now spreading the gospel of opinion morality not just as a replacement
for traditional concepts of right and wrong, but as a superior
ideology and the culmination of the Marxist maxims espoused during the leftist heyday of the 1960s and '70s. Political correctness among the tech oligarchs is a key weapon for
the Left, who have reached an implicit deal with the wealthy
Silicon Valley class not to turn their information warfare
skills against them and indeed have emerged as cheerleaders
for them. The tech oligarchs return the favor by subsidizing
leftists in funding nonprofit organizations and follow their
lead in voicing politically correct views on politics, what
Anton calls "socio-intellectual money laundering."

As a result, conservatives' efforts to woo the Silicon Valley titans by emphasizing sympathetic views on free market
entrepreneurship, less government regulation, and other
themes have failed to resonate. The tycoons there also failed
to oppose the crushing tax burden imposed by both the federal and California governments and seem to have no interest
in trying to change policies that would allow them to keep
more of their money. Thus the wealthy in California effectively were co-opted into supporting the leftist agenda in a
region that represents one of the most important financial
engines and a major target of liberal left takeover plans.

• • •

The transformation of American society through political correctness was the work of self-declared progressives and liberal left political activists who systematically implemented what Democratic presidential nominee Barack Obama, five days before his election in 2008 as the nation's first African American president, promised would be a fundamental transformation of America. "We are five days away from fundamentally transforming the United States of America," Obama said. "In five days, you can turn the page on policies that put greed and irresponsibility on Wall Street before the hard work and sacrifice of folks on Main Street. In five days, you can choose policies that invest in our middle class, and create new jobs, and grow this economy, so that everyone has a chance to succeed, not just the CEO, but the secretary and janitor, not just the factory owner, but the men and women on the factory floor."

Astonishingly, Obama would spend five years in office before anyone asked him what he meant by the alarming declaration. During an interview in February 2014 with conservative television host and author Bill O'Reilly, Obama dissembled about the radical-transformation comment. "I don't think we have to fundamentally transform the nation." What? Had the president already achieved his promised fundamental transformation of the American political system? Or was he backing away from the earlier comments? Pressed to explain, Obama insisted that "what we have to do is make sure that here in America, if you work hard, you can get ahead." Good jobs, good wages, public schools that functioned well, and scholarships for less affluent students.

The comment was clearly playing to O'Reilly's working-class roots on Long Island. O'Reilly moved on to another topic after saying he agreed with the president. Obama then fell back on the current liberal lexicon, which is an outgrowth of the anticapitalism of the leftists who influenced him: "We've got to make sure that we're doing everything we can to expand the middle class."

The Left's use of *middle class* is code for fundamentally transforming the country from a free market capitalist system into a socialist or quasi-socialist system where government controls, in Marxist terms, the means of production. Marcuse was among the Left's most important Marxist philosophers who argued that the U.S. government was too strong to be overthrown by traditional means. Thus New Left Marxists adopted his strategy of long-term infiltration into the institutions of America as part of the path for bringing communism to the country. Marcuse used the analogy of the Long March through the institutions by stealing the term from Mao Zedong's epic military retreat in 1934–35, which culminated in Mao's rise to power in China. As Mao stated in 1935, "The Long March is a manifesto. . . . The Long March is also a propaganda force. It has announced to some 200 million people in eleven provinces that the road of the Red Army is their only road to liberation." For American leftists, the Long March is the socialization of the United States under Marxist ideological principles. Marcuse said that on the Long March the militant minority has a powerful anonymous ally in the capitalist countries: the deteriorating economic-political conditions of capitalism.

If Marcuse is the Karl Marx for the rise of politically correct socialism in America, Saul Alinsky is its Vladimir Lenin. Alinsky, who died the same year Marcuse penned *Counterrevolution and Revolt,* produced a generation of Marxist radicals who followed the prescriptions for taking power he laid out in his 1971 book, *Rules for Radicals.* According to Alinsky, the book is "concerned with how to create mass organizations to seize power and give it to the people; to realize the democratic dream of equality, justice, peace, cooperation, equal and full opportunities for education, full and useful employment, health, and the creation of those circumstances in which man can have the chance to live by values that give meaning to life." Alinsky's utopian vision was the same as the one held by communist dictators who turned normal nations into killing fields for most of the twentieth century. But Alinsky joined a school of neo-Marxists who believed the realization of communism would not come from armed, violent revolution but through gradual infiltration and subversion of existing institutions. As Alinsky put it:

A Marxist begins with his prime truth that all evils are caused by the exploitation of the proletariat by the capitalists. From this he logically proceeds to the revolution to end capitalism, then into the third stage of reorganization into a new social order of the dictatorship of the proletariat, and finally the last stage—the political paradise of communism.

In August 2008, Alinsky's son, David Alinsky, wrote a letter to the *Boston Globe* hailing the Democratic National

Convention at which Obama was chosen as the nominee, for having "all the elements of the perfectly organized event, Saul Alinsky style."

As David Alinsky put it:

Barack Obama's training in Chicago by the great community organizers is showing its effectiveness. It is an amazingly powerful format, and the method of my late father always works to get the message out and get the supporters on board. When executed meticulously and thoughtfully, it is a powerful strategy for initiating change and making it really happen. Obama learned his lesson well. I am proud to see that my father's model for organizing is being applied successfully beyond local community organizing to affect the Democratic campaign in 2008. It is a fine tribute to Saul Alinsky as we approach his 100th birthday.

The fact that it took more than five years before Obama was questioned about his promise of American transformation remark can be traced to a liberal left political bias within the establishment news media, which viewed Obama as one who in sports terms would be called a franchise player. He was not just the best player on the progressive team. He was the player who was so important that an entire team would be built around him. In the eyes of the liberal elite political and media establishment, Obama as the franchise political player had to be protected from political opponents at all costs. Thus the *New York Times*, considered the most important newspaper in America, *never provided a full vet-*

ting of the young community organizer from Chicago prior to his election as president. A July 7, 2008, piece in the *Times,* headlined "Obama's Organizing Years, Guiding Others and Finding Himself," mentions that Obama's community agitation group, Developing Communities Project, was influenced by Alinsky. But the *Times,* rather than describing Alinsky as a radical leftist, summarized him as having "viewed self-interest as the main motivation for political participation," and not Marxist ideology, as Alinsky actually advocated. According to the article, Obama shunned Alinsky's confrontation tactics but followed his formula of meticulously planning for meetings with people in power. There was no mention of *Rules for Radicals* or other Alinsky Leninist political action plans. The only other passing reference to Obama and Alinsky in the *Times* appeared on August 25, 2008, and sought to present Obama as somewhat centrist and "squarely in the liberal mainstream of the Democratic Party," yet also having a "sense of ideological elusiveness." The article described Obama as a "communitarian" exposed to that view from the Alinsky-influenced group. (Communitarianism is a social system built on small self-governing communities.) Thus the importance of Alinsky, his politics, and his rules for radicals to take power was all but obliterated from national public discourse. There were no further references to Obama and Alinsky in the *Times* news pages during his entire administration.

The Left's ideological narrative successfully suppressed discussion of Obama's Alinsky views and the subject remained off-limits for the establishment news media during most of the 2016 presidential campaign, which involved another Alinsky acolyte: Hillary Clinton. In 2014, two years before launching her run for the White House, letters were made public between Clinton and Alinsky. "Dear Saul," she wrote, "when is that new book [*Rules for Radicals*] coming out—or has it come out and I somehow missed the fulfillment of Revelation?"

"You are being rediscovered again as the New Left–type politicos are finally beginning to think seriously about the hard work and mechanics of organizing," Clinton wrote on July 8, 1971, from Berkeley, California, adding that she had survived law school with "my belief in and zest for organizing intact." Clinton was working at the time for the leftist law firm of Treuhaft, Walker & Bernstein, whose clients included Black Panther militants. Her admiration for Alinsky was deep. When she was a twenty-one-year-old student at Wellesley College, her political science thesis, "There Is Only the Fight . . . : An Analysis of the Alinsky Model," lauded the Chicago communist. The paper praised Alinsky but made clear that poverty was not the result of a lack of money but a lack of power—a key Marxist tenet. Clinton's paper concluded by placing Alinsky alongside Martin Luther King, Walt Whitman, and Eugene Debs, the five-time Socialist Party candidate for president from 1900 to 1920.

Regarding the Left's Long March through the institutions, Clinton would say in her 2003 biography, *Living History*, that her fundamental disagreement with Alinsky was that "he believed you could change the system only from the outside. I didn't." In other words, Clinton was convinced at an early stage in her political career that the Long March strategy advocated by Marcuse was the key to successful socialist revolution. As president, Clinton can be expected to go beyond Obama in carrying out a covert leftist takeover of the U.S. government.

For an anticipated Hillary Clinton presidential administration, the pattern has been set for information warfare operations against the American people, as shown in the Obama White House in its campaign against opponents of the Iran nuclear deal.

Further evidence of the radical agenda under Obama was on display at the Justice Department during his administration, involving a dangerous program promoted by liberal civil liberties groups in 2009 that exposed the identities of CIA officers to hardened al Qaeda terrorists held at the Guantanamo Bay, Cuba, detention facility. The prison under Obama had become a rallying cry for the liberal Left, who regarded it as a symbol of American injustice. For the Left, holding terrorists at the Cuban prison was characterized as a grave American injustice left over from the administration of President George W. Bush. Despite critics' claims to the contrary, both Bush and his administration had acted legally and constitutionally in holding terrorists captured on the battlefields of the post-9/11 war on terrorism.

The CIA launched a counterintelligence investigation in

the spring of 2010 after the discovery of twenty color photographs of CIA officers inside the cell of Mustafa Ahmed al-Hawsawi, a Guantanamo detainee who was one of the financiers of the September 11 attacks. The photographs showed CIA interrogators and had been supplied by the terrorists' defense lawyers. Behind the scenes, civil liberties opponents of the Cuban prison hatched a plan that involved exposing the identity of the CIA interrogators as part of a legal ploy that might fairly be called graymail. Graymail is a legal tactic that involves threatening to publicly identify sensitive information as a way to dissuade prosecution. Here it appears the groups planned to expose covert CIA operatives who had interrogated the terrorists held at Guantanamo as a way to force the military tribunal against the terrorists to be called off.

The effort was part of an American Civil Liberties Union–backed program called the John Adams Project. Investigators hired by the project worked to track down the CIA operatives and covertly photograph them. The photos were passed to defense lawyers for the terrorists, who then turned them over to the detainees. The ACLU and the John Adams Project did not deny a role in supplying the photographs but denied any lawyers working to represent Guantanamo detainees had compromised the security of CIA personnel. Both groups asserted that they had operated within rules set by a military judge. But the photographs given to the terrorists showed CIA officials in public places and clearly indicated that they had been taken by private investigators. It is a federal crime to publicly expose the identity of covert CIA personnel. The 1982 Intelligence Identities Protection

Act makes it a crime to expose secret intelligence officers. The law was passed after CIA defector Philip Agee engaged in a public campaign of exposing undercover agency officers. CIA officials blamed the 1975 assassination of Richard Welch in Athens on the leftist operation to publicly expose CIA officers around the world. The legislation was designed to prevent a repeat of such killings.

Justice Department lawyers, including some who had been affiliated with the liberal ACLU and John Adams Project, opposed the CIA investigation and challenged a CIA counterintelligence "Tiger Team" that was set up to investigate the security breach. The team asserted that the compromise had placed the agency officers' lives in danger. To try to tamp down the internal dispute, the Justice Department brought in U.S. attorney Patrick J. Fitzgerald from Chicago. After his arrival, several Justice Department officials, including Donald L. Vieira, chief of staff of the Justice Department's National Security Division (NSD) and counselor to the assistant attorney general for national security, recused themselves from the CIA–Justice Department probe. The reason for the recusal was not made public. But a U.S. official close to the controversy told me that some in the Justice Department had worked in the past as advocates for the detainees in nongovernmental organizations and were suspected of being tied to the CIA officer photos found in the Guantanamo inmate's cell. Asked why he recused himself, Vieira, now in private practice, declined to say, but insisted in an email that what was reported about the case in the past was not accurate.

CIA sources familiar with the internal dispute revealed to me that during a heated meeting at CIA headquarters on March 9, 2010, CIA officials clashed with Justice Department lawyers who were supporting the John Adams Project. The discussion centered on the wording of an interagency memorandum that was to be used to brief President Obama and senior administration aides on the photographs found in one terrorist's prison cell. Justice officials opposed the language, which cited the grave dangers to the CIA personnel if their identities were leaked from Guantanamo to al Qaeda terrorists through their lawyers. The memo was being prepared for White House National Security Council aide John Brennan, who later became CIA director. The CIA won the argument and the language was kept in. Fitzgerald prevailed, and several Justice Department lawyers, including Vieira, stepped aside from any role in the probe. "They have put the lives of CIA officers and their families in danger," a senior official close to the investigation told me, referring to the detainees' lawyers and their supporters. For the liberal Left, the danger to the CIA officers was less important than advancing the politically correct agenda of closing the prison in Cuba. A senior Pentagon official expressed disgust that Justice officials and the civil liberties activists had shown more concern for the imprisoned al Qaeda terrorists than the security of CIA officers. "By the time this is over, they will be building monuments to the terrorists," the official told me.

For the military, Obama closed out his final year in office with a reputation for imposing his radical liberal left agenda on the armed forces. His appointees at the Pentagon unleashed a series of damaging policies that compounded earlier harm resulting from nearly $1 trillion in defense spending cuts imposed during the president's tenure. Several conservative military leaders had their careers cut short, among them Marine Corps general James Mattis, commander of the frontline U.S. Central Command whose gung ho spirit had earned him the nickname Mad Dog Mattis. Under Obama, some eighteen commanding officers of various military units were fired or forced into retirement under politically correct Pentagon policies.

Politically correct information warfare policies under Defense Department political appointees went so far as to force military leaders to alter war plans to include false dire warnings about the alleged danger of climate change, despite thin evidence that global warming in any way would affect future operations. The bogus concern over climate change came as the military had been so weakened under Obama policies that it was forced to abandon the decades-long policy of being ready to fight two wars simultaneously. By 2016, American military capabilities to prevail in a single conflict had atrophied significantly. Yet the Pentagon called climate change an "urgent and growing threat" in 2015, and a year later a directive to all commanders from Secretary of Defense Ashton Carter struck a new tone of ridiculous political correctness: "Incorporate climate change impacts into plans and operations and integrate DoD guidance and analysis in Combatant Command planning to address climate change–related risks and opportunities across the full range of military operations, including steady-state campaign planning and operations and contingency planning." Military officers and enlisted who had joined the services to defend the nation and fight and win the nation's wars were instead finding themselves forced to spend valuable resources on fruitless campaigns designed to wage war against the weather.

The liberal left deception of "white privilege" also was forced upon the military by the Pentagon agenda. Military units, in a policy mirroring the Communist Party commissars of the Chinese People's Liberation Army, hired speakers to present the negative history of the white race in America. The public interest law group Judicial Watch revealed in army documents it obtained that "white privilege" training was held at Fort Gordon, near Augusta, Georgia, for four hundred soldiers. The training included a PowerPoint slide that stated, "Our society attaches privilege to being white and male and heterosexual. . . . Race privilege gives whites little reason to pay a lot of attention to African Americans."

As seen in the knee-jerk reaction to the Orlando shooting, liberal agitation for tighter gun control impacted the Pentagon. An Obama executive order directed the Pentagon to begin research and development on "smart gun" technology, designed to restrict the firing of guns to their owners through biometrics or PIN numbers.

Under the liberal feminist agenda of the Obama administration, halting sexual assaults in the military became the services' highest priority, prompting many soldiers to question whether their fundamental mission of fighting and winning America's wars had been altered. The hysteria over sexual assaults—surveys at the Pentagon on the number of sexual assaults were contradicted by private studies showing the Defense Department had vastly overstated the problem—led to the false prosecution of an air force sergeant who faced 130 years in prison for allegedly making sexual advances at Minot Air Force Base, in North Dakota. The soldier was found to be not guilty of all sex charges and the victim of an out-of-control politically correct atmosphere among commanders at the base. Not content with integrating women into frontline combat units, and despite open opposition to the move from the U.S. Marine Corps, which regarded the shift as undermining training and fighting ability, the Pentagon took the even more radical and potentially more disruptive step of allowing sexual transgenders to remain in the service. In the past, sexual deviancy was viewed as undermining good order and discipline and grounds for dismissal. The army revealed in budget documents that soldiers would have the right to "self-identify" as whatever sex they preferred. "Instead of preparing for transgenderism and related social experiments, our troops should be concentrating on combat readiness," said Elaine Donnelly, who directs the Center for Military Readiness. "The military is a resilient institution, but strong leadership in the next administration will be needed to restore its strength and morale."

The navy in particular seemed to run aground under the Obama administration's political correctness policies. Obama's navy secretary, Ray Mabus, delighted in naming warships for liberal left civil rights and labor activists.

As shown earlier, the most significant left liberal information warfare operation under the Obama administration was directed against the American public and government to obfuscate the Iranian nuclear deal in 2015. Again, "[w]e created an echo chamber," declared Ben Rhodes, Obama's inexperienced foreign policy adviser and former speechwriter, who spent eight years as the White House deputy national security adviser for strategic communications. Rhodes made the remark in the revealing interview with David Samuels, who reported in a *New York Times Magazine* piece on how Rhodes helped bamboozle the American public about the Iran nuclear deal during negotiations in 2015. Using lies, half-truths, and deception, Rhodes orchestrated a propaganda Wurlitzer of news reporters and liberal experts to promote the Iran deal. "They were saying things that validated what we had given them to say," he said.

The political agenda of the liberal Left in the United States is destroying the fabric of American society. It is the culmination of the New Left Marxism of the 1970s and is embodied in two politicians who dominated the early decades of the twenty-first century: Barack Obama and Hillary Clinton.

Angelo Codevilla, a conservative national security strategist, believes liberal left progressivism currently in fashion already ignited what he terms an imperial revolution that has subverted constitutional government. "In fact, the 2016 election is sealing the United States' transition from that republic to some kind of empire," he warned in an essay published by the Claremont Institute a month before the election. A bipartisan ruling class of both left and right is using political correctness to advance its ideological agenda based on the concept of antidiscrimination to do away with American traditions and freedoms. Arbitrary power is replacing the rule of law and the defense of constitutional freedoms.

For example, Americans' rights guaranteed in the Declaration of Independence and codified in the Bill of Rights have been transformed into government-defined civil rights according to liberal political dictates. Religious freedom, free speech and free assembly, keeping and bearing arms, freedom from warrantless searches, and other rights are natural rights, and securing those rights for Americans has been what the United States was built on. Yet the U.S. Civil Rights Commission, reflecting the liberal progressive revolutionary fervor, wants to limit the foremost of those rights. The commission stated in a September 2016 report that "religious exemptions to the protections of civil rights based upon classifications such as race, color, national origin, sex, disability status, sexual orientation, and gender identity, when they are permissible, significantly infringe upon those civil rights." Further, the report states that Americans' rights under the Declaration of Independence and the Bill of Rights should not be allowed, noting that "the phrases 'religious liberty' and 'religious freedom' will stand for nothing except hypocrisy so long as they remain code words for discrimination, intolerance, racism, sexism, homophobia, Islamophobia, Christian supremacy, or any form of intolerance." The terms used by the commission are all buzzwords adopted by the mavens of political correctness.

Codevilla warns that the future under this liberal progressive transformation is bleak:

> In today's America, a network of executive, judicial, bureaucratic, and social kinship channels bypasses the sovereignty of citizens. Our imperial regime, already in force, works on a simple principle: the president and the cronies who populate these channels may do whatever they like so long as the bureaucracy obeys and one third plus one of the Senate protects him from impeachment.
>
> Electing either Hillary Clinton or Donald Trump cannot change that trajectory. Because each candidate represents constituencies hostile to republicanism, each in its own way, these individuals are not what this election is about. This election is about whether the Democratic Party, the ruling class's enforcer, will impose its tastes more strongly and arbitrarily than ever, or whether constituencies opposed to that rule will get some ill-defined chance to strike back. Regardless of the election's outcome, the republic established by America's Founders is probably gone. But since the Democratic Party's constituencies differ radically from their opponents', and since the character of imperial governance depends inherently on the emperor, the election's result will make a big difference in our lives.

The Democratic Party will continue its drive to impose the revolutionary agenda aimed at transforming America. For the Republican Party, it is in turmoil and must regroup in the

coming years from the ashes of its failure to heed traditional-
ist Americans' desire to block the progressive transformation.

In many ways, the politically correct ideology poses an
existential threat to the long-term health of the United States
and must be countered with an information warfare program
that uses truth to expose false and destructive ideas and operations.

9

INFORMATION AMERICA

We Have Met the Enemy and It's *Not* Us

The single biggest failing on the U.S. side in
the war of ideas is that there is no institution
tasked with and responsible for the conduct of
it — only individual, sporadic initiatives.
—ROBERT R. REILLY,
FORMER DIRECTOR, VOICE OF AMERICA

Historians will look back on the administration of President Barack Obama as a dark period in American history. The power and prestige of the country, diminished by a leader who viewed the United States as an imperialist and racist power to be weakened, will take decades to recover. At the same time the country was being damaged from within, the power of hostile foreign states and other powers grew at an unprecedented rate. Instead of a global environment often referred to as Pax Americana, in which the United States is a leading force for peace and stability, the world is being ravaged by America's enemies, who are promoting a dark vision of statism, centralized power, harsh controls on freedom, and, for Islamic terrorists, the nightmare of a global, Muslim-inspired theocratic empire in which all those who do not share its precepts are enemies to be converted or destroyed.

There is hope, however. The damage wrought by Obama can be undone and must be repaired if the nation is to survive as the founders envisioned and to remain the land of the free and the home of the brave.

"America is great because she is good, and if America ever ceases to be good, she will cease to be great." That quotation, frequently attributed to Alexis de Tocqueville's nineteenth-century classic, *Democracy in America,* presents a fundamental truth about the United States of America. Never before in American history has the threat to national survival been as great as it is today. The war America confronts this time is an information war, spanning an array of methods and platforms. From China's Three Warfares—legal, psychological, and media warfare—to Russia's use of sophisticated, KGB-like information warfare, disinformation, and hybrid war, to Islamism's deadly hydralike spread through social media, the United States is under twenty-four-hour ideological assault.

The ill-fated quest of the administration of President Barack Obama to transform America into what he views as a country more admired around the world backfired terribly. Instead, the "Apologize for America" administration has produced the exact opposite of its intended goal. American friends and allies around the world today are alienated and disenfranchised by a president who instead has curried favor with America's enemies and would-be adversaries.

The creation of a new organization I call Information America is urgently needed to conduct a wide-ranging program of offensive and defensive information warfare to promote and protect constitutional democracy, liberty, rule of law, freedom of press and religion, and free markets.

This program must systematically confront and defeat the increasing Information Age lies and disinformation about America—not only abroad but inside the country, where a fundamentally anti-American ideology espoused by utopian liberal leftists has become pervasive and reached heights of power not seen before in U.S. history.

The weapon of choice used by this Information America system is simple: telling the truth—about America, and about its enemies, using modern, intellectually grounded and sophisticated communications tools and techniques. The stakes in today's information warfare have never been higher, and ultimately the survival of our free and open society is in the balance. In the information sphere, as General Douglas MacArthur said of conventional warfare, there is no substitute for victory. And these information activities and counter-activities must be built on a moral clarity of purpose, amid an increasingly immoral and value-neutral world.

America is threatened today as never before. Enemies foreign and domestic have been attacking in the information sphere, seemingly at will. The nation's wealth and power are being aggressively challenged by states like China, Russia,

Iran, and North Korea. The Islamic State terrorist group, successor to the perpetrator of the September 11, 2001, attacks on New York and Washington, is expanding from its bases in the Middle East into Europe, North Africa, and Asia with little resistance, despite limited military attacks on its leaders and facilities in the Middle East and North Africa. Islamic State supporters by 2016 had begun killing Americans inside the United States, and the danger will continue to increase because the American security apparatus appears helpless against the religiously charged ideology of the Islamic State. The reason is simple: killing Islamist enemies, while important in warfare, ultimately is insufficient for winning the war against radical Islamic terror. And make no mistake, it is war. Only a concerted, multitiered ideological and information-based war can bring victory.

Likewise, the failure of American statesmen to counteract the threat posed by Chinese hegemonism in Asia is endangering the peace and security of the world, as China seeks to drive the United States out of the region. Like the Islamic State, the Chinese must be fought and defeated on the ideological front. Similarly, Russia's Vladimir Putin and the neofascist pan-Eurasian aggression that seeks control over the European continent represent a geopolitical danger that must be confronted and defeated ideologically. In regard to Iran, misguided and self-deluding U.S. foreign policies that attempted to coax the radical Islamic theocratic state to evolve into a nonthreatening regional power likewise have utterly failed.

Instead, the current policy of appeasement has produced

even greater dangers to world peace and stability. Again, the solution to the Iranian threat must be built on ideas and implemented through information warfare operations that can produce a lasting peace. North Korea is an increasingly dangerous and erratic nuclear weapons state that repeatedly threatens to unleash a nuclear war. It too must also urgently become the target of American information warfare designed to mitigate the danger.

The first step in solving the problem is to recognize America is under attack from enemies waging strategic information warfare. This problem was addressed in a 2012 study produced by the U.S. military's Joint Chiefs of Staff and ordered by U.S. Army general Martin Dempsey, chairman of the Joint Chiefs. Dempsey had called for the military to study the lessons learned from a decade of war on terrorism. The fifty-page report found the ten-year period following the World Trade Center and Pentagon attacks and subsequent U.S.-led military operations in Afghanistan, Iraq, and elsewhere *lacked a strategic understanding of information warfare needed in the war on terror.* For a decade, "the US was slow to recognize the importance of information and the battle for the narrative in achieving objectives at all levels," the report concluded, adding that "it was often ineffective in applying and aligning the narrative to goals and desired end states." The failure on the information battlefield was characterized by a lack of leadership and resources that needed to focus on using information "as an instrument of national power."

According to the report:

> *The proliferation of the Internet, social media, and personal electronic devices caused the paradigm of communication to shift: it was no longer possible for the military to tightly control and limit information. While the military was slow to adapt to these developments, the enemy was not, developing considerable skill in using these new means of communication to their own ends. In addition, the enemy was frequently unconstrained by the truth: for example, they could feed false information to the media through the use of news stringers on fast-dial from an insurgent/terrorist cell phone. This allowed the enemy to make the first impression, an impression that could be difficult or impossible to overcome, even when false. For example, a premature detonation of an improvised explosive device (IED) in Kandahar City, [Afghanistan] which resulted in many civilian casualties, was quickly (and falsely) reported to be a Predator [drone] strike. Though not true, years later, locals still believed the casualties came from a coalition airstrike.*

The report's conclusion was a stark admission that for a decade of conflict in the early years of the Information Age, the most powerful military in the world had been unable to grasp the strategic importance of information warfare—how to wage it and how to battle against it.

The State Department was no better. As mentioned earlier, the disbanding of the U.S. Information Agency in 1999 and its placement within the State Department's undersecretariat for public diplomacy and public affairs dealt a near-fatal blow to America's strategic messaging in both the war on terrorism and against other adversaries. The ineffective messaging capability, mainly conducted by the poorly run Voice of America and other quasi-official radio outlets, coincided with the explosion of information technology around the globe.

American efforts to counter strategic information warfare have been failing for the fundamental reason that current government leaders have ignored a key reality: the United States has been declared an enemy combatant targeted by foreign information operations. The first step in addressing the threat is to clearly understand the nature of these new, unconventional dangers. Once those threat agents engaged in information warfare are clearly identified, they must be designated as enemy combatants in information war. Upon clearly identifying enemies, the next step will be to identify what Prussian general Carl von Clausewitz called each enemy's "center of gravity," the strategic pillar upon which the enemy is conducting information operations. As Claremont Institute intelligence specialist Angelo Codevilla noted, "competent regimes make war in ways that bring them peace, above all internally."

"[S]ince regimes and circumstances differ," Codevilla wrote, "so do centers of gravity and the foci of wars. Knowing yours and others' centers of gravity is the key to understanding the kind of peace you need, the kinds of wars you must and must not fight, and the way you must fight them.

Hence, self-preservation's prerequisite is to shed any sense of entitlement to your peace, to be ever conscious of how your regime might be undone."

For war and peace in the Information Age, this is the crucial strategic imperative and one requiring extensive study and understanding.

Finally, once the enemy's center of gravity is located, information-based attacks must be used with clear purpose—achieving a victory that results in peace as defined by the United States and the desired end state, where the attacking enemies no longer pose threats.

The current liberal political agenda has hampered America's ability to wage information warfare as a result of misguided policies that emphasize total transparency in foreign messaging aimed at countering Islamic terrorism—the only current information warfare operations marginally being conducted. Current government policies also have limited the use of so-called soft power, as opposed to hard military force. Soft power includes public diplomacy tools for information operations. This approach of limiting soft power operations under politically correct restraints has not worked and never will work. The United States must develop a large-scale, comprehensive program of information warfare that uses the full panoply of tools, such as propaganda, political action, psychological warfare, and other means.

Contrary to conventional wisdom, propaganda and political warfare are not un-American activities used only by dictatorships or authoritarian states. The American Founding Fathers resorted to information warfare in winning independence from Britain. As information warfare expert J. Michael Waller notes, the Founding Fathers employed an array of public diplomacy, propaganda, counterpropaganda, and political warfare as instruments in the struggle for freedom from British rule. "John Adams, Samuel Adams, Benjamin Franklin, Alexander Hamilton, Thomas Jefferson, and George Washington recognized that the opinions and perceptions of foreign governments, publics, and armies mattered, and they used information operations as instruments of first resort in the American Revolution," Waller told me.

"Hopelessly outmatched against the world's most formidable military power, the American founders compensated asymmetrically with public diplomacy, propaganda, counterpropaganda, and political warfare," Waller said. "They never used those terms—all came into vogue as we know them in the twentieth century—but they employed all the measures, integrating them with domestic politics, secret diplomacy, intelligence, and warfare with decisive strategic effect."

Public diplomacy is defined by the U.S. government as efforts "to promote the national interest and the national security of the United States through understanding, informing, and influencing foreign publics and broadening dialogue between American citizens and institutions and their counterparts abroad." Counterpropaganda is the active effort to neutralize enemy propaganda. Political warfare is the use of aggressive and coercive political means to achieve objectives. Psychological operations, or psyops, are military activities to convey information and indicators to foreign audiences to influence emotions, motives, objective reasoning, and ultimately the behavior of foreign governments, organizations, groups, and individuals. Under liberal politically correct policies, the military was forced to abandon even the term *psyops,* which was considered too aggressive for the mavens of the Left. Instead, military psyops were transformed into the politically correct term *military information support operations,* or *MISO.*

Massachusetts's colonial statesman Sam Adams was a master at political warfare. Adams was a follower of English philosopher John Locke and mounted relentless negative political or ideological attacks that would be followed up by offering positive alternative solutions—all designed to keep the enemy on the defensive. "Adams strategically integrated the negative and the positive with political action both at home and, when necessary and possible, abroad," Waller explains.

It is these kinds of lessons that must be learned from the founders and applied to our Information Age foes.

To achieve victory for America, the comprehensive strategic plan for Information America must be able to reach all levels of society, government, and the private sector with truthful information.

The first step in restoring America's unique greatness and bringing unity to the homeland is to create dedicated organizations—public, private, and joint public-private endeavors—that will be used to aggressively dispel the widespread lies and disinformation about America, its history, and its contemporary activities. Again, I call this new program Information America and envision the effort as an upgrade to the disbanded U.S. Information Agency. This is an Information Age system of organizations and groups, both governmental and nongovernmental, devoted to promoting the United States of America and to countering information warfare against the country, which is spread with electron speed due to advances in information technology.

Robert R. Reilly, a former USIA official and senior fellow at the American Foreign Policy Council, correctly identified the disbanding of USIA and its absorption by the State Department as a setback in U.S. efforts to wage a war of ideas. "The State Department should not have been expected to do diplomacy and public diplomacy, as they sometimes conflict," Reilly told me. Public diplomacy often seeks to reach foreign audiences over the head of their governments and this can complicate diplomatic relations. The two functions should not be colocated in the same agency. "In short, since the disbanding of USIA, there has been no central U.S. government institution within which policy, personnel, and budget could be deployed coherently to implement a multifaceted strategy to win the war of ideas over an extended period of time," Reilly says. "As a result, as Secretary [of State Hillary] Clinton said, the U.S. is largely absent from the field." The broadcasting arms, led by VOA, are run by part-time employees with little experience, and its programming has been dumbed down from American promotion to entertainment featuring pop music that does little to influence Arab publics and in fact encourages anti-Americanism.

The objective of Information America is to promote the best that America has to offer, both to the American people and to the world. It will be driven by fundamental concepts that the blessings of liberty and prosperity America enjoys should not be limited to America, but shared with the world. The guiding principle for the narrative of Information America is that the most effective weapon in the war of ideas is truth. Information America will be structured into two components, based on new media and old media, corresponding to today's media environment.

Currently, the U.S. government is unable to conduct this function effectively, its bureaucracy having been highly politicized by decades of liberal ideologues who have inculcated those in its ranks under a dominant political culture that prevents portraying America fairly or accurately. Details on how best to construct this new organization will be crowd-sourced among private sector and government experts and specialists—the best and brightest—to produce the best ideas and concrete plans of action. If Information America is made one of the U.S. government's highest national security priorities, the program will be funded and staffed at robust levels. A key requirement is presidential leadership.

With the Obama administration soon to be relegated to the dustbin of history, the damage done to American prestige and power under Obama's leadership must be reversed. No more apologizing for America's past or present. America must be held up to the world as the last, best hope for humankind.

Given the current disarray within the federal government, two lines of effort will be required: government and private sector, nonprofit and for-profit. American business and industry leaders and other philanthropists must be educated to understand the urgent need to support and invest in this vitally needed project. The simple truth is that new weapons of information warfare are needed on the digital battlefield to preserve and defend the nation. The message to American leaders both public and private is simple: support Information America programs because the nation is engaged in an existential fight that requires action to defend and support the American ideal.

This project is an urgent priority. America's enemies have carefully gauged the weakness of the current leadership in the country and see America as a dying empire, along with what many view as the decline of Western civilization in Europe. Decades of lies and distortions about America are reshaping perceptions.

INFORMATION AMERICA PROJECTS

To prevent America's defeat in the ongoing and accelerating global information conflict, what follows are a number of proposed programs and projects to be carried out under Information America.

The New Active Measures Working Group: As sought by the Senate Intelligence Committee, Information America will reestablish and modernize the Active Measures Working Group, but for use beyond just Russian information warfare. The new Active Measures Working Group will also conduct counter-disinformation activities against an array of enemies, notably China. Information America, while strictly adhering to a charter of telling the truth, will seek to learn from our adversaries by adapting similar programs used by enemies and retooling them according to American values and guidelines. Research and analysis on information warfare programs and activities by Russia, China, Iran, North Korea, and other adversaries will inform its programs and activities, such as China's use of the Three Warfares: legal, psychological, and media.

The Social Media Development Project: Based on Moore's law, that technology power is doubling on a regular basis, Information America will seek to study and anticipate new and emerging social media platforms likely to replace dominant current social media like Twitter and Facebook. In fact, research should be conducted by national laboratories aimed at producing new social media platforms designed specifically to support the goals and objectives of Information America—a commitment to the American ideals of freedom, democracy, and free markets—while seeking to protect and defend the country against hostile states that seek to use information attacks against us.

The Big Data Project: Data mining is emerging as a cutting-edge tool in the Information Age. Tom Reilly, chief executive officer of the Palo Alto, California, firm Cloudera, believes data mining can be an extremely valuable tool in supporting information operations.

"I think cybersecurity itself is over–written about, but

information warfare is not," Reilly told me. "Big data analytics can play a big role in information warfare by arming the global intelligence community with insights from cyberspace social communications."

Big data technology already is widely used in both government and the private sector for a variety of purposes. For example, banks and telecommunications companies are leveraging data-crunching technology to gauge what is called social sentiment. Companies like Coca-Cola and General Motors are closely listening and analyzing the massive amount of communications on the Internet, whether in Facebook or Twitter or in various discussion forums. The practice reveals who is listening, who is talking, and what they are buying.

The same technology can be applied to listening to America's information adversaries to identify who are the key influencers. These can be targeted in campaigns of sophisticated information warfare operations to influence the influencers. Big data will be one of the major weapons for operations, targeting, agent penetration, and influence operation in strategic information warfare.

Through big data, an exquisite picture of foreign information threats will be obtained, a critical first step in understanding the threat.

China too is aggressively using big data, as the hacks of the U.S. Office of Personnel Management and Anthem health care revealed. Currently in China some 20,000 to 30,000 projects are under way devoted to analyzing big data on the Chinese Internet and exploiting it for both commercial and information warfare purposes.

"With big data analytics you can learn who the influ-encers are, what is being said, who is listening, who's re-communicating, how fast is news propagating, and what is the sentiment of it," Reilly says. "We can determine who are the enemy instigators and who are the positive and influential responders. Big data analytics can provide unprecedented insight into the online world of social influence and enable authorities to interpret, respond, and counteract potential emerging threats."

Big data will prove to be one of the most significant stra-tegic force multipliers in today's hyperconnected Informa-tion Age.

The Hollywood Project: America since the 1930s has been admired globally in large measure because of the content of its motion pictures that accurately portrayed America as the best the world had to offer. Whatever its past shortcomings, the United States remains a great nation characterized by a people who love freedom, equality, and independence.

Unfortunately today, as the result of the liberal left cul-tural subversion, a large portion of American films portray the most negative and base aspects of American life. With cliché-like frequency, American films denigrate the U.S. military, American corporations, American intelligence agen-cies, and the government writ large as corrupt and evil—all themes in line with the anti-American ideology of the liberal Left. Hollywood, of course, must remain free to produce whatever films it wants. However, a parallel, pro-American, patriotic film industry must be created to counteract the lies and distortions being promoted by the dominant liberal left film industry. Backed by American philanthropists, wealthy technologists, and others, Information America will seek to create film companies that produce feature-length films and documentaries with the aim of providing a balance to the often extremely negative portrayals of the United States so prevalent in many sectors of Hollywood.

Additionally, Information America programs will seek to push back against enemy states like China that are seeking to buy into and ultimately control the content of American movies in ways that would support Beijing's communist information warfare narratives. China already is swaying the movie industry. As part of its information warfare program, China's Dalian Wanda, a real estate conglomerate, has purchased major U.S. movie studies, including Legendary Entertainment and Paramount studios, along with the AMC, Hoyts, and Carmike theater chains. The takeovers have raised fears that Beijing is seeking to censor topics and exert propaganda control over American movies. In 2011, the American movie company MGM bowed to Chinese government pressure during the remake of the movie *Red Dawn,* which was initially planned to show a fictional American guerrilla resistance force fighting a Chinese military invasion of the United States. But under pressure from Beijing the company altered the story in the late stages of production by replacing Chinese military forces with North Korean troops. Such rank appeasement must be resisted.

Adapting the Chinese model but using democratic and free market means of persuasion, Information America advocacy specialists will seek to appeal directly to film industry leaders and producers to get them to realize that in the current international security environment, anti-American portrayals and depictions in movies are not only untruthful but also destructive of America's peace and long-term survival. For those film companies bent on promoting false and negative stereotypes, a boycott system should be considered that would reinforce the point.

The "Hamilton" Project: Similar to the Hollywood project, this Information America program will focus on revitalizing and protecting broader American culture. It will be based on the demonstrated appeal of the wildly popular Broadway musical *Hamilton*, which premiered in 2015. The musical portrays the life of American Founding Father Alexander Hamilton. Its popularity demonstrates that the liberal left anti-American narrative can be broken and that the greatness of America's history can be shown and celebrated in a highly artistic musical format.

The Semantics/Terminology Project: Information America will challenge liberal left language subversion and seek to take back the narrative of constraining language and semantics. Left liberal advocates promote an ideology of political correctness, as shown, that is based on New Left anti-Americanism and must be countered. Language fascists among New Left Marxists and their Long March through the institutions of America, mainly within universities, must be exposed and countered by disseminating accurate and true information. Marxist and false terminologies must be challenged aggressively on a systematic basis, and Information America will use educational tools to inform and correct publics about the threat posed to the American way of life by false and misleading terminology. Clarity of terminology in debate is an urgent requirement. The academic discourse remains captive of the Marxist Left. This program will expose and reject the nomenclature of the anti-American Left and provide a more accurate lexicon that will assist in bringing about honest public debate on issues of critical national importance.

The Cable News Project: One of the top priorities of Information America will be the creation and operation of a new cable and satellite television news outlet. The broadcasts will be high quality, well funded, and staffed with television professionals in multiple languages, twenty-four hours a day. This is an urgent requirement and needed as an international counterweight to the negative portrayals of all things American by such outlets as Doha-based Arabic cable and satellite station Al Jazeera television, Russia's Kremlin mouthpiece RT television, and state-run China Central Television (CCTV). This program would not be needed if privately owned American cable networks had devoted more resources to critical issues related to promoting American ideas and values and countering hostile foreign propaganda. Information America television will be a pro-American, truth-providing news, information, and entertainment outlet designed to show the best of America, and when necessary aggressively counter the lies and disinformation about the country. Anticipating critics' charges that this cable news outlet will lack credibility because it will be regarded as a government propaganda organ can be countered by establishing clear rules and guidelines for broadcasts under fairness principles, and by oversight from a board of experienced journalists.

The Lawfare Project: Information America will establish domestic and international nongovernmental legal organizations that will be employed to engage enemies on the legal battlefield, using lawfare and similar legal tools and institutions. An example was the July 2016 ruling by the United Nations Permanent Court of Arbitration in The Hague, which ruled against China's expansive and illegal claims to owning 90 percent of the South China Sea. A concerted network of nongovernmental legal organizations will engage the Chinese directly to counter legal aggression.

The Democracy Promotion Project/Human Rights Promotion Project: Current government efforts to promote democracy have failed. For example, as a result of pro-China, business-oriented American policies, an antidemocratic "Beijing consensus" was developed by China and is being used to expand Chinese influence and control around the world as part of information warfare operations. Despite the overwhelming desire for democracy and freedom around the world, China's model of antidemocratic development is gaining ground in the international informational battle space over American and Western efforts to promote democracy. China has attempted to alter and in some cases has subverted foreign governments, mainly in the developing world, by promoting its false version of "socialist democracy"—rule by a single dictatorial party. Additionally, Russia's neofascist authoritarianism can be turned around and transformed into a democratic system through an effective program of democracy promotion against Putinism. Iran and North Korea also must face the full force of American information operations in promoting peaceful evolution from radical Islamist theocracy in the case of Iran, and totalitarian communism in the case of North Korea, toward less threatening democratic social and political systems in both countries.

A Democracy Revolution subproject also would build on the prodemocracy movements that emerged during the 2010s across the world. The objective would be to assist future revolutions against dictatorial regimes by preparing now to promote a comprehensive system of transition to democracy programs tailored to each individual country. This program will be designed to avoid a repeat of the Obama administration's disastrous failure in 2009 to support the aspirations of reformers in Iran—as a result of Obama's self-centered desire to appease an enemy in pursuit of a dangerous nuclear accord. Even though the reformers backing the Green Revolution may not have been democratic reformers, supporting their Green Revolution would have been an important step in ultimately overthrowing the Islamist mullahs in Tehran who continue to kill Americans or support the killing of Americans by proxies.

The Military Information Warfare Program: The U.S. defense establishment must take the gloves off and develop comprehensive, modernized, and upgraded programs of information warfare theory and practice for U.S. military forces. These programs must be integrated within every military command and unit, and must become a significant element of all military training. Current military information warfare programs remain hamstrung by political correctness ideology, which has kept the role of information warfare subordinate to traditional conventional warfare. This must change as future wars will be network-centric and nonkinetic and dominated by information warfare. Military conflict using traditional arms and weapons will not disappear. But the value of military conflict as a tool for achieving strategic political objectives will be greatly diminished as new and innovative ways of using cyberwarfare and nontraditional influence and soft power information warfare are developed, refined, deployed, and used. As General MacArthur remarked in his famous West Point farewell address: "The soldier above all other people prays for peace, for he must suffer and bear the deepest wounds and scars of war. But always in our ears ring the ominous words of Plato, that wisest of all philosophers: 'Only the dead have seen the end of war.'"

Learning and applying information warfare must be made one of the highest priorities of the military. Failure to do so will result in defeat in the next conflict.

The Intelligence/Covert Action Program: The U.S. government urgently needs to modernize U.S. intelligence agencies' use of covert action and information warfare as a major tool of statecraft. Intelligence agencies once had formidable information warfare capabilities but as a result of liberal left policies have completely lost this capability in a true intelligence operations sense. As the result of the politicization of American intelligence agencies over the past two decades, the capability of conducting effective intelligence-based information warfare has been diminished to near zero, despite advances in technical cyberwarfare techniques. Cyberwarfare must be closely integrated with content-based information warfare to achieve victory in international conflict, and most important, to bring peace on American terms.

Information America represents hope for the future. Americans of all walks of life must recognize that this new organization will be an important first step in restoring the greatness of America and expanding the light of liberty and freedom worldwide.

CONCLUSION

Solutions for a New Age

What follows is an outline of the strategic information warfare threats that are the front lines of today's global information environment, outlined earlier. They include a series of proposals for a new information warfare strategy and operations based on the strategy to mitigate the threats. These represent an urgently needed starting point for developing concrete policies and programs for both government and the private sector.

The central recommendation is the creation of a new institution called Information America, derived from the U.S. Information Agency of the past and adapted to the threats and opportunities of the twenty-first-century Information Age. This new institution must be a hybrid entity combining the best features of government, with funding resources and powerful intelligence capabilities that can be combined or coordinated with the capabilities of the private sector, which generally is more effective at operating in innovative and practical ways. Where the public and private sectors can interact directly, programs and initiatives can be conducted jointly. The overriding requirement is a firm and clear commitment to promoting and defending America's founding ideals of liberty, democracy, free markets, and traditional concepts of morality.

SOCIAL MEDIA

Social media is not an enemy. It is a powerful tool with great potential for information warfare. The center of gravity for social media is technology and the masses of data it produces. Twitter, Facebook, and lesser offshoots rely heavily on proprietary technology, much of it open source, that is targeted by enemies, including China and Russia, who are seeking to exploit social media for nefarious purposes. Social media companies and the technology titans that control them must be enlisted to support programs that confront the growing information warfare threats against America. In information warfare, as in conventional warfare, the most reliable way to keep the peace is to prepare for war. Many of today's social media companies remain in the dark about the ongoing information war threats and opportunities, and thus remain vulnerable to information attacks and foreign influence operations. Left liberal politicization of social media has produced a neo-anarchist trend among many leaders of America's robust high-technology sector that must be reversed. As shown in Facebook's censoring of conservative content and Twitter's selective banning of conservative users, social media can be misused for antidemocratic and ultimately totalitarian purposes.

iWar Policy Proposal One: Information America Social Media Program. This effort will begin with a series of nationwide debates on social media, carried out physically and online with the goal of producing private sector, voluntary Information Age guidelines for social media to define the enemies, such as efforts by Russia and China to stifle Internet freedom. Clear guidelines are needed to identify the activities of the Islamic State terrorist group and other violent extremist organizations as enemies that should not be permitted to utilize social media for recruitment, training, fund-raising, and other operations. Communist China and its global information warfare network, and the antidemocratic, neofascist regime of Vladimir Putin's Russia, also must be clearly identified as enemies to free and open social media. Social media and the Internet that carries it must be enshrined globally under First Amendment principles adapted to the Information Age. Enemies of freedom and democracy must be blocked from using social media through technology and data mining.

CHINA

The People's Republic of China represents the greatest long-term threat to American national interests. China has been engaged in across-the-board information warfare against the

United States as its main enemy, while at the same time using strategic deception to play down its true intentions. China has become an enemy because its information aggression threatens America's peace. The notion of the nuclear-armed communist dictatorship in China rising to become the world's leading global power must be rejected. Furthermore, the nature of China's role as an information warfare adversary must be clearly identified and confronted. Government and private sector elites have damaged American national security for decades since the 1980s by following policies designed to redefine China as a nonthreatening, "normal" member of the international community when in reality China remains a revolutionary antidemocratic and protototalitarian force that seeks not just regional control but ultimately international expansion beyond Asia.

China's center of gravity is the dictatorial Communist Party, whose membership numbers 88.76 million. Information warfare waged openly and covertly against the ruling party will aim to produce a free and democratic China, or at a minimum a reformist and noncommunist system that poses less of a threat to the United States.

iWar Policy Proposal Two: Free China. China's communist rulers recognized in the early 1980s that the economics of Marxist-Leninist ideology were false and thus began initiating quasi-capitalist reforms. The Marxist-Leninist sociopolitical system remains, however. It is a collective dictatorship by the leaders of the ruling Communist Party and a military force loyal not to the nation but to the party. The contradiction between the economic reforms and the Leninist nature of the system is inherently destabilizing and has resulted in the emergence of the current neofascist state. Unless altered, Chinese internal contradictions will increase over the next several decades and produce extreme dangers that range from regional military conflicts to the risk of global thermonuclear war. The United States must use information warfare against China with the end state of producing a noncommunist, democratic-oriented political and social system—democracy with Chinese characteristics would suffice. This program will require attacking and defeating China's Three Warfares— legal, psychological, and media—by exposing the programs and counterattacking with truthful information. Under current Chinese information attacks, the United States is facing eventual defeat in the new conflict from an onslaught of Chinese cyber and influence warfare schemes and programs. The democracy transformation project will create a democratic Chinese government in exile, as well as a program of information and influence from overseas Chinese in ways that will produce democratic political reform inside China. This democratization program must be among the highest priorities of both the U.S. government and the private sector since China represents the gravest long-term danger to America.

A Chinese government in exile was first proposed by the late Constantine Menges, a senior official within the Reagan administration, as outlined in his 2005 book, *China: The Gathering Threat.*

A concrete program was developed by Michael Pillsbury, a former Reagan administration defense policy maker and longtime Pentagon consultant on China. Pillsbury's formula for Information Age policies toward China includes uniting Americans in understanding the threat; building a virtual coalition of nations opposed to China; influencing debates within China between hawks and reformers; and, most important, providing concrete support to prodemocracy reformers—unlike the failure to do so by the George H. W. Bush administration and its successors after the party crackdown on prodemocracy protesters in Beijing's Tiananmen Square in 1989.[*]

RUSSIA

Russia emerged from the collapse of the enemy state of the Soviet Union in 1991 and the victory of the West in the Cold War as a potential democratic state aligned with the West. Unfortunately, Russia today has become an enemy that threatens American peace. Misguided policies under successive U.S. administrations resulted in Russia turning into a hostile revanchist state run by a former officer of the KGB, Vladimir Putin. Under Putin, Russia has been aggressively building up its nuclear forces and poses the greatest strategic nuclear threat to the United States. Putin and other Russian leaders have adopted a dangerous and destabilizing new military doctrine to go along with the modernized nuclear force

---

[*] For more information, see Michael Pillsbury, *The Hundred-Year Marathon: China's Secret Strategy to Replace America as the Global Superpower* (New York: Henry Holt, 2015).

that seeks to use nuclear weapons and conflict as a way to win a future conflict. Known as "escalate to deescalate," the Kremlin doctrine has increased the danger of global thermonuclear war.

iWar Policy Proposal Three: Russia Democratic Transformation Program: As with China, the United States must employ aggressive and sophisticated information warfare techniques to counter Russian information warfare, by aiming at the center of gravity of the revanchist regime: Putin and the network of cronies in government and the commercial sector. The Russian leader and the military and political officials he has placed in power speak openly of the United States as the main enemy in this information conflict. The enemy in Russian information warfare must be clearly identified and a plan of action developed and implemented that, using advanced information warfare techniques, will produce a peaceful transition from a Putin administration to a democratic reformist regime. A central element of the program will be an aggressive counter-cyberwarfare program directed against Russia's formidable cyberwarfare networks.

ISLAMIC STATE

The center of gravity for the Islamic State terrorist group is its alien and abhorrent Islamic ideology, as promulgated in the doctrine and teachings of the so-called caliph Abu Bakr al-Baghdadi. Islamic State terrorists and their supporters are

America's most immediate enemy. The United States must alter its policy and recognize that killing Islamic State leaders, choking off funds, and slowing the recruitment of Islamic fighters, while important measures, will never lead to the defeat of the Islamic State, and thus will never produce peace and an end to terrorist attacks. The purpose of war is to inflict such heavy costs on enemies they no longer maintain the will to fight. This can be accomplished only by attacking and destroying Islamic State ideology. That alone will produce defeat for the group.

Instead of the current efforts to counter the Islamic State ideology by relying on foreign Muslim-majority governments, the United States must take the lead in first clearly understanding the ideology and then developing specific programs to defeat it, by discrediting it as un-Islamic. "It is easier to kill radical Islamic jihadists than to eliminate their Islamist ideology," says Patrick Sookhdeo, one of Britain's leading experts on jihadist ideology. "It is ideology that gathers resources and recruits new fighters to replace those who have been killed. Kill the ideology, and the terrorism-inspiring movement withers and dies."

iWar Policy Proposal Four: Strategic Information Warfare Against the Islamic State. The model for the ideological defeat of Islamic jihadism was demonstrated by President Ronald Reagan, who challenged the liberal dominant foreign policy that dealt for decades with the Soviet Union as mainly a competing social system. Declaring the Soviet Union an "evil empire," Reagan set in motion a series of policies, both open and covert, that resulted in the downfall of the communist empire. Similarly, the Islamic State can and must be defeated on both the ideological plane as well as through military and intelligence means. This can be accomplished by adapting the same principles and programs used during the Reagan administration against the Soviet Union, adapted now to ideologically attacking and defeating the most violent terrorist group on the planet. This will require a large-scale American-led program to expose the lies and deception inherent in Islamist ideology and offer a moderate religiously based alternative. A series of Centers for Nonviolent Faith will be created that will bring together religious scholars of all faiths to work together on plans to reform Islam to end its terrorist-supporting religious practices. This program will be implemented under a long-term strategic plan with the United States funding and supporting these nongovernmental organization interfaith centers. The centers will be in key countries—the United States, Britain, Egypt, Iraq, Afghanistan, Pakistan, India, and Indonesia—and will bring together religious scholars and experts from different faiths under the central operating principle that no God-centered religion condones the killing of innocents or the use of suicide in conflict. The central objective will be to define political Islam as un-Islamic.

As former U.S. government counterterrorism officials Richard Higgins and Stephen Coughlin have noted, currently in the United States the Islamist enemy is under the direction of Muslim Brotherhood Islamist front groups that control the narrative. It is supported by the liberal left narrative that regards Islamism as progressive.

POLITICAL CORRECTNESS AND THE LIBERAL LEFT

The liberal Left and its policies in America are destroying the fabric of the country. Political, racial, and religious tensions reached unprecedented levels during the 2010s as the nation's diverse population was turned against American values and traditions by liberal activists bent on promoting policies of resentment, retribution, and socialist transformation. The enemy, as shown earlier, is political correctness. Counter–information warfare programs must be developed and implemented that will attack and counter political correctness, first recognizing that it poses a threat to America's peace. The political Left continues promulgating a false narrative, widely accepted throughout media, academia, and government, that America is an evil, racist, and repressive state that must be taken apart and replaced with a statist system that would impose "social justice"—defined as government-led efforts to redistribute wealth from rich to poor, while punishing all in society that benefited from so-called white privilege. This destructive vision must be soundly rejected. Political freedom is absolutely essential in the United States, but as Supreme Court justice Robert H. Jackson noted in a 1949 free speech case, "the Constitution is not a suicide pact."

iWar Policy Proposal Five: A Counter–Political Correctness Program. This program will employ a public information campaign that uses truth to expose lies. The central idea is to hold up to the light of public sunshine all the central tenets of the destructive liberal left agenda couched in political correctness. One method will be to host nationwide public debates on the problem of political correctness, in cities and town and on campuses. Through such debates, the true nature of the destructive tenets of political correctness will be exposed and rejected as harmful to America's traditions and values.

This program can rely on elements of Information America as well as private sector programs funded by philanthropists.

Falsehoods and lies that are allowed to affect both government and the private sector must be exposed and rejected. As conservative columnist R. Emmett Tyrrell Jr. notes, tradition must be made a major element in the American experience. As Tyrrell exquisitely wrote:

> One thinks of our unique history, with our colonial heritage, George Washington and the war against King George III, the brilliant period of our Founding Fathers, our Civil War and Abraham Lincoln's Emancipation Proclamation. Then came our appearance on the world stage with spectacular contributions to science, sports, industry, commerce and popular culture, to say nothing of the defense and advancement of democracy, freedom and equality. Ours is a great history and we should have a rich tradition, but somehow we have failed the traditions that recall American history and values.

In fact, there are Americans denying our traditions. I am talking about the so-called liberals who sneer at American traditions and peel away at them: the tradition of Christmas, the tradition of Thanksgiving, July 4th and all the traditions attacked by political correctness.

IRAN

The Islamic Republic of Iran has proclaimed itself an enemy of the United States since the Islamic Republic was created in 1979. As long as Iran continues to regard America as such, there should be no relations or engagement with this leading state sponsor of international terrorism. The nuclear deal carried out by the Obama administration must be recognized as based on the false assumption that negotiating with hard-line Islamist extremists in Tehran will lead to better relations and a less threatening Iran. The nuclear deal must be rejected and a campaign of information warfare must be waged with the goal of ousting the Iranian Islamist regime and replacing it with one that is free and democratic.

As shown in these pages, Iran poses a direct threat to U.S. peace through its nuclear program and its long-range missiles, which will almost certainly directly threaten American security by 2020.

Iran remains the world's leading state sponsor of terrorism and until its support for terrorism ceases, there can be no peace between the Islamic Republic and the United States. Through Barack Obama and his administration concluding the international agreement with Iran on its nuclear program, American security has been undermined. The agreement released more than $100 billion in frozen, pre-1979 assets to the Iranian regime that will be used by Tehran to continue killing Americans, directly through the provision of arms and explosives to terrorists, and indirectly through Iranian proxy groups like Hezbollah. Iran's center of gravity is its brand of Islamist ideology.

iWar Policy Proposal Six: Transform Iran Project. The Obama administration made a strategic blunder in 2009 by failing to support reformers in the so-called Green Revolution in Iran, who had risen up against the mullahs controlling the country. The Green Revolution was an opportunity to bring about the demise of an enemy that is increasing in power and influence, the Islamist regime in Tehran. An information warfare program targeting Iran will use truthful information warfare tools and digital warfare weapons to expose the Islamist regime as a threat to both regional and world peace, and to counter the apocalyptic ideology behind the Islamists in power. The objective will be to foment a democratic revolution in Iran and replace the theocratic regime with a pro-Western, democratic one.

NORTH KOREA

The North Korean regime of Kim Jong Un is an abomination. The United Nations has concluded that the communist regime is guilty of crimes against humanity throughout three generations of dynastic dictators who should not have been allowed to prosper and remain in power into the twenty-first century, much less arm itself with a growing arsenal of nuclear weapons and intercontinental-range missiles that can deliver them. North Korea represents an unconscionable failure on the part of the civilized world, which has permitted the regime to persist through decades of totalitarian repression. This failure is mainly the result of its fraternal communist ally China making sure the Kim dynasty continues to boost Beijing's regional fortunes by maintaining a buffer from the extraordinary free and prosperous system in South Korea. The Kim regime must end and its rulers be held accountable for its crimes. This can be done through an aggressive program of information warfare designed to bring about the peaceful overthrow of the Kim regime and its absorption into the free and open society of South Korea. The first step must be that China, as North Korea's main patron and supplier, is held accountable for the crimes of North Korea.

iWar Policy Proposal Seven: Regime Change in North Korea. North Korea is an enemy because it has armed itself with nuclear weapons and missiles while repeatedly threatening to use those weapons against the United States and its allies. The center of gravity for North Korea is the Kim dynasty. An information warfare program against North Korea will begin with the Western development of information infrastructure in the country and then through provision of large numbers of information systems, computers, and smartphones. The regime will seek to use technology to control this new infrastructure but will be unable to do so, because of the ingenuity of the Korean people. Once the infrastructure is in place, information warfare operations can be carried out that will expose the horrors and crimes of the regime and reveal the prosperity and freedoms outside the backward state.

The program will include co-opting Kim Jong Nam, the out-of-power brother of North Korean supreme leader Kim Jong Un, and conducting information operations that will seek to install the brother as a replacement for the current leader.

These programs reflect the kinds of operations and activities that can be carried out once enemies are clearly defined and the means of achieving victory over them, through information warfare means, are developed.

Some in Congress have recognized the need to prepare the U.S. government for strategic information warfare. In 2008, then-senator Sam Brownback introduced legislation that would have created a new National Center for Strategic Communications, modeled after the USIA. The new center would have engaged in promoting American ideals and countering disinformation. The measure was never passed and died after Congress adjourned that year.

By 2016, prompted mainly by the Republican-led Congress, others in the U.S. government had begun to realize the urgent need for information warfare tools to prevent losing ground to hostile states that remain highly advanced in the field compared to the United States. One solution was offered by the Senate Select Committee on Intelligence. The annual intelligence agency authorization bill for fiscal 2017 contained draft language that would require the president to reestablish a new Active Measures Working Group–type organization focused on the Russian information warfare threat. The legislation defined active measures as covert influence operations using front groups, covert broadcasting, media manipulation, disinformation and forgeries, funding of agents of influence, incitement, and offensive counterintelligence, assassinations, or terrorist acts.

The new committee would be made up of the director of national intelligence, secretaries of state, defense, and the Treasury, the attorney general, energy secretary, and FBI director, along with other key officials. The mission: "To counter active measures by Russia to exert covert influence over peoples and government by exposing falsehoods, agents of influence, corruption, human rights abuses, terrorism, and assassinations carried out by the security services or political elites of the Russian Federation or their proxies," the legislation states. This revived group would be an important first step in creating American information warfare capabilities.

As shown in these pages, America's status as a superpower engaged in advancing the traditional ideals of liberty and democracy has been severely eroded through the rise of enemies, ranging from the immediate danger of al Qaeda and its evolution into the ultraviolent Islamic State, to the failure to support a prodemocratic Iranian revolution, to the disastrous policies of appeasement toward Russia, which produced a deadly new revanchist Russia. Shortsighted policies encouraging the rise of the nuclear-armed communist dictatorship that is China and then attempting to address it with an anemic policy of shifting toward the East, called the Asia Pivot, has provided little support to embattled Asian friends and allies greatly concerned by the threat posed by China. America is facing disarray and remains in urgent need of leadership.

Relations between America and its two main enemies, China and Russia, have reached dangerous levels. China has transformed from a rising nuclear power into a country that is systematically trying to orchestrate the decline of the United States, while driving the American military farther and farther from Asia in a bid to create a geopolitical power shift aimed at forcing the states of the region to kowtow to Beijing's demands. Russia devolved from a nascent, pro-Western state with democratic aspirations to the new fascism of Vladimir Putin, who is adapting neo-Soviet KGB and Red Army tactics to restore the Soviet model of power over what Moscow calls the "Near Abroad"—the former Soviet republics and eventually Eastern Europe.

The Islamism threat has metastasized by the failure of secular, politically correct government policies and a leadership that has been rendered incapable of waging information warfare against Islamic extremists—the ultimate solution to a global problem. The failure of successive administrations since 9/11 to wage ideological war on Islamism has forced the United States into expensive and seemingly endless military and intelligence operations that produced successful programs of killing terrorist leaders while doing almost nothing to stop the spread of Islamic jihadism and its ideology, which is creating terrorists who are adaptive and easily self-replicating, like a mutating and increasingly virulent virus.

The task before us is daunting. But Americans have risen to such challenges in the past. Information warfare presents both challenges and tremendous opportunities for bringing about transformation and ultimately peace. The challenge must be met with nothing less than victory.

ACKNOWLEDGMENTS

This book is in many ways a culmination of decades of experience working as a journalist covering national security affairs. During those many years I have been extraordinarily fortunate to have worked with a great many people within government and in the private sector who provided tremendous assistance in uncovering facts behind some of the most important news stories. To them I am deeply grateful.

Among those who provided valuable assistance on the subject of information warfare are Kenneth E. deGraffenreid, Jim Fanell, Sebastian Gorka, Katharine Gorka, John Lenczowski, J. Michael Waller, Michael Pillsbury, Rich Higgins, Patrick Poole, Joe Myers, Michael Rubin, Stefan Halper, Tom Reilly, Brad Johnson, Robert R. Reilly, Angelo Codevilla, Phillip Karber, Mark Sauter, Chris Farrell, and Rowan Scarborough. Special thanks to former CIA officer

Duane "Dewey" Clarridge, a great American intelligence hero who passed away in April 2016.

I would like to thank my colleagues at the *Washington Free Beacon* for their support, especially Chairman Michael Goldfarb, Editor in Chief Matthew Continetti, and President Aaron Harison. Thanks also to my colleagues at the *Washington Times*, including President and CEO Larry Beasley, Chairman Thomas McDevitt, Executive Editor Chris Dolan, and Michael Jenkins, head of the *Times'* parent company. Thanks also to my agent, Joseph Brendan Vallely.

INDEX